LAND, POWER, AND POVERTY

THEMATIC STUDIES IN LATIN AMERICA

Series editor: Gilbert W. Merkx,
 Director, Latin American Institute,
 University of New Mexico

THE POLITICAL ECONOMY OF
REVOLUTIONARY NICARAGUA
by Rose J. Spalding

WOMEN ON THE U.S.–MEXICO BORDER:
RESPONSES TO CHANGE
edited by Vicki L. Ruiz and Susan Tiano

THE JEWISH PRESENCE IN LATIN AMERICA
edited by Judith Laikin Elkin and Gilbert W. Merkx

POLICYMAKING IN MEXICO: FROM BOOM TO CRISIS
by Judith A. Teichman

LAND, POWER, AND POVERTY:
AGRARIAN TRANSFORMATION AND
POLITICAL CONFLICT IN CENTRAL AMERICA
by Charles D. Brockett

PINOCHET: THE POLITICS OF POWER
by Genaro Arriagada. *Translated by* Nancy Morris

SEARCHING FOR AGRARIAN REFORM IN LATIN AMERICA
edited by William C. Thiesenhusen

THE CHILEAN POLITICAL PROCESS
by Manuel Antonio Garreton. *Translated by* Sharon Kellum

LABOR AUTONOMY AND THE STATE IN
LATIN AMERICA
edited by Edward C. Epstein

ASSEMBLING FOR DEVELOPMENT:
THE MAQUILA INDUSTRY IN MEXICO
AND THE UNITED STATES
by Leslie Sklair

Additional titles under preparation.

LAND, POWER, AND POVERTY

AGRARIAN TRANSFORMATION AND POLITICAL CONFLICT IN CENTRAL AMERICA

revised edition

Charles D. Brockett

Routledge
Taylor & Francis Group

LONDON AND NEW YORK

First published 1991 by Westview Press, Inc.

Published 2018 by Routledge
52 Vanderbilt Avenue, New York, NY 10017
2 Park Square, Milton Park, Abingdon, Oxon OX14 4RN

Routledge is an imprint of the Taylor & Francis Group, an informa business

Copyright © 1991 Taylor & Francis

Library of Congress Cataloging-in-Publication Data

Brockett, Charles D., 1946–
  Land, power, and poverty: agrarian transformation and political
conflict in Central America/Charles D. Brockett.—Rev. ed.
    p. cm.—(Thematic studies in Latin America)
  Includes bibliographical references.
  ISBN 0-8133-1269-8
  1. Agriculture—Economic aspects—Central America. 2. Land use—
Central America. 3. Land tenure—Central America. 4. Land reform—
Central America. 5. Elite (Social sciences)—Central America.
6. Poor—Central America. 7. Central America—Rural conditions.
I. Title II. Series.
HD1797.B76 1990
333.3′09728—dc20   89-78172
                                                                         CIP

ISBN 13: 978-0-367-00420-0 (hbk)
ISBN 13: 978-0-367-15407-3 (pbk)

*For Sharon
Aaron and Kate*

Contents

Contents

Preface

This study represents the confluence of two previously separate projects. The first concerns the political crisis that has engulfed Central America since—to pick a somewhat arbitrary starting point—the beginning of the end for the Somoza dynasty in Nicaragua in the late 1970s. The second is the tragic persistence of hunger generally, and in Central America specifically.

Eventually, I came to realize that these were different starting points leading me to the same story: a series of socioeconomic transformations occurring over the course of centuries that have advantaged some groups but that have created and perpetuated the disadvantage of others. This book is not intended to tell all of that story; instead, its focus is on the aspects concerned with rural life. Central American societies are still primarily rural, and they were substantially so in the not-so-distant past. The changes that have occurred in the region's rural areas are not only central to understanding the causes of widespread hunger and malnutrition; they also are fundamental to comprehending the politics of the last few decades, including revolution, civil war, reformism, and repression.

Students of Latin American politics are necessarily led to appreciate how closely political life is connected to its socioeconomic context and to realize the importance of viewing politics from a historical perspective. Sadly, much of the North American discussion of contemporary Central America has not been enlightened by these perspectives, especially when its subjects are the causes of the region's conflicts or possible solutions to them. This work is presented in the hope of underscoring the importance of perceiving Central America in light of its own history, especially the development of its fundamental socioeconomic structures. It is offered with the conviction that a sensitivity to this history is necessary, if not sufficient, for the achievement of solutions that facilitate the realization of peace and justice.

Although my training is as a political scientist, this study makes extensive use of the works of anthropologists, economists, historians, and sociologists. Considerable effort has been made to integrate the vocabularies of a number of disparate disciplines, fields, and schools of thought into one language intelligible to all, including undergraduates. Similarly, I have attempted to write a theoretically informed work—and one that offers its own theoretical contributions—without becoming diverted by issues and debates tangential to my primary objectives.

This is a work of synthesis. I have been impressed by the quantity and quality of field studies, published and unpublished, available on particular aspects of Central American life. At the same time, I have been disappointed by the lack of good works of interdisciplinary synthesis, on individual countries and especially for the region as a whole. Because this is a work of synthesis, my debts are substantial. As the reference section indicates, I have made use of a great number of studies by both Central American and North American scholars. A study such as this one is dependent on the quality of libraries and the helpfulness of librarians. During separate summers of research, I developed significant debts to the staffs at the following institutions: the University of North Carolina at Chapel Hill; the University of Denver; and, at the University of Wisconsin at Madison, the Land Tenure Center, the main library, and the agricultural library. Research on a more limited basis was undertaken at the libraries of Duke University, the University of Tennessee at Knoxville, and Vanderbilt University. The crucial financial support for my summer research ventures was provided by several grants from the University of the South Faculty Research Fund.

My debt to Robert Trudeau is substantial. His encouragement and example over many years were critical to my decision to undertake this effort, and his suggestions on the organization of Part I were almost all incorporated, with a substantial improvement as the result. Robin Gottfried also offered useful advice for portions of the manuscript. Gilbert Merkx, the editor of this series, provided many good suggestions that helped me to produce a more coherent volume. Laura de la Torre Bueno's superb copy-editing eliminated many errors and helped to add some grace to my prose. Earlier versions of parts of this study were presented as papers at professional meetings and published in academic journals (Brockett 1984a, 1984b, 1987a, 1987b). My understanding and treatment of the issues discussed here have been substantially strengthened by the comments of a number of panelists and reviewers; to them I again express my gratitude. I am pleased to distribute credit widely but do accept full responsibility for any of this work's shortcomings.

This book is dedicated to my wife, Sharon, and my children, Aaron and Kate. Their love, confidence, and support have inspired and sustained me throughout the project.

CHAPTER 1

Introduction: Agrarian Transformation and Political Conflict

The extraordinary concentration of land·ownership and the entrenched position of a small but powerful land-based elite have long been regarded by both reformers and revolutionaries in Central America as primary causes of the impoverishment of the rural majority and as fundamental obstacles to the sustained, just development of their societies. Agrarian issues such as land use and distribution have consequently been central to the political rhetoric and platforms of progressive movements and to their policies—and even survival—when they are in power. For example, agrarian reform programs and proposals were major catalysts of the overthrow of progressive governments in Guatemala in 1954 and Honduras in 1963. More recently, contrasting agrarian reform programs were at the heart of the different developmental models pursued in the early 1980s by the governments of El Salvador and Nicaragua.

More conservative groups in Central America also have been preoccupied with agrarian issues. Since the days when the region was a Spanish colony, the profit-generating sector of the economy has been oriented toward the export of agricultural commodities. Whether in the nineteenth century or in the post–World War II period, most conservatives (as well as many others) have favored the expansion of agricultural exports as the preferred model of economic development, especially when they have had direct interests in this expansion themselves (for example, as landowners or commercial groups). Historically, elites attracted to this agro-export development model have been concerned with securing sufficient land and labor to implement the model successfully. They have invariably been able to utilize public policy to achieve their goals.

For their part, the rural majority have seldom been in a position to determine development policy, even its rural components; instead, they have been the subjects of policy and, too often, its victims. Especially during those periods when export agriculture has expanded rapidly, peasants have been thrown into unequal competition against more powerful interests for control of fertile land. They were even coerced at times into laboring for those interests. Peasants have resisted their dispossession and subjugation across the centuries, but ultimately with little success. Since the 1970s, the conflict and resistance have intensified, especially in Guatemala, El Salvador, and Nicaragua. But now the peasant cause has been embraced by armed revolutionaries who have found support from some politicized peasants. As a result, government counterinsurgency programs have targeted innocent peasants on a number of occasions, a form of repression that has been especially ferocious in Guatemala and El Salvador.

Agrarian structures, issues, and conflicts, then, play a central role in contemporary Central American politics. Accordingly, an understanding of these factors is essential to the comprehension of the causes of the contemporary crisis in the region and to the determination of adequate and viable solutions. This study divides the pursuit of such an understanding into two parts. Part I discusses the major transformations that have created contemporary agrarian society and evaluates their impact on the lives of the rural population. Part II examines, country by country, the political response of peasants, political movements, and governments to postwar agrarian change. The fundamental purpose of this section is to compare, within and between countries, the adequacy of governmental responses to the challenges presented by the upheaval of recent decades in rural society.

Although there are a number of exceptions, this book begins on the general, regionwide level and becomes more specific to individual countries as it proceeds. During the colonial period, what are now the countries of Costa Rica, El Salvador, Guatemala, Honduras, and Nicaragua were unified under an administrative structure headquartered in Guatemala. Many of the central political conflicts of the nineteenth century were generated by contradictory impulses toward national autonomy on the one hand and regional unity on the other. Because of their small sizes and their proximity, the various Central American countries have been subjected to many similar influences. Discussion at the regional level will often be most appropriate, for Part I, but care will be taken to distinguish country-specific patterns where appropriate. Part II has a more explicitly political focus; since variations among countries are more prominent here, the discussion is organized by country. Several manifestations of regional characteristics, including both similarities and differences among countries, are provided in Table 1.1, which gives current demographic data for the region.

TABLE 1.1
Demographic Profile

Country	Population[1] 1950	Population[1] 1985	Rural Population (as percentage of total) 1950	Rural Population (as percentage of total) 1985	Infant Mortality[2] 1950	Infant Mortality[2] 1980
Costa Rica	.80	2.52	67	51	87.3	20.2
El Salvador	1.86	4.86	64	49	81.8	42.0
Guatemala	2.79	7.96	75	67	100.1	65.9
Honduras	.1.37	4.37	69	60	65.4	95.0
Nicaragua	1.06	3.27	65	43	76.7	97.0

NOTES: 1. In millions.
2. Infant deaths in first year per thousand live births; 1950 figures are for 1950–54.
SOURCES: Population and rural populations: 1950: Herring 1964:820–827. 1985: Preliminary estimate, IDB 1986. Infant mortality: UN 1964:527–529, 1985:344.

AGRARIAN TRANSFORMATION

The primary focus of Part I is the transformation that occurred in rural Central America after World War II as a result of the rapid spread of commercial, especially export, agriculture. Although the region had produced for international markets since the colonial period, before the midtwentieth century most peasants[1] toiled for their own subsistence outside of the market economy. They neither purchased agricultural inputs (such as seeds or fertilizer) nor produced more than at most a minimal amount for commercial markets. Until recently, Central American agriculture was accurately characterized as dualistic: multitudes of peasants worked small plots, essentially for their own consumption, alongside of large, often huge, estates that produced for consumption in urban centers and overseas. Outside of the banana enclaves owned by foreign enterprises, most of these large haciendas operated under neofeudal conditions, using both land and labor inefficiently.

As a result of numerous interrelated changes such as the opening of new international markets, technological innovations, and the increased availability of credit, traditional agricultural structures and practices have altered substantially in recent decades, alterations that will be detailed in chapter 3. Haciendas have become commercial farms as new incentives encourage established landowners and new investors to pursue opportunities for financial gain. Sharecroppers have been replaced by wage laborers, while large commercial enterprises devoted to such export commodities as cotton, sugar, and beef have spread throughout the countryside. Similarly, small and medium-sized landholdings producing for urban markets have become more commonplace. The market economy, then, has penetrated rural society. Through this commercialization of agriculture, the share of the region's land, farms, and production that is devoted to commercial sales has increased.[2]

Although this transformation is unique in its scope, when it is placed in a historical perspective it becomes clear that it is the latest in a series of similar agrarian changes that extend all the way back to the Spanish Conquest of the sixteenth century. As chapter 2 makes clear, patterns have persisted across the earlier transformations that can be used as guides to that of the contemporary period. The essential dynamics in the present are invariably difficult to perceive because of our proximity to them; the past can help us to find our way.

Across the centuries, the results of the agro-export development model have been much less than its promise, as chapters 2 and 4 thoroughly discuss. As often as they have invested their profits in developmental enterprises, elites have used them for the purchase of luxury goods imported from industrial countries. Sometimes the profits have been returned even more directly to the affluent trading partners, either because Central American elites protected their gains in foreign banks or because the production and export of a crop was controlled by First World multinational companies to begin with. Furthermore, the expansion of export agriculture has often had a direct, negative effect on the lives of rural people. From the colonial expansion of cacao and indigo exports to the coffee boom of the nineteenth and early twentieth centuries and on to the spread of commercial agriculture after World War II, peasants have lost their land to more powerful interests that have wanted it for export production. Systems of domination have been created to coerce labor from peasants so that the export crops could be produced. When land and autonomy have been lost, domestic food production has usually suffered, resulting in an inadequate food supply for the rural poor. Rather than bringing progress for all sectors of society, then, the expansion of export agriculture in Central America has resulted for many rural people in an adverse and often devastating disruption of their lives.

Part I concludes with an evaluation both of the commercialization of agriculture and of the agro-export development model in Central America. A fairly extensive literature has documented that, in situations of great inequality, the promotion of commercial agriculture through the adoption of modern productive technology exacerbates that inequality.[3] Moreover, a substantial debate has developed concerning the economic and social consequences of the agro-export development model,[4] a debate that is perhaps more evenly balanced because of the perceived relative successes of countries such as South Korea and Taiwan. The evidence presented in Part I raises serious questions about the viability of the agro-export development model for countries with substantial rural inequality and underdeveloped domestic markets.

The most fundamental purpose of this study is to clarify the agrarian causes and dimensions of the crisis in Central America that has so concerned the United States for the past decade. Central America entered the postwar period with most of its population living in terrible poverty, and with the possibilities for improvement in the quality of life constrained by gross and rigid inequalities in social structures. Although the agrarian transformation of the following decades provided new alternatives and promises for some Central Americans, it actually diminished economic security for many others. As a result, substantial pressures developed on governments in the region to address the needs of millions of desperate people. The response to those pressures has been a primary determinant of the political conflicts each country faced since the late 1970s.

POLITICAL CONFLICT

The agrarian transformation of the postwar period changed the lives of most rural people in Central America, in many cases substantially. Their reactions have taken many forms, from passivity to migration to political activity. Some rural people have benefited from the changes of the last decades and have organized in order to defend and advance their interests. These groups include not only large producers but also farmers with medium and small commercial operations. The major concern of this study, though, is the rural majority; that is, peasants with insufficient land or none. Despite frequent stereotypes to the contrary, a significant degree of grassroots political activity has occurred in the region, especially in the 1970s, when peasants organized in response to the threat they experienced from the postwar transformation.

There is a substantial body of literature concerning the sources of peasant passivity, politicization, and mobilization.[5] The following model, abstracted from this scholarship, is used in Part II to guide the analysis of peasant mobilization and demobilization in each of the Central American countries. It is generally uncontested that peasants in this region, like those elsewhere throughout the Third World, have traditionally been politically passive. A typical review of the literature points out that "peasants are conservative . . . [and] difficult to organize.... They tend to be passive, feel politically powerless, and lack interest in politics" (Mathiason and Powell, quoted in Booth and Seligson, 1979:30).

More controversial has been the explanation for this passivity. The interpretation that corresponds most closely to the Central American experience is the one increasingly given by scholars: peasants' inaction, distrust, and suspicion are fundamentally the results of generations of repression and

exploitation. This reality is well captured by Huizer's (1972) concept of a
"culture of repression" (pp. x, 19, 27, 52–61; also see Paige 1975:26–27;
Schwartz 1978:247–248; Scott 1985:317–345; and Singelmann 1981:35).
The passivity of Central American peasants in the past was not due to their
lack of awareness of their oppression. As Brown (1971) has pointed out,
"there is probably enough despair, anger, perceived relative deprivation and
'consciousness' to start an uprising in most any traditional rural community
in Latin America on any given day" (p. 194). Self-assertion is dangerous,
however, for those with little power, wealth, or protection. Successful
peasant mobilization requires, at a minimum, two changes in social relations.
First, traditional patronage relationships must be weakened, for they are the
personalized manifestation of peasants' subordination within the status quo
(Brown 1971:192–194; Huizer 1972:18–19; Singelmann 1981:135–138;
White 1977:329). Second, new ties of solidarity must be forged among the
peasants themselves (Singelmann 1981:138–140; White 1977:244, 500–
506).[6]

There have been two major agents of such changes in social relations:
economic transformation and outside organizers.[7] The commercialization of
agriculture has diminished economic security for many rural people while
eroding traditional patronage relationships. As a consequence, this socioeconomic change has increased the incentives for mobilization while reducing
one of its major constraints (Migdal 1974:14–21, 135–138; Scott
1976:176–201, 1985:236–240; Singelmann 1981:125; White 1977:180–
182). To the extent that the commercialization of agriculture transforms
individualistic small landholders into wage-earning farm laborers working in
teams, it also facilitates rural organizing (Paige 1975:25–40). Finally, the
more rapid the economic change (Migdal 1974:252–253) and the more
fundamental the corresponding alteration of social relations (Paige 1983),
the greater the probability of successful peasant mobilization.

Nevertheless, some rural people have benefited from the spread of
commercial agriculture. Their newly gained economic security can reduce
their vulnerability to traditional elites and patrons while fostering a desire for
enhanced roles in society. Under certain conditions, then, newly secure
peasants join their economically insecure counterparts as forces for change.

Significant peasant mobilization seldom is self-generated. Outside
organizers, including religious workers, union organizers, revolutionary
guerrillas, political party activists, and development workers, have been
especially important to the political changes of recent decades in the Central
American countryside; accordingly, their role is stressed throughout the
individual-country chapters of Part II. Such organizers help to break down
the domination of traditional patrons by offering alternative sources of
economic assistance and protection (Migdal 1974:208–211, 228–232;

Singelmann 1981:134–140, 163; White 1977:244–245, 301, 344, 401). They are able to promote peasant mobilization not only because of their organizational expertise but also because they can facilitate the transformation of attitudes from those of powerlessness manifested by the isolated individual to those of solidarity and strength that are made possible with collective action (White 1977:244, 500–506).

The actual form that peasants' activity will take depends, of course, on a number of variables. Whether they will organize peaceful marches, initiate land seizures, support insurgents, or become revolutionaries depends, in part, on internal factors such as the depth and scope of their discontent, the level of their organization, and their perception of the legitimacy of the regime and system. Equally important are external conditions, especially the response of government and private elites to peasant mobilization. Substantial attention is given in Part II to the agrarian policies of the five Central American governments. Possible responses are numerous and include repression (minor to systematic), symbolic action, distributive policy (e.g., technical services, land colonization programs, etc.), regulatory policy (e.g., commodity pricing levels), and redistributive policy (e.g., extensive land redistribution). Particular attention is given here to the frequent reliance by governments and rural elites on repression and to the various approaches to agrarian reform.

Several attempts at agrarian reform have been made in Central America during the postwar period, but there have been great variations among them, especially in scope and the seriousness of intent.[8] The conception of agrarian reform used here has been left broad and loose in order to encompass these diverse approaches.[9] Some reforms have envisioned major alterations in tenure relations, while others have required little disruption in prevailing structures; some have been central to the purposes of committed popular governments, while others appear to have been primarily symbolic actions intended to pacify a restive peasantry.

Through this diversity, three general patterns emerge. In Guatemala, a substantial reform effort in 1944–54 was followed by counterreform and repression—a repression that reached extraordinary levels in the late 1970s and early 1980s. A second pattern occurred in Honduras and Costa Rica, which have pursued intermittent, moderate reforms over more than two decades. Finally, Nicaragua and El Salvador share the pattern of elite obstruction of agrarian reform until the end of the 1970s. Hated tyrants were overthrown in both countries in 1979, transforming not only domestic political life but also regional politics. The Nicaraguan insurgency, nurtured in rural areas, regarded agrarian issues as fundamental. Once in power, the Sandinista government made agrarian reform central to its program for the transformation of society. Similarly, the agrarian reform initiated in El Salvador in 1980 has been perhaps the most significant action taken by a

Salvadoran government in recent years. Its objectives and especially its implementation have been major sources of controversy within both El Salvador and the United States.

This study includes no separate chapter or section on the influences of other countries. The intent is not to minimize their role; on the contrary, the book's organization is a reflection of the extent to which Central American affairs continue to be permeated by international linkages.[10] Consequently, the impact of foreign influences is a major topic throughout this study. Central America has been tied to the international economic system through agricultural exports since the early colonial period. To a significant extent, Part I tells the story of the increasing impact of this connection up to the present time. Other aspects of the internationalization of Central American agriculture are also examined in depth, such as the role of foreign actors in promoting the agrarian transformation of the contemporary period. Part II documents the critical role that the United States has played in agrarian politics in Central America in recent decades, from promoting certain peasant organizations and guiding and financing some agrarian reform programs to working to destroy others.

By the end of this study, it should be clear that no lasting stability can be created in Central America without significant change in the social structures that have created and perpetuated incredible levels of poverty and suffering for much of the region's rural population. Given the strength of these structures and of the elites who are advantaged by them, such change requires substantial popular mobilization as well as committed governments. It also should be clear, however, that in Central America such movements and governments invariably have encountered the stiff resistance of the United States. Accordingly, the last chapter and the study conclude with a discussion of the role and interests of the United States in Central America.

NOTES

1. The terms "peasant" and "peasantry" will be employed loosely in this study. Their use here will generally conform to the authoritative definition in the Latin American context provided by Landsberger and Hewitt (1970) of the peasant as "any rural cultivator who is low in economic and political status" (p. 560). This usage does not assume any particular set of values or agricultural practices. Often in the present study more descriptive terms will be used, such as "rural people," "small farmer," "wage earner," "sharecropper," "plantation worker," and so on. For a good description of traditional peasant agricultural practices in Central America prior to World War II, see Tax (1963:47–49); for various types of agricultural practices in the 1950s at several locations in the region, see Dozier (1958).

2. The commercialization of agriculture, of course, is part of the larger process of the capitalist transformation of agriculture, or the development of agrarian capitalism. This trans-

formation involves not only penetration by the market economy and the profit motive but also the restructuring of class relations as, for example, sharecroppers are replaced by wage laborers (a process often referred to as the "proletarianization of the peasantry"). Because this study focuses on the first set of transformations but gives only limited attention to the second, "the commercialization of agriculture" is a more accurate characterization of the transformation under examination. The expansion of export agriculture obviously is generated by the profit motive, but it can occur with little disturbance to precapitalist class relations (as will become clear in chapter 2). For a good discussion of the theoretical issues involved in the capitalist transformation of agriculture in Latin America, see Arroyo (1978), Duncan and Rutledge (1977), and de Janvry (1981).

3. On the relationship between rural inequality and capitalist modernization, see Barkin (1982), Feder (1977), Griffin (1978), Hewitt de Alacantara (1973–74, 1976), de Janvry (1981), and Pearse (1980).

4. For discussions of the agro-export development model, see Adams and Behrman (1982), Goldberg (1981), Hillman (1981), Kent (1984), Lappé and Collins (1978), and Payer (1975).

5. Most helpful for this study have been the following: Booth and Seligson (1979), Brown (1971), Huizer (1972), Migdal (1974), Paige (1975), Scott (1976, 1985), Singelmann (1981), and White (1977). For reviews of some of this literature, see Colburn (1982) and Skocpol (1982); for reviews combined with case studies of Guatemala and Peru respectively, see Paige (1983) and McClintock (1984). For a thorough elaboration of a model similar to the one sketched here, see Tilly (1978).

6. Singelmann (1981) points out that

> vertical exchanges and dependencies between campesinos and landlords have tradi-
> tionally been reinforced by coercion, economic pressures, social organization, political
> structures, and psychocultural configurations. On the other hand, horizontal solidarity
> among campesinos has been mitigated by these same factors as well as by relevant
> dimensions of the socioeconomic organization within their community. Vertical
> exchanges and a relative lack of horizontal solidarity thus reinforce the traditional
> pattern of domination in rural Latin America. (p. 117)

7. These are usually discussed as competing explanations (e.g., Paige, 1983); here they are incorporated into a more complete interpretation. Moral economists have highlighted the importance of subsistence crises, while political economists have tended to give greater emphasis to the role of outside agents.

8. Among the many comparative studies of agrarian reform that include at least some Latin American cases, see Alexander (1974), Barraclough (1973), Dorner (1971), Ghose (1983), Grindle (1986), King (1977), Tai (1974), and Tuma (1965). Other useful studies of agrarian reform include Barraclough (1970), Berry and Cline (1979), Dorner (1972), Herring (1983), Jacoby (1971), de Janvry (1981), and Smith (1965).

9. Some argue that agrarian reform is meaningful only when it involves significant land redistribution and the provision of adequate supportive services, such as technical assistance and credit. Others, especially government officials in the region and in the United States, have found value in more limited programs, such as colonization and land titling programs. In order to be inclusive, *agrarian reform* is understood in this study to mean changes brought about by public policy in land distribution and/or land tenure relations. Such changes will vary from the narrowly distributive to the broadly redistributive.

10. Although these linkages point up Central America's dependency, an explicit "depen-dency" approach will not be taken here for reasons well stated by Evans (1985), who claims that the label is likely to disappear for the following reasons:

The term now carries too much theoretical baggage. . . . [Its] hypotheses served a useful intellectual purpose in early polemics with modernization theorists. They provided the 'anti-thesis' that facilitated the more sophisticated hypotheses of current works. But these hypotheses do not represent the ideas of those currently working in the historical-structural tradition, and the most effective way of disavowing them is to shed the label. (p. 185)

PART I

Agrarian Transformation

CHAPTER 2

Agrarian Transformation
Before 1950

The fundamental cause of the current crisis in Central America is the system of domination elites established over the centuries in order to pursue their material goals.[1] The objectives of Part I are to outline the essential features of the historical development of this repressive social order and to assess its human consequences. The central organizing concept is that of an agrarian transformation; that is, a major change in the organization of agrarian society.[2] The results of the transformations that occurred before 1950 limit present possibilities; they are important determinants of the demands faced by contemporary society, of the resources available for meeting those demands, and of the distribution of political power that constrains possible solutions.

This chapter begins with brief descriptions of indigenous Central American society, of the devastating impact of the Conquest, and of the creation of the colonial agrarian system. Following national independence in the early nineteenth century, socioeconomic change continued at a slow pace until the liberal reforms and the coffee boom of the second half of the century, both of which will receive substantial attention. The final topic of this chapter is the coming of the great banana companies and the creation of banana enclaves around the beginning of the twentieth century. A major purpose will be to assess the impact of the agrarian transformations of each period on the lives of rural people.

The objectives of development-oriented Central American elites have been constrained across the centuries by the availability of markets, land, and labor. Elites often have sought their wealth through the development of primary—usually agricultural—exports. Adequate foreign markets, though, have been a recurrent problem for four centuries. Sufficient land and labor have also been problematic, but over these factors elites have had more control. Central to most of the transformations of the past has been the expropriation of land and labor from the peasantry in order that elites might pursue their objectives. While the implementation of the agro-export development model in Central America has brought great wealth to some, for much of the peasantry it has represented the loss of land, food supply, and autonomy.

PRE-COLUMBIAN CENTRAL AMERICA[3]

Pre-Columbian Central America was a meeting and mixing ground for Indian peoples from Mexico, the Caribbean, and South America. As a result of migration, wars of conquest, and trade, many different linguistic and cultural groups had been created and had settled in the area. These various Indian groups are usually divided into two types: those of the higher Meso-American culture and those of the less advanced groups of South American ancestry. The former occupied the more hospitable areas of what is now Guatemala[4] and the western portion of Honduras, as well as the Pacific coast of Nicaragua and northern Costa Rica. The remainder of Central America is more tropical and less conducive to settled agricultural communities. Although the Indians in these latter regions did raise some crops, especially corn and tubers, they were just as likely to pursue fishing, hunting, and gathering activities. Their descendants can still be found today in Caribbean Nicaragua and the proximate part of Honduras. Historically isolated from the rest of their countries and living in remote, "undesirable" surroundings, they continue to resist incorporation into national life. The contemporary manifestation of this tension is the conflict between the Sandinista government and the Misquito Indians.

Before the Conquest, northern Central America had a substantial population living in well-developed, complex societies. Many of its inhabitants were descendants of the great Mayan civilization, whose core was in the lowlands of the Petén region of northern Guatemala, in western Honduras, and on the Yucatán Peninsula. The accomplishments of this civilization in science and mathematics, art and architecture, and commerce and construction often rivaled those of contemporary Europe. Although it had been in a long decline before the Conquest, its influence continued throughout the area.

As civilizations developed and declined in the Mexican plateau, Indians migrated into Central America from the north, usually intermixing with the indigenous populations they subjugated. One notable example was a group that arrived in the Guatemalan highlands about 1250, mixed with the local population, and adopted the local language by which they became known. The Quiché Empire then expanded through conquest until it reached its peak two centuries later with a total population of about one million people.

The Quiché and similar groups were organized into stratified societies. Nobles lived in cities supported by the agricultural production of vassals. Production techniques were often relatively advanced; for example, cacao groves of thousands of trees requiring careful attention were cultivated along the Pacific coast. A substantial commerce was maintained within the empire as well as with other regions. The Quiché overextended their empire, however. After 1450 subject tribes were in revolt, and in the years leading up to the Spanish invasion the Quiché were involved in a number of protracted wars.

Tribal divisions and warfare were only some of the factors facilitating the Spanish Conquest of Central America. Lacking immunity to many potentially lethal European diseases, the indigenous population was often weakened, physically and psychologically, by infections that invaded in advance of their European carriers. "Infamous for his cruelty and inhuman treatment of his foes" (Morley 1983:576), Pedro de Alvarado entered the area in 1524 with a small band of men and quickly subjugated the area in behalf of the Spanish Crown and personal fortune.

THE IMPACT OF THE CONQUEST[5]

It is now generally acknowledged that in 1492 the population of the Americas was greater than that of Europe. The sizable population of Central America, however, was quickly reduced by epidemics that were but the first in a series that swept the region throughout the colonial period. The large population of the Caribbean lowlands of Guatemala and Honduras soon disappeared. The Indians of Honduras and Nicaragua (and to a lesser extent those of El Salvador and Guatemala) were further decimated by a second horror: slavery. Able-bodied adults were enslaved and exported to labor in Panama and Peru. When the slave trade ended by 1550, "there were simply no Indians left to send" in Nicaragua and Honduras (MacLeod 1973:54). The most recent scholarship suggests that the population of the colonized areas of Nicaragua was reduced to about one-fortieth of its pre-Conquest numbers, while in Honduras it was reduced to less than one-twentieth its previous size, as it was along the Pacific coast of Guatemala. Although the decimation was less in the Guatemalan highlands, the rates were still extraordinarily high:

anywhere from four-fifths to seven-eighths of the population disappeared (Newson 1982; 1985:44).

Where indigenous communities were more advanced and productive, most notably in Guatemala, the conquerors superimposed themselves at the top of the existing social structure, redirecting tribute into their own hands. The direct labor of Indians was also obtained through the *encomienda* system (from *encomendar*, "to entrust"). Large numbers of Indians were "entrusted" to conquerors in reward for their services and in order that they might be "civilized" and Christianized. The usual result was virtual slavery.

The tragedy the Central American Indians suffered was of terrible proportions. Whole villages disappeared. In others, much of the remaining population was enfeebled and became incapable of producing an adequate food supply. Consequently, to the horrors of conquest, enslavement, and disease was added famine. The plight of the Indians provoked many in the clergy and Spanish Crown to action. Although impossible to enforce, the New Laws of 1542 banned the *encomienda*; soon slavery was prohibited as well. Theoretically, Indians were now free vassals; not surprisingly, however, they were reluctant to sell their labor to the Spaniards. The colonists accordingly evolved new systems of domination to attempt to insure for themselves an adequate labor supply. Especially important to that end were the concentration of villages and the *repartimiento*.

Because of the decimation of the Indian population and the ever-present threat of rebellion, some social restructuring was necessary in order to maintain both order and access to sufficient labor after the first few decades following the Conquest. Crucial to the accomplishment of these objectives was the resettlement of the Indians in centralized villages during the 1540s. This objective was accomplished by bringing Indians from outlying areas to more central villages and by moving groups to new areas and creating new villages. Over four hundred years later and for many of the same reasons, descendants of these Indians would once again be subjected to a similar resettlement program in Guatemala, as will be discussed in chapter 5.

The *repartimiento* (from *repartir*, "to divide up") provided another effective way to guarantee a labor supply. Each Indian village was to fill a labor quota, generally one-quarter of the men between sixteen and sixty in the village each week. In practice, however, the demand was often greater in both numbers and duration. Indians were assigned to work not only in religious and public institutions but also for private individuals, sometimes at long distances from their homes. Consequently, their ability to produce subsistence for their own families was diminished, heightening their susceptibility to the periodic epidemics. The travails of the Indians under this system are well portrayed in the account of a contemporary observer:

They go to the farms and other places of work, where they are made to toil from dawn to dusk in the raw cold of morning and afternoon, in wind and storm, without other food than the rotten or dried-out tortillas, and even of this they have not enough. They sleep on the ground in the open air, naked, without shelter. Even if they wish to buy food with their pitiful wages they could not, for they are not paid until they are laid off. . . .

So the Indian returns home worn out from his toil, minus his pay and his mantle, not to speak of the food that he brought with him. He returns home famished, unhappy, distraught, and shattered in health. For these reasons pestilence always rages among the Indians. . . . The Indians will all die out very quickly if they do not obtain relief from these intolerable conditions. (quoted in Sherman 1979:207)

THE SEARCH FOR EXPORTS[6]

The primary motive governing the creation of the Spanish colony in Central America was the enrichment of the Crown, colonists, and colonial administrators. In the early years this was achieved through what MacLeod (1973:63) aptly terms "looting"; that is, the expropriation of slaves and surface gold. Once these resources were exhausted, however, new sources of wealth had to be discovered. Many commodities were tried, but with little success.

The cacao trade was the first to be developed successfully, in part because its development was just a few steps beyond looting. Large cacao orchards were maintained by the Indians on both coasts before the Conquest. Cacao beans were used for money and in religious rituals, while the beverage produced from them was an aristocratic drink. Following the Conquest, Central America continued to supply cacao to Mexican Indians. Chocolate caught on in Europe, and a demand was created for the region's first transatlantic agricultural export. This demand was met in Central America by production primarily along the Pacific coast extending from north of present-day Guatemala down to western El Salvador.

Outside of the Salvadoran region, the cacao plantations were taken over by the Spaniards with Indians forced to provide the labor. Weakened by the demanding work, they were vulnerable to disease and died in great numbers. The colonists in their greed compounded the problem by forcing the conversion of too much land to cacao production. Lacking land and time, the Indians were unable to raise sufficient food; a serious famine resulted in 1570. To meet their labor needs, the colonists then brought Indians down from the highlands to work on the plantations. Not only did the new arrivals experience the same problems as their predecessors, but their stress was aggravated by the difficulty of adjusting to a very different climate. The highland Indians apparently died as fast as they could be replaced.

In El Salvador the effects were similar, though the Indian villages retained ownership of their orchards, some of which numbered up to fifteen thousand trees. Here the colonists obtained their wealth through unfair trade practices and tribute demands. Initially the Salvadoran Indians enjoyed some benefits from the cacao boom; but as time passed they too suffered from disease and famine, and their production fell as a result of depopulation. Nonetheless, these villages were able to preserve their relative independence, making the southwestern part of El Salvador the one place in that country where an indigenous culture persisted. Browning (1971:65) accords this situation substantial significance in explaining why Salvadoran peasant rebellions of the late nineteenth century and the major uprising of 1932 (see chapter 7) were centered in this region.

By the close of the sixteenth century the cacao boom had ended. High death rates prevented the maintenance of an adequate labor supply. Cacao production required specialized knowledge, knowledge possessed not at all by the Spaniards and by fewer of the Indians as time passed. The Indians had little incentive to preserve or replenish healthy orchards. Essentially, then, the existing orchards were plundered rather than cultivated by the Spaniards. As the orchards were depleted, so was the soil. When cacao production arose elsewhere, the Central American colonists were therefore unequal to that competition.

As Central America's cacao boom turned into a bust, the search for alternative export crops accelerated. Various possibilities were tried, but attention throughout most of the colonial period centered on a dye extracted from the leaves of the indigo plant. Despite sufficient suitable land to create a prosperous indigo industry, commercial hopes were constantly frustrated by both scarce labor and insufficient markets. Indigo production did not have the year-round labor requirement of cacao production, but for a few months the labor demands were heavy. Indigo planters relied on a variety of techniques to insure a sufficient labor suply, but it was a constant challenge both because of depopulation and because of colonial laws. Some regulations were general in scope, affecting all of colonial society in an effort to halt the most grievous exploitation of the Indians. Others were directed specifically at the indigo works because of the reputation they soon gained as death traps. For example, one priest wrote in 1636:

> I have seen large Indian villages . . . practically destroyed after indigo mills have been erected near to them. For most Indians that enter the mills will soon sicken as a result of the forced work and the effect of the piles of rotting indigo they make. . . . As most of these wretches have been forced to abandon their

homes and plots of maize, many of their wives and children die also. (quoted in Browning 1971:73)

Regulations, however, could be ignored, and officials bribed. More intractable was the problem of markets. The early–seventeenth-century acceleration of indigo production along the Pacific coast from Nicaragua to Guatemala was stifled by 1630 because of the inability of Spain, then in economic decline, to stimulate a healthy trade. Since the beginning of its empire, Spain had attempted to prevent trade between its colonies and other countries. Consequently, when European demand for indigo increased at the end of the seventeenth century, direct Central American access to those markets was possible only through contraband trade, and even this alternative was constrained by inadequate transportation. Although indigo exports did increase through much of the eighteenth century, in Central American eyes the dye's full potential was never reached during the colonial period.

Insufficient export development was not the only agricultural problem facing colonial society, nor even the most serious. As disease and famine depleted Indian numbers while the size of the Spanish population continued to climb, an insufficient food supply became an increasingly serious problem in the late sixteenth century. It was aggravated, of course, when Indians were forced to cultivate nonfood commodities. With this twin failure of the colonial economic system, many colonists were forced to leave the cities, some departing the region altogether but most taking to the countryside. It was at this time that the haciendas so characteristic of the area first developed.

The expansion of the hacienda had both positive and negative ramifications for the Indians. Up to that point they had been exploited for their labor, but they had confronted only minimal competition with their use of the land. Now, as colonists found urban life too expensive and turned to the countryside, Indians began to lose land to their conquerors. This loss was felt most seriously in those areas close to cities and trade routes and where the climate was most hospitable to the colonists. As Spanish penetration of these regions hastened Indian depopulation, they soon became *ladino* (non-Indian in culture) if not *mestizo* (racially mixed) in composition. Significant autonomy and continuity with the indigenous past, then, were retained by Indian peoples only in areas that were remote and/or inhospitable: in the tropical Caribbean lowlands from northeastern Honduras to Panama, in the high mountains of parts of Honduras, and most importantly in the western highlands of Guatemala.

Even in the highlands, the impact of the Conquest and colonial structures was extensive through depopulation by death and enslavement and though the enforced destruction of various aspects of traditional culture. Furthermore, highland Indians were forced to pay tribute to the Crown and the local colonial governments; as late as 1748, over 80 percent of royal revenues came from tribute (Wortman 1982:146). Some of the most seriously eroded and sterile soils in Guatemala today are located in the highlands. Where Indians were forced to pay their tribute in wool products, the excessive demands led to the overgrazing of sheep, thereby resulting not only in soil destruction but also in an insufficient food supply, even though the population was only one-half of that at the time of the Conquest (Veblen 1978).

Because village life left Indians vulnerable to oppressive tribute demands and the excesses of the *repartimiento*, the hacienda provided many Indians with an alternative—if not attractive, at least less burdensome. Hacienda owners were often rich in land and sometimes in labor, once depopulation reversed, but they usually lacked capital and markets. Until markets could be found (a discovery that was centuries in coming for many), there was little incentive for efficient use of the land. As economic life stagnated in the seventeenth century, many haciendas slipped into a semifeudal existence.

One exception to this pattern was Costa Rica, whose atypical characteristics today can be traced back to its unique colonial development. Its indigenous population, less numerous than those elsewhere in the region to begin with, was largely exterminated by the pandemic of 1576–81.[7] Lacking a labor supply and any exploitable mineral wealth, as well as remote from the cities of the colonial administration, Costa Rica attracted few colonists. Those who did settle in this area had to farm for themselves, usually on a subsistence basis. Consequently, Costa Rica's central plateau was slowly populated by the "yeoman farmer, independent, self-sufficient, and poor" (Seligson 1980a:7).

In summary, when the Spaniards invaded Central America, the region was rich in resources that they could exploit in order to materialize their goals. Soon, however, the indigenous population was decimated by disease, both because it lacked immunities and because of overwork, periodic famines, and the psychological impact of sudden subjugation. The effect of the colonial agrarian transformation on the rural population, then, was devastating, ranging from the widespread loss of land, culture, and autonomy to death on an extraordinary scale. As a result, access to an adequate labor supply was a constant preoccupation of rural elites throughout the colonial period and continued as a major concern into the twentieth century. The colonists came to the region not with the intention of retiring to a sleepy pastoral life, but with the goal of self-enrichment. The expansion of agricultural exports has always been constrained, however, by limitations on the ability to produce and market on a competitive basis goods desired by others, especially people in the more developed countries.

COFFEE AND THE LIBERAL REFORMS[8]

Central America gained its independence in 1823. Some aspects of life changed then, but economic structures that had evolved over the previous three hundred years remained intact. The major exports at the time, and for the next few decades, were the two dyes, indigo and cochineal (a red dye produced from insects that thrive on the leaves of a particular type of cactus; it took seventy thousand insects to yield one pound of dye). Inadequate earners of foreign exchange even at their peak, these agents were made anachronistic by the development of coal-tar dyes at midcentury. Consequently, the search for new and better exports was seen as imperative. Its result was the development of a booming coffee economy that transformed the lives of many rural inhabitants.

Coffee had received some governmental promotion during the colonial period, but inadequate transportation retarded its development as a trade item then and in the decades immediately following Independence. Costa Ricans were the first to increase their production as completion of the Panama Railway in 1855 facilitated transportation of their coffee to growing European markets. Impressed by their example, Guatemalans expanded their plantings, and coffee became their leading export by 1870. The revolution hit El Salvador in that decade and Nicaragua in the next; in Honduras, coffee has been largely a post–World War II development. These and other longitudinal and comparative trends are portrayed in Table 2.1, which gives for each country coffee production figures from 1885 to 1914 and coffee export figures from 1909 to 1945. The impact of the coffee boom was substantial everywhere in the region, though once again the Costa Rican experience needs to be differentiated from that of its neighbors.

Guatemala

The initial expansion of coffee growing in Guatemala was due to market stimulation without the support of the Conservative government, which was allied with the cochineal interests. This lack of support was a primary factor leading to a revolution in 1871 by the other leading party in the nineteenth century, the Liberals, and to the presidency of Justo Rufino Barrios. His rule had been unsuccessfully anticipated earlier in the 1830s, during the Liberal administration of Mariano Gálvez. Unlike Conservatives, the Liberals in Central America sought in the nineteenth century to create modern societies in place of the anachronistic structures of colonial society. The privileged position of the Church was to be destroyed, and the isolation of the Indians ended. Liberals tended to see Indians as an inferior race blocking the develop-

TABLE 2.1
The Central American Coffee Boom

Period	Costa Rica	El Salvador	Guatemala	Honduras	Nicaragua
A. Coffee Production, 1885–1914[1]					
1885–90	24.5	17.1	39.3	4.1	9.3
1890–95	26.9	29.5	49.7	4.4	12.6
1895–99	31.1	17.2	64.0	2.3	9.0
1900–04	45.7	47.2	67.9	2.6	18.5
1905–09	31.1	64.3	80.0	2.5	19.9
1910–14	30.9	66.6	106.3	.9	18.1
B. Coffee Exports, 1909–45[2]					
1909–13	28.4	64.6	86.6	1.1	19.0
1914–18	31.1	75.2	84.6	1.1	22.9
1919–23	31.3	83.8	95.6	1.1	25.8
1924–28	38.3	97.4	103.4	3.0	32.7
1929–33	49.6	112.8	96.4	3.4	29.1
1934–38	51.2	119.4	104.2	3.6	33.7
1939–43	46.4	116.2	99.6	3.7	30.9
1944–45	44.8	133.2	110.5	5.1	28.0

NOTES: 1. Average annual production within each period, reported in millions of pounds. The coffee year is not equivalent to the calendar year; for convenience years are listed here as, for example, 1885–90 rather than 1884/85–1889/90.

2. Average annual exports within each period, reported in millions of pounds.

SOURCE: Condensed from Torres Rivas 1971:283–287.

ment of the nation. Under both Gálvez and Barrios, they tried to dilute the indigenous presence by encouraging European and North American immigration and by assimilating Indians into a free market system. Given Central America's marginal position in the world economy and their own espousal of the doctrine of comparative advantage, Liberals were strong believers in the expansion of agricultural exports as the best route to developing a prosperous society.

Gálvez acted too quickly, however, provoking not only a Conservative reaction but also a peasant rebellion that brought the Conservatives back to power, a position they retained for over three decades. Conditions were more conducive to the Liberal program in 1871, and Barrios was more politically astute. The new government undertook the direct promotion of coffee growing through financial incentives, infrastructure development, the dissemination of agricultural information, and land and labor reforms. The program was successful as coffee production and exports skyrocketed. The new coffee elite was enriched, and associated commerical interests and service providers benefited as well; much of the peasantry, however, lost once again.

Prime coffee-growing land is at moderate elevations, but most such land was already densely settled in Guatemala (as it was in the rest of the region) by subsistence peasants. Consequently, in areas coveted for coffee growing, Indians often lost their communal lands as land titling reforms were instituted to foster coffee growing and to promote and protect the European concept of private property. This notion was alien to the indigenous societies of Central America. Generally in these cultures, private use of village property for family sustenance was frequent, and access to such plots even inheritable; however, the land continued to be understood as belonging to the community. Private property titles, by definition, were not available to communal lands (including Church lands, which also were confiscated). Although some Indians were able to protect their interests, many others were coerced or cheated out of theirs in what McCreery (1976) has called "a massive assault upon village lands" (p. 457).

Equally critical to the dreams of the coffee growers was the labor of the Indians. The potential for coffee export expansion was great, but the limiting factor was an inadequate labor supply. Rather than providing the necessary financial and other incentives to attract workers, the growers depended on coercion. Initially, they relied on the *mandamiento*, an updated version of the *repartimiento*. The use of Indians as needed by farmers was reaffirmed by President Barrios in 1876 since, as he stated, otherwise all efforts would be doomed to failure because of the "deceit of the Indians" and negligence (quoted in Whetten 1961:119). This system was inadequate, however, and it was outlawed in 1894 to be replaced by debt labor, which was regulated through legislation passed in 1877 and 1894. These acts legalized and rationalized a system requiring workers to labor for employers to whom they were indebted until the debt was paid. The creation of indebted workers was usually easier than the discharge of their debts. For example, one observer pointed out,

> It used to be customary during times of labor shortage to imprison large numbers of Indians for small offenses, especially for drunkenness, and to impose heavy fines. Obligadores from some plantation would pay this fine . . . and the Indian was turned over to the plantation to work off the debt. (quoted in Dessaint 1962:339)

Particular victims of this system were the poorer Indians, who had little or no land other than the communal lands. The appropriation of those lands left many of them helpless in the face of the determination of elites to coerce an adequate labor supply through debt labor and, later, the vagrancy system.

The lifetime bondage of Indians to the coffee *finca* (farm) often resulted from an initial grant of a substantial (to them) sum of credit, which they were never able to pay off. Upon their deaths, the debts were transferred to their sons. As one government official later admitted, the 1894 law kept the Indian in a "status similar to slavery" (quoted in Jones 1966:153). Nonetheless, growers still complained of labor shortages, which they believed could not be alleviated without compulsion.

A more pervasive system of coercion was created in 1933 as debt labor was prohibited and replaced with a vagrancy law. To work is an obligation, that law stated, and the amount of work one had to provide depended upon the amount of land one owned. The obvious target and victim was the Indian with little or no property. Indians were forced to provide their labor for 100 to 150 days a year to someone who would give them the opportunity to discharge their debt to society. As Jones (1966) observes, the law's "main object was to shift the basis of regulation of Indian labor from the obligation of the laborer to work to pay his debts to an obligation to work whether he was in debt or not" (p. 162). This law was abolished in 1945 as one of the first targets of the progressive Revolution of 1944.

The developmental model pursued in Guatemala effectively turned the countryside into a forced labor camp for much of the Indian population. Such a system of domination necessarily contaminates the rest of society. A system so based on coercion is inherently predisposed toward reliance on coercion as the preferred method of dealing with dissent and challenge. The following description of Guatemala in 1918, during the twenty-two-year rule of Manuel Estrada Cabrera bears chilling resemblance to the Guatemala of six decades later.

> The administration firmly maintains its authority by means of a large standing army and police force, and promptly and mercilessly checks the slightest manifestation of popular dissatisfaction. An elaborate secret service attempts, with a large measure of success, to inform itself fully of everything which occurs in the Republic. Supposed enemies of the party in power are closely watched. ... Persons who fall under suspicion are imprisoned or restricted in their liberty, or even mysteriously disappear. The ruthless execution of large numbers of persons, many of whom were probably innocent, have followed attempts to revolt or to assassinate the President. This reign of terror is approved by many influential natives and by the majority of the foreigners in the country on the ground that only a very strong government can prevent revolution and maintain order; and there is no doubt that the life and property of foreigners, at least, has been safer in Guatemala than in some of the other Central American countries. (Munro 1918:53–54)

El Salvador

The peasantry was more accessible in El Salvador since it had become substantially *ladino* during the colonial period, and its accessibility increased as the country's population almost tripled between 1878 and 1931. As government officials encouraged coffee production after mid-nineteenth century, a major preoccupation was the coffee-growing potential of the one-quarter of the national territory that still was held communally and invariably devoted to the production of basic food crops.

The Liberal government's first attack on these lands was a decree in 1878 mandating that access to common lands was no longer a right and that private title to such lands could be received upon the cultivation of specified (export) crops. Many villages attempted to comply with the law, but they were constrained by the capital requirements of coffee, which are considerable compared to those of other crops. Development-minded elites were impatient, however, and by decrees in 1881 and 1882 the common lands were abolished. Some small and medium-sized farms did emerge through this transformation; primarily, though, the land was consolidated in the hands of a small number of growers with holdings substantial enough to make them the backbone of the small oligarchy that ruled El Salvador until recently—the fabled "fourteen families," actually seventy-five families in fourteen groups (Dunkerley 1982:7). Peasants did resist; there were a number of uprisings in the next few decades, but they were successfully repressed.

The expansion of coffee holdings continued through the next several decades. The 1920s were a notable period of growth until coffee prices crashed along with the world economy at the end of the decade. The impact of this conversion of land to coffee growing is well described in contemporary accounts. For example, the following account by a journalist concerns the Indians in the southwestern part of the country, close to the cacao- and indigo-growing regions discussed earlier.

> The conquest of territory by the coffee industry is alarming. It has already occupied all the high ground and is now descending to the valleys, displacing maize, rice, and beans. It goes in the manner of the conquistador, spreading hunger and misery, reducing the former proprietors to the worst conditions—woe to those who sell out! (quoted in Durham 1979:34)

Nicaragua

Except for its retarded development, the spread of coffee cultivation in Nicaragua manifested most of the characteristics just described for its neighbors. Here more than in the other countries, coffee expansion was limited by poor transportation and by civil wars. Even more problematic was the meddling of the United States and Great Britain in the country's affairs. The liberal cause in Nicaragua was severely damaged by its association with the U.S. adventurer William Walker, who fought his way to the presidency in 1856. Following his forced departure the next year, the Liberals were out of power until 1893, when José Santos Zelaya established his rule. Once again, though, foreign interference led to a Liberal setback; the United States government was centrally involved in Zelaya's overthrow in 1909 and in subsequent efforts to keep his political heirs out of office. This active intervention by the United States in behalf of Conservatives was a critical factor in retarding the development in Nicaragua of a modernizing agrarian bourgeoisie such as was then occurring in Costa Rica, El Salvador, and Guatemala (Deere and Marchette 1981:44). Even after it developed, the Nicaraguan coffee elite still was unable to gain control of the state because of the creation and perpetuation of the Somoza dynasty, which again was a manifestation of substantial U.S. interference (Paige 1985:94).

Fortunately for coffee growers, some of the Conservative presidents before Zelaya were willing to adopt portions of the reforms elsewhere identified with the Liberals. An agrarian law in 1877 directly attacked communal and public lands, specifying that they be sold, with first option going to those who worked them. Neither this requirement nor one establishing size limits on purchases was always followed. Many peasants in Nicaragua occupied prime coffee land, and they often lost it as a result of the flouting of the law. Thousands of Indians rose up in rebellion in 1877, some fighting for nine months. In the end they lost, thousands of them were killed, and fierce repression followed. Their defeat facilitated even further loss of land to coffee planters.

New land became available under Zelaya as Church lands were expropriated and national lands sold. Conservative governments between 1910 and 1920 continued the sale of national lands, some of which were worked by small and medium-sized farmers with no legal titles, who were accordingly expelled. Some of these peasants were able to get their lands back when the nationalist rebel army of Augusto Sandino established control over parts of the northern region of the country during the late 1920s and early 1930s. They were the primary victims of the rural repression by the National Guard that followed the Guard's assassination of Sandino in 1934.

Costa Rica

Costa Rica was populated in relatively large proportion by independent small farmers, and it was they who initiated the coffee boom there. Their ability to meet the expanding European demand was limited by labor shortages, however. The family farm could produce only so much without additional help, which generally was not available. A partial alternative was provided in the midnineteenth century by the importation of newly invented processing machinery that allowed the rapid expansion of production. Relatively high wages also were offered in order to attract help during harvesting. As the decades progressed, labor shortages became less of a problem as population increases, high land prices, and some bankruptcies created a growing landless rural population. The development of the coffee economy in Costa Rica, then, was pioneered by the yeomanry (especially those who were already better off), and it fostered the development of a strong rural middle class. This brings us one step closer to understanding the uniqueness of Costa Rican political life today.[9] Nonetheless, even in Costa Rica the expansion of coffee production for export markets was still associated with land concentration, a decline in food production, and social stratification.

Summary

The expansion of coffee production in Central America, then, had a differential impact upon various social groups. A wealthy agrarian bourgeoisie was created in each country by the export boom, while many peasants (especially Indians) lost their access to land and were coerced, by the marketplace and/or by force, to supply their labor to others. Some of the most fertile land was switched from raising basic food crops to producing for export, with deleterious effects on food supplies. One scholar's careful study of this process in an Indian region of Guatemala led him to the following characterization, which applies almost equally well to the coffee-growing regions of El Salvador and Nicaragua: elites created and "controlled a virtual fascist state" (Carmack 1983:243).

As coffee exports increased and export earnings climbed in each of the countries, a substantial amount of money entered the region. Some of it was productively employed, in such areas as public works, education, and the beginnings of a textile industry. Contrary to Liberals' dreams, however, coffee earnings did not spark an industrial revolution. Much of the profit paid for imports to meet the rising consumerist aspirations of the elites and the growing urban middle sectors, while substantial amounts were reinvested abroad (Woodward 1976:163–164). Many of the merchants who handled the coffee trade were of foreign origin, as in fact were many of the owners of the coffee *fincas*, especially in Nicaragua and Guatemala. In a number of cases, then, the coffee boom benefited Europeans and North Americans attracted to the region, not Central Americans. In Guatemala, for example, a slump in coffee prices in 1897 left a number of native planters bankrupt and unable to prevent their German creditors from taking over their *fincas*; by 1914, 170 German planters produced almost one-third of the Guatemalan coffee crop (Jones 1966:207).

The unsettling experience of world market slumps, like the coffee crisis of 1897, reinforced the commitment of government officials and commercially oriented farmers to diversify export production. Dependence on the export of essentially one commodity obviously leaves a country highly vulnerable to world market fluctuations, over which it has little control or influence if it is a minor producer; and Central America has never produced more than 15 percent of the world's coffee. Finding a new export proved to be much easier this time, however, than it had been during the past four centuries.

THE COMING OF THE BANANA COMPANIES[10]

Few issues concerning the history of Central American political and economic life have generated more intense controversy than the role of the great United States banana companies. To some, the story is one of heroic entrepreneurs struggling against tremendous odds and risks to bring civilization and economic opportunity to the inhospitable tropical lowlands of the Caribbean coast. In pursuit of their vision and their self-interest, some lost their lives, others went broke, but some made vast fortunes. In the process, they provided good jobs and relatively high incomes for tens of thousands of Central Americans, built schools and hospitals, and provided much-needed export earnings for the underdeveloped countries of the area.

Others see the story instead as that of two U.S. corporations (United Fruit Company[11] and Standard Fruit Company[12]) gaining monopoly power over what had been a developing domestic industry through their control of shipping and marketing operations, their more highly developed business skills, their larger size, and their ruthless practices. Through corruption and political intrigue, backed at times by U.S. military power, the banana companies were able to obtain from vulnerable Central American governments extraordinary concessions that allowed them to capture and maintain control over an important sector of the region's economy and vast sections of its countryside.

Actually, there is little essential contradiction between these two very different stories. Although the first has validity, much of it is irrelevant to an evaluation of the role of the fruit companies in Central America. The most important questions such an evaluation must explore are first, the relative weight of the positive contributions of the companies and their negative consequences, and second, the relationship between this cost-benefit analysis and the benefits enjoyed by the companies themselves. The systematic exploration of these questions is still to be performed; what follows is a brief account of the evidence that is available.

The development of the banana industry in Central America is intimately tied to the building of railroad lines in the region, though this relationship varies somewhat from country to country. Railroad building in Costa Rica led to the banana industry, while in Honduras the relationship was essentially the opposite. In Guatemala, an existing rail line facilitated the expansion of United Fruit operations. Bananas are grown in Nicaragua, but their importance has been considerably less; they are unimportant in El Salvador.[13] In addition to their obvious importance as an infrastructure necessary for development, railroads were an important symbol of modernity in the second half of the nineteenth century. Central American countries wanted railroads for both reasons. They were willing to pay a high price, and they generally did, both in bad loans and in the alienation of extraordinary amounts of land to foreign interests. Costa Rica's first loans with European bankers left it with a debt of £2.4 million, even though it actually received only about half a million (Seligson 1980a:51). Honduras ran up a debt in the late 1800s of almost £6 million to pay for a rail line that was incompetently built and left uncompleted. Yet Honduras actually received only about three million, and about one-half of that amount was paid out to bankers (Ross 1975:78). The country was unable to pay off the loans, and by 1926 high interest charges had increased the debt to an incredible $125 million (Kepner and Soothill 1967:104–105).

Costa Rica contracted in 1870 with the famous railroad builder Henry Meiggs to construct its line. He then turned the contract over to his nephew Henry Meiggs Keith, who in turn brought in his younger brother, Minor, to help with the job. The project faced much greater hardships than foreseen, and Henry soon died in the effort (as did a younger brother later). Work plodded on more slowly than expected, and consequently the line was more expensive than planned. Minor Keith's banana-growing enterprise was founded in order to provide the railroad with income while work continued on construction of the segment from the Caribbean coast to the central plateau and its coffee groves, which were intended to be its major cargo. Keith's banana-growing efforts coincided with rising prices in the United States as demand continued to exceed supply. By 1890 his Costa Rican operation was the largest banana producer in the world. In 1900, the year after United Fruit was formed through Keith's merger with other interests, that company owned almost a quarter of a million acres in six countries; by the end of 1918, it owned or leased one and one-quarter million acres of land and operated about a thousand miles of railroad lines (Wilson 1968:118,

196). This land came very cheaply, much of it free of charge. Costa Rica signed the Soto-Keith Contract in 1894, under the terms of which Keith committed himself to finish the railway and to absorb the attendant £2.4 million debt. In return, Costa Rica granted him eight hundred thousand acres of state lands in any part of the country he chose, a ninety-nine-year lease on the railroad, a twenty-year exemption from land taxes, and an exemption from import duties for construction materials related to the railroad project. While the inducement was excessive, Costa Rica did get a railroad linking its inland capital with the Atlantic Coast.

The Honduran experience, by contrast, was less fortunate. Before the turn of the century, there were hundreds of small banana producers in Honduras (as there were in Costa Rica) who sold their produce to U.S. trading interests. The Honduran government, however, desired to expand the banana industry rapidly and retained hopes of constructing a railroad to the capital, which was separated from the Caribbean Coast by a rugged, mountainous terrain. Government officials believed that foreign capital and technicians would be necessary to achieve both goals, and the banana companies seemed to them to provide the solution. At the same time, the U.S. interests were ready to expand from trading bananas to producing their own supplies on their plantations. Within a short period of time, three of these interests came to dominate Honduran production: United Fruit, Cuyamel (which was bought out by United in 1930), and Vacarro Brothers (which became Standard Fruit).

Honduras offered the companies concessions similar to those granted United Fruit in Costa Rica as incentives to encourage them to expand their operations into the country. Especially notable were generous land grants in return for railroads the fruit companies were to construct. By 1924, United's two subsidiaries possessed 400,000 acres, at least 175,000 of them obtained without cost as subsidies for railroad construction. The Honduran intention was that the rail lines serve national needs by linking interior cities to the coast, but the thousand miles of tracks the banana companies did build were designed to serve their needs instead. Each company's coastal enclave was laced with tracks that did not penetrate into the interior nor even link adjacent enclaves. Because of the vulnerability of the weak Honduran government to its ambitious and omnipresent foes, the companies were often able to manipulate the political process to obtain deadline extensions or stifle attempts to institute meaningful sanctions for noncompliance (Kepner and Soothill 1967:140–152).

Honduras had intended to prevent the banana companies from developing larger enclaves. The lands granted were in alternating lots, with those in between them retained by the nation to be rented to Honduran citizens for a small fee. The banana companies later bought many of these leases from the citizens, however, thereby expanding and consolidating their holdings.

Guatemala demonstrates a third pattern in the relationship between bananas and railroads. A substantial amount of railroad construction had been completed there before the first concession was obtained by United Fruit in 1907, some of it in the region (inland from Puerto Barrios) in which its holdings were located. But the line fell sixty-one miles short of the capital, Guatemala City, and in 1904 the energetic Minor Keith obtained a contract for its completion. In return, he received control of the entire line, including the Caribbean port facilities at Puerto Barrios. This enterprise changed its name in 1912 to International Railways of Central America and obtained the rest of Guatemala's railroads, about two hundred miles of track in the western part of the country. Given Keith's interest in both, it is no surprise that mutual preferential treatment existed between IRCA and United Fruit, nor that the latter eventually absorbed the former.

From today's perspective, the huge tracts granted to the banana companies often look shocking. At the turn of the century, however, the Caribbean lowlands were largely unsettled and were viewed by most Central Americans (especially urban elites) as inhospitable to civilized habitation. Population densities were still quite low; the common belief was that Central America was blessed with a bountiful land supply. Therefore, unlike the coffee planters or the growers of new export crops after World War II, the banana companies could gain enormous land holdings without making much impact on land tenure patterns or rural class structures. But once land pressures developed in the postwar period, the size of those holdings became both a significant obstacle to meeting the land needs of a growing population and a pressing political issue, as will be discussed in Part II.

As their operations expanded, the companies hired thousands of workers, making them the largest employers in each of the countries. They provided important job opportunities for workers displaced when the expansion of coffee growing resulted in diminished food supplies in Costa Rica, in Guatemala, and even in El Salvador, as Salvadorans migrated to the Honduran banana fields. Wages paid by the U.S. banana companies have almost always been higher than those offered by domestic employers, and at a relatively early date the companies began to provide housing, educational, medical, and recreational facilities. Nevertheless, workers have had a number of reasons for serious discontent, including inadequate pay, extortionist company-store prices, poor working conditions, and racism. Organization in behalf of workers' interests has been facilitated by the collective nature of their work, and in each of the countries the banana workers' unions have been at the forefront of unionizing efforts. Their activities have had an impact on both rural and national politics, especially in Guatemala and Honduras, as will be discussed in later chapters.

The most important issue in the impact of the fruit companies, however, is their contribution to the development of the Central American economies through the generation of export earnings. As discussed in previous sections of this chapter, across the centuries Central American elites had seen the diversification and expansion of agricultural exports as the key to their own enrichment and their countries' development. The banana companies were welcomed to the region with generous concessions because of the promise they offered of achieving these goals.

It is uncontroversial today to assert that in the first decades (say, up to 1940), this contribution was much less than it should have been. Indeed, United Fruit's public relations director of the early 1970s admitted as much, writing that the "values of the era allowed the company to take without giving back in reasonable proportions" (McCann 1976:160). Nor did the presence of the banana companies stimulate the development of the local economies to the extent that might be expected. Despite their substantial infrastructure, many company operations were impermanent. When forced by disease or declining productivity to relocate, the entire operation, including even the railroad tracks, often would be moved to the next area to be cultivated.[14]

In addition to the wages the companies paid, their direct contribution to the domestic economy was based on goods and services purchased domestically and on taxes and duties paid. Generally, though, the needs of the companies were met by imports from the United States. Indeed, since the banana enclaves were isolated from the rest of the country, large portions of the workers' wages were spent in company stores that sold imported goods. Although duties on these imports were an important generator of income, they were reduced by concessions that let the companies import duty-free materials necessary for construction. "Necessity" has often been interpreted broadly; United Fruit was still successfully importing liquor duty free into Costa Rica in 1970, arguing that it was necessary for the improvement of labor relations (Seligson 1980a:61).

Potentially more important were the export taxes that could be levied on the bananas as they left the country. As part of the initial package of inducements, however, the companies were usually guaranteed a number of years of operations free from any export duties; United Fruit in Costa Rica, for example, had an exemption lasting until 1910. Once taxes were levied on the exports of the foreign-owned banana companies, the rates were substantially below those paid by domestic coffee growers. In 1928 the export tax on bananas in Guatemala was 1.97 percent of total valuation, while it was 8.7 percent on coffee; in Costa Rica the comparable figures were 1.4 percent for bananas and 11.8 percent for coffee (Kepner and Soothill 1967:213). Eventually, the companies were hit with other taxes, such as various types of land taxes. From 1918 to 1927, United Fruit in Costa Rica annually paid $2,000 on its vast uncultivated lands; in Guatemala its 1929 land tax was $6,500 (Kepner and Soothill 1967:214). As late as 1952, one study estimated that United Fruit's tax bill in Guatemala was still one-half of what it would have been without the exemptions granted in the original contracts (Adler, Schlesinger, and Olson 1952:124).

Such generous concessions proved to be very difficult to amend. The banana companies grew to be the largest landowners, employers, and generators of foreign exchange in the three countries. They were huge, stable, profitable, and backed by the government of the United States. The Central American governments, by contrast, were weak, unstable, and chronically short of revenues; in fact, when facing insolvency, the Honduran government often accepted loans from Standard Fruit. Central American officials were understandably apprehensive about pressuring the companies to contribute more for fear that they might respond by asserting their substantial economic leverage, perhaps cutting back on exports or production or even shifting operations to other countries. Such fears were reinforced by action on a number of occasions, as when United Fruit in 1930 successfully persuaded Costa Rica to modify proposed changes in the export tax by threatening to withdraw from the country (Kepner and Soothill 1967:79–80) or when in Honduras in 1920 United and Cuyamel threatened lockouts in support of Vacarro (Standard Fruit), which was experiencing serious labor difficulties (Karnes 1978:67). Furthermore, the historical record is full of examples of the companies using their substantial power and income to intervene directly in Central American politics in order to protect their interests.

The position of the banana companies was reinforced by the fact that the period of their expansion in Central America (the first third of the century) corresponded with the most interventionist stage of United States policy toward the region. The U.S. government did not always back the position of the companies, but its military penetration of the region generally, and specifically incidents of its military support for the companies, had an obvious effect on Central American governments. Public officials were reluctant to press confrontation with the companies when the U.S. Navy appeared off shore.

Domestic elements conspiring to overthrow a Central American government invariably dreamed of the advantage to be gained by enlisting the support of a banana company and/or the United States to their cause. As a result of the dominating position of the companies and of the U.S. government (whose military forces occupied Honduras and Nicaragua), Central American politics had little autonomy. A somewhat extreme example makes the point well: A loser in the 1923 Honduran presidential election launched a revolt, with the support of United Fruit, against the government, which had substantial financial ties to Cuyamel Fruit. The following year, U.S. troops were landed to protect lives and property, a role that soon brought them into armed conflict with the United Fruit–backed rebels. The conflict was then mediated by the U.S. State Department (LaFeber 1984:62).

Slowly the dominating position of the banana companies eroded. Central American governments stabilized; their economies grew; urban middle sectors expanded; and the nationalist voice became more prominent in domestic politics. The United States government became less overtly interventionist by the 1930s, while a new generation of business managers came to leadership who had greater concern for the image of their firms, both at home and abroad. As the configuration of power altered, contracts and taxes were amended to be less disadvantageous to the Central American countries. Accordingly, the evaluation of the economic contribution of the banana industry to Central America since about 1940 is complex.

As a preface to the discussion of the recent period, it is important to keep in mind that the erosion of the companies' dominant position has been slow and relative; they continue to enjoy a substantial ability to protect their interests through their economic leverage in the three countries. The prime example, of course, is United Fruit's role in the overthrow of the progressive government of Guatemala in 1954, to be discussed in chapter 5. More recently, a $1.25 million bribe paid by United Brands to Honduran officials in 1975 was successful in minimizing a proposed increase in the banana export tax (United Nations Economic Commission for Latin America [UNECLA] 1979:72–95, 139–150). At another level, reports in the early 1970s (Baer 1973:44–45) and mid-1980s (*Central America Report* [CAR] 1986:114) pointed out that the countries are still cautious in their fiscal negotiations with the companies because of the relative ease with which production emphasis can be shifted from one country to another. Because of their vulnerability, between 1978 and 1985 each of the region's three major banana-exporting countries lowered or eliminated taxes levied on the multinational companies (CAR 1986:114).

There have been several empirical attempts to evaluate the economic impact of the banana companies in Central America relative to their profits, but all are methodologically inadequate.[15] Furthermore, even complete access to the companies' accounting statements, as Clairmonte (1975) points out, "tells us very little of net profits in view of the integrated nature of the[ir] operation" (p. 141). Until recently, each company controlled the railway and shipping lines it utilized, and therefore profits could be hidden under transportation costs. Another illustration of this difficulty is provided by a former United Fruit official. McCann (1976:40) explains that in 1952 the company's three hundred stores generated a 16 percent gross profit of almost three million dollars, in itself, he claims, an understatement of actual profits. Yet after the accounts were juggled, the books showed an operating loss of about fifty thousand dollars for the stores. In sum, a conclusive statement well grounded in empirical analysis cannot yet be made concerning the economic impact of the banana companies relative to their gains.

There is, however, some useful evidence concerning foreign exchange earnings. The annual percentage of export earnings converted to local currency (a measure of the proportion of fruit company earnings benefiting the local economy) fluctuated between 40 and 65 percent in Honduras from 1961 to 1974, with the average for the period at 53 percent (Ellis 1983:204). This evidence is reinforced by a 1966 Alliance for Progress estimate that about half of foreign exchange earnings from bananas were converted into local currency for direct expenditure in Honduras.

Foreign exchange earnings have been depressed, though, by declining real prices for bananas on the world market. The real retail price of bananas fell 44 percent in the United States and 59 percent in West Germany between 1950 and 1972 (Clairmonte 1975:135). But higher real prices and expanding markets would not represent a great windfall for the banana producers because only a small portion of what the foreign consumer pays comes back to the producer. Clairmonte (1975:138–139) estimates that growers get only about 11.5 cents for each dollar spent by foreign consumers, while retailers' gross costs amount to 31.9 cents. Even when all other domestic costs (e.g., transportation) are added, only a quarter of the price paid by the consumer is generated in the banana-producing country. Given the nature of the Central American banana industry, most of even that small amount is incurred by U.S.–based multinational corporations, not by domestic growers or businesses. For such reasons, a recent study by the Economic Commission for Latin America (UNCEPAL 1979:116) came to the following conclusion:

> Given this uneven balance of bargaining capacity the benefits derived from the [banana] industry were appropriated mainly by [transnational corporatons]. The linkages with the domestic economy and the tax revenues extracted by the host governments were relatively insignificant.

CONCLUSION:
EXPORT AGRICULTURE AND
COMPARATIVE ADVANTAGE

The history of rural Central America is marked by tension and at times conflict between two different conceptions of the role of the land. The first

sees it as provider and as source of security. Often the human-land relationship takes on religious overtones; in any case, the attachment is invariably
strong. The other view values the land for its commercial possibilities: the tie
is functional. The first conception is obviously that of peasants everywhere,
while the second is characteristic of both rural and urban elites with commercial and/or developmental goals.

Because domestic commercial possibilities were minor following the
Spanish Conquest of Central America, profit-minded colonists not surprisingly turned their attention toward the world market. As theirs was a
conquest society, the structures they created exploited for their enrichment
not only the land but also the indigenous people. This domination and
exploitation of the native population reinforced the bias toward export
agriculture because too few in society benefited sufficiently to promote the
development of stronger domestic markets. After Independence, this rigidly
unequal social structure continued, and along with it the bias toward export
agriculture. While elites placed great hopes on export diversification and
expansion and made efforts toward these goals, basic food production
received little attention and fewer resources. Instead, the land and the labor of
the peasantry continued to be valued by development-oriented elites for their
commercial potential.

The bias toward commercial export agriculture was justified in the
nineteenth century by the spread of liberal ideology, which was in part a
manifestation and defense of the expanding international capitalist economic
system. Adam Smith's "invisible hand" rationalized both the external and the
internal components of that system. Internationally, the doctrine of comparative advantage taught that the mutual wealth of nations would be
maximized by free trade between countries that specialized in the production
of those commodities for which they enjoyed a relative advantage. In the
years between Independence and the Great Depression, this theory was
understood (largely without controversy) to mean that Central America
should concentrate on the development of exportable agricultural products.
The capital accumulated through such trade would in turn promote internal
development that eventually would permit a country to reach the point where
it would become self-sustaining. The invisible hand, then, also worked its
magic at home; while elites were obviously pursuing their own self-interest in
developing export agriculture, the fruits of their efforts would eventually
spread through all of society.

This chapter's brief survey of agrarian transformations in Central America from the Conquest to World War II has demonstrated that the actual
results of the implementation of the agro-export development model during
this period were much less than promised. The dependence of Central American economies and governments on the export earnings of a few agricultural

commodities left them tightly bound to, and therefore vulnerable to, an international economic system over which they had only the most minimal influence. The revenues obtained from the expansion of agricultural exports have been less than desired and expected, and the amount of capital actually employed in promoting further development has also been substantially less than anticipated.

Furthermore, the negative consequences of the great agricultural transformations of the past have been substantial. The expansion of export crop production during the colonial cacao and indigo booms and the coffee boom of the late nineteenth century had a devastating impact on the peasantry it affected. During the first transformation, the land and labor of Indians were expropriated, with death the frequent result. The coffee transformation extended the domination of the agro-elite as more lands were confiscated and coercive labor systems were expanded and tightened. For the affected peasantry, the results were a further loss of land, autonomy, and food supply. In Central America, then, the model might more correctly be termed "the repressive agro-export development model"; it has been most repressive in Guatemala and El Salvador and least so in Costa Rica.

Because bananas are grown in what used to be remote areas, their initial cultivation did not have similar adverse consequences. Once land pressures did develop, however, the banana companies' enormous land holdings (obtained at little or no cost) contributed to a rapidly expanding pool of landless peasants. The foreign companies have made a number of important contributions such as helping to eradicate tropical diseases, developing railroads and ports (those under their control), and building schools and hospitals. But their tremendous size gave them a dominating political position that allowed them to make minimal financial contributions to the Central American countries, especially during the first third of the century, while reaping great profits. Furthermore, the continual involvement of such giant enterprises in domestic affairs served to distort Central American politics and to retard the region's political maturation.

When following World War II development became an even greater imperative in the region, the diversification and expansion of agricultural exports was once again believed by many to be the key to realizing Central America's aspirations.[16] Although the developments of the previous four hundred years were not encouraging, the renewed reliance on export agriculture should not be surprising. A small (though now larger) elite still controlled economies too underdeveloped to stimulate independently their own rapid development. And the same ideological beliefs continued to rationalize the defense of privilege and the pursuit of self-interest as fundamental to the achievement of the greater good.

38 LAND, POWER, AND POVERTY

NOTES

1. For similar but much briefer arguments, see Weeks (1986) and Woodward (1984) on Central America and Grindle (1986:25–46) on Latin America as a whole.

2. Such a change may or may not be sufficiently qualitative to constitute a change in the mode of production. The more general concept of an agrarian transformation is utilized in this study to avoid the problematic and tangential controversies associated with assessing changes in the mode of production in rural societies.

3. Helpful in preparing this section were Fox (1978), Harrison and Turner (1978), Linares (1979), Morley and Brainerd (1983), Orellana (1984), West and Augelli (1976), and Woodward (1976).

4. To facilitate discussion, geographical references will utilize post-Independence national boundaries.

5. Especially useful in preparing this section were MacLeod (1973) and Sherman (1979); Herring (1964), MacLeod and Wasserstrom (1983), Newson (1982, 1985), Orellana (1984), Woodward (1976), and Wortman (1982) were also consulted.

6. This section draws heavily on MacLeod (1973); also useful were Browning (1971), Seligson (1980a), Smith (1956), Woodward (1976), and Wortman (1982).

7. For further information on Costa Rican Indians, see the special issue of *América Indígena* (1974), Hall (1985:32–50), and Saenz Maroto (1970).

8. For Costa Rica, this section drew on Gudmundson (1983) and Seligson (1980a); for El Salvador, on Browning (1971) and Durham (1979); for Nicaragua, on Wheelock Román (1980). More resources are available on Guatemala: see Cambranes (1985), Carmack (1983), Dessaint (1962), Griffith (1965), Jones (1966), McCreery (1976, 1983), Mosk (1955), Naylor (1967), and Whetten (1961). For discussions of the entire region, see Torres Rivas (1971) and Woodward (1976).

9. Although Costa Rican politics are unique in the region, the difference should not be overstated. Of the first forty-four presidents after Independence (through 1982), thirty-three were descendants of three families. Just one of these families (the Vazquez de Coronados) has given the nation eighteen presidents and 230 parliamentary deputies (Dunkerley 1982:8).

10. The best-known positive accounts of the role of the United States banana companies are May and Plaza (1958) and Wilson (1968), while their leading critical counterparts are Bauer Paíz (1956) and Kepner and Soothill (1967). Also useful in preparing this section were Baer (1973), UNCEPAL (1979), Ellis (1983), Karnes (1978), LaBarge (1968), LaFeber (1984), Ross (1975), Seligson (1980a), Strouse (1970), and Woodward (1976).

11. The United Fruit Company was formed in 1899 through the merger of the Boston Fruit Company, several other trading and marketing companies, and Minor Keith's Costa Rican operation. It became United Brands in 1970 after being taken over by the AMK Corporation (a story well told by McCann, 1976). An uncritical but most readable account of its fascinating pioneering days is told by Wilson (1968). A third U.S. agribusiness giant, Del Monte, entered the Central American banana industry in 1968 to avoid a United Fruit takeover effort. United Fruit is legally enjoined in the United States from absorbing competing banana companies.

12. Standard Fruit was built by the Vacarro brothers and was named after them until 1923. Between 1964 and 1968 it was absorbed by Castle & Cooke. A scholarly history of the company is provided by Karnes (1978).

13. As Karnes (1978) notes, "Generally, Nicaragua has played a minor role in the banana industry, but periodically the land is 'rediscovered,' its prospects exaggerated, and its problems and previous failures ignored" (p. 119).

14. The impact of this impermanence still in the 1950s in Honduras was described this way by one observer:

Probably more development would evolve along the route of the railway if people knew that it would remain. There is an overdependence and complacency because of the Fruit Company being around, and there is no incentive to establish roots because it may soon be gone, together with all of its facilities. (Dozier 1958:42)

15. The most favorable judgment is provided by May and Plaza (1958:118–120, 157–158), who claim that United Fruit's dividends for operations in six countries in 1954–55 were only 11.4 percent, not "immoderate by any standards" (p. 120). This study has limited usefulness, however, because of its short time span and omission of relevant data. Its shortcomings become clear when the study is compared to the highly critical evaluation of United Fruit's contribution to the Guatemalan economy during 1950–53 by Bauer Paíz (1956:328–331), minister of labor and economy during that period. The more complete data compiled by Bauer Paíz, though again covering only a short period of time, indicate profits for that period averaging 47.6 percent. A contrasting view of United Fruit's impact on Guatemala for 1946–53 is provided by LaBarge (1960). Using data sets as extensive as those of Bauer Paíz but with a different focus, LaBarge (1960:25) claims that United Fruit's operations added 2.5 percent annually to Guatemala's gross national product during the period examined. The conclusions of these two studies, of course, are not mutually exclusive.

16. The expansion of the internal market through the development of the Central American Common Market to promote industrialization was the important alternative during this period.

CHAPTER 3

The Postwar Transformation of Central American Agriculture

The desire of public and private elites in Central America to find new agricultural exports intensified after World War II. The traditional export commodities of coffee and bananas (and minerals in Nicaragua and Honduras) had enriched some people and had brought sorely needed capital to the region. They had not, however, promoted sufficient development of the region's economies. Each of the countries remained at a low level of economic development, with most of the peasantry living at subsistence level. Furthermore, both of the major export crops had faced years of difficulties. The price of coffee fell with the Great Depression, by 80 percent relative to the price of gold. The important markets of Europe were closed by the war and remained shut for a period after its end. Eventually, prices began to climb, even rapidly, but they peaked by 1954 as overproduction once again plagued the world's coffee producers. Banana cultivation had long been troubled by devastating diseases that often required the abandonment of huge sections of plantations. Furthermore, the banana sector continued to be controlled by the United States fruit companies.

A revolution of rising aspirations hit urban Central America by mid-century. The region's economic growth, even if less than desired, had created a growing middle sector and a limited industrial working class. These groups wanted an improvement in their standard of living, and they hoped it would be dramatic and soon. Accordingly, rapid economic development was an imperative for them. On occasion, middle-sector groups were able to participate directly in the formulation of public policy when popular movements brought progressive governments to power, as happened in Costa Rica and

Guatemala in the 1940s. At other times, such groups were able to influence policy as the social base of dominant political institutions—such as the military in El Salvador and the political parties in Honduras—became more inclusive in the postwar period. As the influence of the middle sectors increased, many elites came to share their commitment to economic development, viewing an expanding economic pie as the solution that would satisfy the rising aspirations of those below them without sacrificing their own material advantages (Anderson 1961).

Once again many people saw the diversification and expansion of agricultural exports as the keys to the region's development, and for essentially the same reasons as in earlier periods. Hopes also were placed on industrialization, but internal markets were too small and underdeveloped to promote sufficient economic development; they remained so even with the development of the Central American Common Market during the 1960s. Furthermore, internally oriented growth strategies collided with the seriously skewed distribution of such key resources as land and with the systems of labor domination that had evolved over the centuries. Strategies based on export agriculture not only avoided these constraints but in addition were congruent with existing socioeconomic structures and their attendant ideologies. The primary constraint on export agriculture had always been external, especially as structures for controlling the internal problems of land and labor were developed during the colonial and coffee transformations. Once international postwar recovery began, the external limitation, too, seemed to vanish with the expansion of foreign markets. Furthermore, new international agencies had been created that came to Central America with advice and financial credits to assist in the quest for economic development. Soon great expanses of land were given over to the production of the new export commodities, cotton, sugar, and beef.[1]

NEW EXPORTS AND THE DRIVE FOR DEVELOPMENT

Honduras has traditionally been the least developed of the Central American countries, largely for geographical reasons. Its mountainous terrain is the region's most difficult to traverse, and its central location has made it a frequent site of conflict between the region's contending forces from the early nineteenth century up through the 1980s. As the least developed of the five countries, Honduras provides a good illustration of the forces at work in the early postwar period. The portrait of these forces then will be given more detail by a brief examination of Nicaragua, which at that time stood ahead of the other countries (with the exception of Costa Rica) on most indicators of socioeconomic development.

Until after the war, the Honduran government had played virtually no role in the nation's economy with the exception of its various dealings with the banana companies, discussed in the previous chapter.[2] Except for the banana enclave, largely isolated from the rest of the country, Honduras was still characterized by a traditional, dualistic agricultural economy: a subsistence peasantry alongside large landholdings utilizing land and labor inefficiently. Indeed, a study mission to the country in the early 1950s characterized the prevailing level of agricultural development as being "as primitive as can be comprehended within the meaning of the term 'agriculture'" (Checchi 1959:52).

At the same time, though, other international study missions were laying the framework for the transformation of Honduran agriculture. Advisors from the International Monetary Fund played an important role in drafting an income tax, which was implemented in 1949, and in the creation of the Central Bank and the National Development Bank in the following year. In 1951, an agricultural extension service was formed under United States auspices and staffed by personnel from both countries. This service in turn stimulated the creation of the agricultural ministry the next year. The income tax provided revenues that could be used for developmental purposes, while the new banks provided the instruments necessary for a direct governmental role in the economy. Construction in the early 1950s of the Pan American Highway through the southern part of the country, along with that of connecting highways to Tegucigalpa in the interior and San Pedro Sula in the northern coastal region, more effectively integrated the country, broadening the internal market and better linking agricultural producers to international markets. At the same time, the government began through the Development Bank to provide credits to encourage the expansion of commercial agricultural production, especially that aimed at the export market. Indeed, Posas and del Cid (1981:87) credit the bank with the creation of an agrarian bourgeoisie in Honduras.

Similar developments occurred in neighboring Nicaragua,[3] where they were earlier, stronger, and closely connected to the personal fortune of the dictator, Anastasio Somoza. As he consolidated his political power from 1934 on, Somoza undertook the completion of the Liberal project in Nicaragua. Through strict autocratic rule, he attempted to modernize the country by promoting economic growth. His efforts were not without self-interest, of course; his family, which in 1934 owned no land, was the largest landowner in the country by the 1950s. Somoza's empire building was equally substantial in the industrial sector. In Nicaragua, unlike Honduras, much of the necessary government infrastructure was in place and therefore ready to take advantage of postwar opportunities. Somoza's agricultural modernization campaign began in 1936. He soon created a ministry of agriculture, an Overseas Trading Company, and a national bank; the last-named became an important source of agricultural credit by 1938. Working through these three institutions, Somoza cooperated with the leading cattlemen and coffee-growers' associations to stimulate agricultural modernization.

The First Round:
Cotton and Sugar

An indication of the change in the Central American agricultural sector during the past few decades is provided by Table 3.1, which gives the percentage change for the area planted in the major export (as well as food) crops between 1948–52 and 1976–78 and between 1948–52 and 1981–83. Two end dates are given because of the many developments in the region since 1979 and because the second set of figures is the less reliable.[4] A few

TABLE 3.1

Agricultural Land Use: Percentage Change in Average Annual Area Devoted to Various Food and Export Crops, 1948–52 to 1981–83[1]

	Costa Rica		El Salvador		Guatemala		Honduras		Nicaragua	
	A	B	A	B	A	B	A	B	A	B
Food Crops										
Beans	−4	26	72	39	111	65	48	48	100	127
Corn	−22	−7	36	46	8	41	53	19	105	76
Rice	204	220	−7	−13	75	25	36	109	14	104
TOTAL FOOD	34	53	35	41	20[2]	42[2]	52	26	92	90
Export Crops										
Bananas	156	156	—	—	264	264	−12	−12	4,100	4,100
Coffee	63	69	31	58	60	59	92	92	57	79
Cotton	600	700	300	152	2,080	1,340	1,400	600	780	34
Sorghum	—	—	36	23	110	84	0	−2	47	32
Sugar	129	143	223	138	419	425	168	323	169	163
TOTAL EXPORT	127	133	71	60	153	133	51	64	219	145
EXPORT as % of FOOD	69	52	27	13	109	65	0	31	66	29

NOTES: 1. Figures are for percentage change in area harvested; A is change from 1948–52 to 1976–78; B is that from 1948–52 to 1981–83. Many of the original data included estimates by either the country or the FAO, especially for 1981–83.

2. Guatemala's total food production also includes wheat.

SOURCE: Calculated from U.N. Food and Agriculture Organization (UNFAO), various years.

explanatory comments are required before this and later tables can be discussed. They include not all crops but only the major ones: beans, corn, and rice as the principal food and bananas, coffee, cotton, sorghum, and sugar as the major exports. Furthermore, the distinction between the two types is not a clean one; all of the export crops are also consumed domestically, especially sugar and in recent years sorghum (which is still primarily fed to livestock, much of which is meant for the export market). Large quantities of corn also are used as animal feed (for example, over one-quarter of domestic supply in Honduras in 1982) and therefore indirectly related to the export market. It should be noted, too, that the lands held by the banana companies are many times greater than the crop sizes reported here would seem to indicate. It has been the companies' traditional (and controversial) practice to hold reserves substantially greater than the land actually planted in bananas or any other crop.

The big increases shown in Table 3.1 for banana cultivation in Costa Rica, Guatemala, and Nicaragua are primarily the result of a resurgence in this crop after the difficult days when plantations were abandoned in the face of spreading disease. Otherwise, the essential pattern is the same in each country: the largest gains are registered by cotton, followed by sugar, regardless of end date. The gains for these two export crops are greater than those for all food crops in every case, with the exception of rice in Costa Rica (a commercial crop there). Consequently, the ratio of land devoted to export crops in comparison to food crops increased. This change has been dramatic, as Table 3.1 shows, especially in Guatemala, Costa Rica, and Nicaragua.

Cotton had received some attention in the nineteenth century as a possible commercial crop, at least in El Salvador, where at midcentury the government offered various financial incentives to potential planters.[5] But conditions were not conducive to its cultivation then nor for the next century. Although the Pacific lowlands of Central America are ideal for cotton growing, diseases introduced at the Conquest, such as malaria and yellow fever, had made them inhospitable to human habitation. Following the decimation of the indigenous people in the sixteenth century, these areas remained sparsely populated up to the mid-twentieth. Their primary importance until then was as a frontier destination for peasants dispossessed of their land elsewhere, for instance by the spread of coffee cultivation on the more temperate mountain slopes. These areas were also the site of large haciendas devoted to low-density cattle ranching.

Technological change was one of the keys to opening up the Pacific lowlands. The development of chemical pesticides and of small airplanes to spray them conveniently over large expanses of territory permitted the management of disease-carrying mosquitoes and of the ravenous enemies of the cotton plant. The construction of highways and feeder roads made the region accessible and facilitated property management by growers who preferred to continue to live in the cities of the interior. Finally, the necessary international markets were available; this was a period of growing demand and rising prices.

Because the Caribbean lowlands are too wet for cotton growing, cultivation spread most rapidly in the three countries with the most extensive lowlands on the Pacific coast: El Salvador, Guatemala, and Nicaragua. Governments eagerly encouraged its expansion, from the progressive administration of Arbenz in Guatemala to the autocratic regime of Somoza in Nicaragua. The result was a cotton boom; between 1950 and 1964 the total area of Central America planted in cotton increased tenfold, especially in Nicaragua, where by the 1960s cotton had become the largest source of rural employment and of foreign exchange earnings.

In later years, though, cotton went through boom-bust cycles driven largely by profit fluctuations. Most cotton is produced on large commercial holdings using modern techniques. Since cotton (unlike coffee or bananas) is an annual crop, its production can be expanded or contracted relatively easily in response to profit possibilities. Many cotton growers have therefore had a more speculative orientation than those found among growers of other export crops. A "get-rich-quick" attitude, especially prevalent during the 1950s and early 1960s, led to an indiscriminate use of pesticides and a lack of attention to soil fertility and conservation. As insect resistance increased and soil fertility declined, input costs climbed because more pesticides and fertilizer were required. Increasing input costs coupled with less attractive cotton prices account for the brake on cotton expansion in the late 1960s, especially in El Salvador (Browning 1971:240–246; Quiros 1973:90–91). Similar forces as well as political factors (to be discussed in Part II), brought cotton production down again in the early 1980s. When commercial farmers have shifted out of cotton production, they have usually turned to corn for urban markets or sugar cane for export. Accordingly, sugar growing has tended to expand most rapidly during the periods when cotton is least attractive, and sugar is now an important crop in each of the five countries.

The expansion of cotton and sugar cultivation did not come at the expense of coffee growing; the amount of land allocated to coffee has continued to increase throughout the contemporary period. One useful way of gauging this increase is to compare the relative fortunes of coffee, still the leading export crop, to corn, by far the most important food crop. The percentage of the increase in land devoted to coffee is greater for both end dates used in Table 3.1 for Costa Rica, Guatemala, and Honduras; and it is greater for the 1948–52 to 1981–83 period for El Salvador and Nicaragua. The greatest expansion of coffee growing came in Honduras, where the amount of land used for it almost doubled. The coffee boom of the late nineteenth century and the earlier decades of this one largely bypassed

Honduras, but following World War II, the development of the coffee sector became a primary concern of that nation's elites. New conditions—political stability, a more adequate transportation system, available credit, and rising world prices—made the materialization of their interest possible. By the late 1960s Honduran coffee earnings were approaching those of Nicaragua, which it surpassed for the first time in 1973.

The major instrument available to governments to promote export development has been the provision of credit, often using capital obtained from international lenders. In some cases laws needed to be changed first; in Nicaragua, for example, reforms in 1941, 1949, and 1952 removed such impediments as a credit ceiling of seventy hectares (Belli 1970:390). As a result, by 1951–52 almost 80 percent of the National Bank lending for agriculture in Nicaragua went to a few hundred producers of cotton, sugar, and sesame (International Bank for Reconstruction and Development [IBRD] 1953:292). More generally, almost two-thirds of total bank loans for agriculture in Nicaragua in 1952 went to coffee and cotton producers; by 1956 cotton growers alone were receiving about the same proportion, as they still were in 1970 (Wheelock Román 1980:204). Similarly in El Salvador, the relevant institutions consistently lent over three-quarters of their credit between 1961 and 1975 to planters of the same two crops (Burke 1976:485).

As previously explained, the National Development Bank in Honduras played a pivotal role in the development of new export crops in that country; in the early 1950s cotton received only 8 percent of the agricultural loans, but a decade later its share had climbed to 48 percent. From 1950 to 1974, the proportion of agricultural credit allocated to cotton and coffee in Honduras varied between 52 and 68 percent (Posas 1979:49).

Cotton has been relatively insignificant in Costa Rica, where the more important new export was beef, as will be discussed below. In the late 1960s the production of coffee and beef received about two-thirds of Costa Rica's total agricultural credits (Kriesberg, Bullard, and Becraft 1970:38). In 1972 the cattle sector in Costa Rica received more credits than the rest of agriculture combined (Barahona Riera 1980:53). The following year it got more than even the industrial sector: 31.4 percent of all national banking system credit went to the expansion of the cattle industry (Guess 1979:44).

Little of the postwar credit in the region went to the smallholder. In El Salvador in the 1970s, for example, large farms received up to 200 percent of the national average of credit per cropped hectare, but the smallest ones received only about 5 percent of that average (Daines 1977:9; also see Adams, Graham, and Von Pischke 1984 and Hatch, Ames, and Davis 1977). Often obtained from international sources such as the United States, agricultural credit has played a leading role in facilitating the concentration of land in the postwar era.

Raising Cattle for Exports[6]

Cattle grazing had been traditional on the underutilized lands of the larger estates of Central America since the early colonial period. Demand for meat was weak, however, because the domestic market was limited in such poor countries. Whether for domestic or minor export trade, cattle were usually sold live by the head rather than by weight. This practice, of course, minimized incentives for improvements in herd quality. Expanding domestic and especially international beef markets have changed the cattle business in Central America during the last few decades into a major commercial operation. Pastures and herds have been expanded and practices modernized. The most important stimulus has been the growth in the United States of demand for "industrial quality" beef. Because Central American cattle are grass fed, their meat is not up to North American "steak" standards, but their meat is most suitable for the fast-food market that has grown rapidly in the United States since the 1950s. The U.S. imported almost no beef in 1960; by 1980 nearly 10 percent of the beef consumed was imported. Although only about one-eighth of this amount comes from Central America (the major suppliers are Australia and New Zealand), this trade has nevertheless become one of the more important earners of foreign exchange for the region.

The development of the Central American cattle industry has received substantial assistance from international actors. One study, for example, estimates that over half of the loans made to the region during the 1960s and 1970s by the World Bank and the Inter-American Development Bank for agriculture and rural development promoted the production of beef for export (Keene 1980:2). More specifically, between 1974 and 1978 World Bank loans included $55.6 million to Costa Rica, $40.6 million to Honduras, and $24.3 million to Nicaragua for livestock development programs; Inter-American Development Bank livestock lending between 1961 and 1977 included $16.8 million for Costa Rica, $4.4 million for Guatemala, $36.9 million for Honduras, and $9.1 for Nicaragua (Shane 1980:36–37, 41–42). Substantial loans from the United States also played a major role by facilitating herd expansion and improvement, building packing plants for the export trade, and so on. Private foreign capital has been involved as well; many of the region's packing plants that are licensed for export are controlled by foreign (not all U.S.) capital. In Honduras, for instance, foreign interests control the two largest plants, which do about three-quarters of the exporting. According to a Honduran scholar of the industry, it was this foreign influence that initiated the beef export industry in his country (Slutzky 1979:166–169).

The development of this trade is portrayed in Table 3.2 as a percentage of total domestic production at five points between 1961 and 1981. As can be seen, during the 1960s the percentage of the region's beef production that was exported more than doubled, from 15 to over 30 percent. In Costa Rica and Honduras it even reached half of all production at times. Even though the figures fluctuate over time and between countries, a common pattern is apparent when El Salvador (where beef exports have been relatively unimportant), is excluded. Exports grow even more rapidly than production at first, and therefore the percentage of beef exported rises as well. Then exports plateau but production continues to increase, so exports' percentage share declines. Nicaragua hit this plateau first, by the early 1970s, followed by Costa Rica and Guatemala later in the decade. In 1981, Honduras had yet to reach this plateau, but it presumably would in the near future.

Clearly, the last few years have not been trouble-free ones for the beef export industry. The United States market has not continued to expand as rapidly as has the Central American export potential. Indeed, U.S. imports peaked in 1979 as beef consumption declined from ninety-two pounds per person in 1977 to an estimated seventy-seven pounds in 1985 (*World Development Forum* 1985:2). Access to the U.S. market is governed by a

TABLE 3.2
Beef Exports: Annual Averages, Selected Periods, 1961–65 to 1980–81

Country	1961–65	1969–71	1972–74	1976–78	1980–81
Costa Rica					
Exports[1]	6.2	17.6	24	33.6	32.2
Exports: Prod.[2]	18	39	44	50	40
El Salvador					
Exports[1]	—	—	.8	5	1.1
Exports: Prod.[2]	—	—	3	17	4
Guatemala					
Exports[1]	.8	14.7	16.6	17.7	17.8
Exports: Prod.[2]	2	28	28	27	21
Honduras					
Exports[1]	4	12.9	16.8	20.3	26.2
Exports: Prod.[2]	16	39	43	41	51
Nicaragua					
Exports[1]	10.8	23.2	23.8	24	23.2
Exports: Prod.[2]	30	39	43	26	25
Central America					
Exports[1]					
Exports: Prod.[2]	15	32	35	33	30

NOTES: 1. Average annual export of bovine meat in metric tons.
2. Exports as a percentage of domestic production.
SOURCES: Calculated from UNFAO, various years; UN, various years.

system of voluntary export restraints that set each country's share of the U.S. market below its export capacity. On a number of occasions since the late 1970s, a country has exceeded its U.S. export quota but found domestic demand at prevailing prices unable to absorb the excess (this has been especially true of Honduras).[7] An additional problem has been pesticide contamination, usually the result of promiscuous spraying by cotton planters. In order to export to the United States, a processing plant must pass periodic inspections. With substantial frequency during the late 1970s and early 1980s, inspectors found pesticide contamination at plants whose permission to export to the United States they then temporarily suspended. Such suspensions have been a particularly serious problem in El Salvador and Guatemala; in the latter, 1980 exports fell almost one-third from the previous year's as a result of pesticide contamination.

Central American officials have attempted to get their quotas increased, but the quota system was established by the U.S. Congress largely in response to the considerable pressures of the U.S. cattle industry, which wanted to restrict access in order to protect prices (Shane 1980:101–104). Because relatively low beef prices have prevailed in recent years, any significant increase in quotas is unlikely unless the market situation changes. As a result of these difficulties, Central American exporters have been looking for alternative markets, with partial success. For example, Guatemala signed an agreement with Mexico in 1980 by which up to 45 percent of its 1981 exports were expected to go to that country, and Venezuela purchased some of Costa Rica's and Nicaragua's beef production in the late 1970s after their annual U.S. quota was filled.

Nontraditional Agricultural Exports Today[8]

A team of agricultural experts counseled the Guatemalan government in 1970 that "the fairly bleak prospects which coffee and cotton are facing on the world demand side make it unlikely that the crops can continue to be the dynamic and propulsive forces in the growth of the overall economy" (Fletcher et al. 1970:49; also see Organization of American States [OAS] 1974:90–91). Their advice was correct and applied not only to these two crops but to bananas, sugar, and meat as well. The region's ability to produce its export crops was far greater than the world market's ability to absorb that production. Furthermore, at the end of the 1970s the real world price for each of these commodities (with the qualified exception of coffee) was below the 1970–74 average; except for sugar, the 1979 real price was also below annual averages for 1965–69 (Kessing 1981:32). Coffee's higher price was due to a frost limiting Brazil's huge exports and therefore was only temporary. Export diversification, then, continues to be a major concern of Central Americans and of international advisors and lenders. The search for new, or "nontraditional," exports includes industrial goods as well as agricultural products, but only the latter are relevant to this study.

Most attention has been given to the cultivation of fruits and vegetables to be sold in the United States, either fresh (during the winter season) or frozen. Efforts have been undertaken by private individuals both on their own initiative and with governmental encouragement. The task has been more difficult than often anticipated, and many efforts have resulted in failure (Belli 1977; Goldberg and Wilson 1974). As Table 3.3 indicates, the greatest successes have occurred in Guatemala, followed by Honduras and then Costa Rica. During the 1970s in Guatemala, the value of the new commodities (largely vegetables) increased over sixfold, and their share of total export earnings increased from 2 to 3.2 percent. While their value also rose substantially in Honduras (where the new crops were largely fruits), their share of total export earnings was 3 percent at both the beginning and the end of the decade. In Costa Rica, by contrast, these new agricultural exports doubled their share of total exports during the decade, though both their total value and their share (1.4 percent) are still substantially below those of the other two countries.

The development and expansion of nontraditional agricultural exports has received considerable assistance from the United States, especially in Guatemala and Honduras. In the late 1960s, according to one account, the U.S. Agency for International Development (AID) encouraged the government of Guatemala to establish an export promotion center and to

TABLE 3.3
Export of Nontraditional Fruits and Vegetables 1970–71 to 1980–81[1]

| | 1980–81 | | Percentage Change to 1980–81 | | | |
| | Total | as % of | From 1970–71 | | From 1974–75 | |
Country	Value	All Exp.	Value	Weight	Value	Weight
Costa Rica	14.0	1.4	775	—	226	—
El Salvador	5.6	0.9	—	—	81[2]	—
Guatemala	42.0	3.2	624	275	527	236
Honduras	22.8	3.0	330	80	269	67
Nicaragua	2.5	0.6	150	−2	56	−3

NOTES: 1. Excludes bananas and plaintains, except for El Salvador. Value in hundreds of thousands of U.S. dollars.
2. From 1976 to 77.
SOURCE: Calculated from UNFAO, various years.

adopt legislation that would provide incentives to attract foreign investors to export industries (North American Congress on Latin America [NACLA] 1974:11–15). An AID loan of $8.5 million made in 1970 was intended to encourage the expansion of seven new commercial crops (vegetables, fruits, and flowers) aimed at regional and international markets (United States Agency for International Development [USAID] 1970). In recent years, a frequent pattern has been for these crops to be grown by small to medium-sized landholders producing under contract to U.S.–based multinational agribusiness companies.

Probably the best known effort in Guatemala is Alimentos Congelados Monte Bello, S.A. (ALCOSA), now a subsidiary of Hanover Brands. ALCOSA was developed with considerable financial assistance from the Latin American Agribusiness Development Corporation (LAAD), which in turn received USAID loans in the 1970s of at least $17 million. LAAD is a private company organized in 1970 to finance and develop agribusiness projects in Latin America and the Caribbean; its shareholders have included Bank of America; Cargill; Castle & Cooke; and Chase Manhattan Bank. Some of its early projects were criticized for promoting upper-status dom-estic consumption or export expansion instead of the interests of the "small man" (Lappé and Collins 1978:423–424). In contrast, ALCOSA was designed to fulfill later AID guidelines to benefit the rural poor. By 1979 it had purchased 11 million pounds of cauliflower, broccoli, brussels sprouts, snow peas, and okra from two thousand farmers, 95 percent of them "very small," for export to the United States (Kusterer, Estrada de Batres, and Xuyá Cuxil 1981:6).

The AID–sponsored evaluations of ALCOSA have been used by critics of multinational agribusiness as supporting evidence for their viewpoint (Lappé and Collins 1978:425–426; Kinley 1982:17–19); however, it should be noted that the most complete evaluation (Kusterer, Estrada de Batres, and Xuyá Cuxil 1981) found that the ALCOSA projects had a number of bene-ficial results, economic, psychological, and social. It is clear that peasants welcomed the new marketing opportunities and that peasant women bene-fited from the employment opportunities at the processing plant (Kusterer, Estrada de Batres, and Xuyá Cuxil 1981: 2–11). But though ALCOSA clearly responded to very real needs, there were significant costs as well. Contracting peasants became dependent on the company for increasingly expensive seeds and fertilizer and for credit. As production increased, so did the company's quality standards. Finally in 1980, supply overwhelmed the company's pro-cessing capacity, so it temporarily suspended purchases, reneging on many contracts. Some three to four hundred of the two thousand contracting peasants took losses for the year, including a majority in two of the four towns studied. They were left with an abundance of cauliflower in place of the corn and beans they had previously planted (Kusterer, Estrada de Batres, and Xuyá Cuxil 1981:17–24).

The development of programs that were intended to benefit the poor directly was characteristic of the "new directions" of the middle to late 1970s. More typical of U.S. policy during the Reagan administration in the 1980s was the expansion of agricultural exports through private enterprise. Early in Reagan's tenure, spokespeople referred to "major policy changes" that "are needed to stimulate agricultural and industrial production, especially for export" (United States, House 1981b:155). This approach was taken up particularly by AID, which began a "private-sector initiative" and created a new Bureau for Private Enterprise.[9]

Honduras probably received the most attention from the United States in this regard during the early 1980s. Previous efforts by the Honduran government to promote exports were characterized by AID as "sporadic and relatively unsuccessful" because, the organization claimed, the Honduran "government has not tried particularly hard to push for increased exports or to attract investors for export operations" (USAID 1984:7). Through "policy dialogue" between the two governments and through AID assistance, the Honduran government in 1983 passed the Export Incentives Law, one mani-festation of its becoming "more committed to altering its policies to favor exports" (USAID 1984:9). In the following year the United States initiated a three-year, $7-million Export Promotion and Services project, similarly aimed at boosting nontraditional, including agricultural, exports by "Honduran entrepreneurs." Intended to provide both technical assistance and foreign exchange, the project is characterized as "a massive technology transfer" utilizing "the accumulated experience of highly experienced trade executives" from the United States (USAID 1984:42). The cost is budgeted at about one hundred thousand dollars per year per advisor. In 1984, AID also established a Honduran Agricultural Research Foundation. Planned to run for eight years at a cost of $20 million, this project will provide applied research activities for both export and food crops (USAID 1985:115, 122–123). Similar kinds of programs have been put in effect and/or proposed in Costa Rica and Guatemala (USAID 1985:44–45, 96, 103).

A prominent role in the expansion of nontraditional agricultural exports in Honduras has been played by the collective farms created by the agrarian reform of the 1960s and 1970s (to be further discussed in chapter 6). Favored by international lenders, including the United States, the World Bank, and the Inter-American Development Bank, these settlements have been valued by Honduran officials for their commercial potential as well as for their ability to attract foreign loans. Government officials have encouraged the cultivation of commercial crops, especially those with export promise (melons have been a favorite). At times, though, encouragement has become coercion; Boyer

(1982:192–194) cites the example of a reform settlement that was refused credits when it attempted to return to basic grain production after growing cotton and melons.

In almost all cases, the Honduran reform projects sell their produce to commercial enterprises, which process and export them. Often these are well-established multinational firms such as Castle & Cooke, United Brands, and more recently, Mitsubishi.[10] Honduran scholars (Posas 1979:70–71, 106–107; Slutzky 1979:39–40) have pointed out how propitious this arrangement has been for the multinationals. The corporations have been threatened by increasing labor militancy since the early 1950s and by land expropriations since the early 1970s. At least in part for these reasons, they have been switching from direct production on their own lands to contract buying from domestic producers. Now themselves freed from the risks of labor conflict and bad weather, agribusinesses have been provided by the reform settlements with a guaranteed source of supply, backed by the Honduran government and partially financed by international donors.

Export Expansion and
Land Use Patterns

The increasing allocation of agricultural land to the production of export crops at the expense of food crops has been reported for each of the Central American countries but not studied systematically for the region as a whole. The following two tables provide regionwide data. The amount of land given over to the basic food crops has increased steadily across the three decades studied, as Table 3.4 indicates, but this increase has not been as rapid as that registered by the major exports. El Salvador already had more land in exports than in foods by the period 1948–52, one measure of the substantial impact of the agrarian transformation associated with the coffee boom. This threshold was crossed in Nicaragua by the early 1960s and in Costa Rica by the early 1970s.

Another view of these trends is provided by Table 3.5, which gives percentage changes in the ratio between the two types of land use for the first two and last two periods studied. An example may be useful to clarify what is measured here: the 69 percent for Costa Rica in the first column represents an increase by that percentage in the share of land devoted to export crops relative to that allocated to food crops from 1948–52 to 1976–78. This figure represents an increase in food crop land of 34 percent and in export crop land of 127 percent.

For 1948–52, Table 3.5 indicates, the trends are essentially the same for

TABLE 3.4
Agricultural Land Use: Area Devoted to Food and Export Crops, 1948–52 to 1981–83[1]

Country	1948–52	1961–65	1971–73	1976–78	1981–83
Costa Rica					
Food	110	161	116	147	168
Export	89	139	182	202	207
Export: Food	81	86	157	137	123
El Salvador					
Food	233	214	258	314	328
Export	242	355	386	413	388
Export: Food	104	166	150	132	118
Guatemala					
Food	644	786	881	774	912
Export	219	429	515	553	510
Export: Food	34	55	58	71	56
Honduras					
Food	344	357	382	523	433
Export	200	207	246	302	327
Export: Food	58	58	64	58	76
Nicaragua					
Food	166	249	323	319	315
Export	128	307	326	408	313
Export: Food	77	123	101	128	99
Central America					
Food	1497	1767	1960	2077	2156
Export	878	1437	1655	1878	1745
Export: Food	59	81	84	90	81

NOTE: 1. Area harvested in thousands of hectares. Many of the original data included estimates by either UNFAO or country, especially for 1981–83. Food crops are beans, corn, and rice (and wheat in Guatemala); export crops are bananas, coffee, cotton, sorghum, and sugar.
SOURCE: Calculated from UNFAO, various years.

all of the countries with the exception of Honduras. The relative share of land given over to export crops expanded substantially to 1976–78 but by a lesser degree to 1981–83. The most dramatic shift for both end dates was in Guatemala, with a 109 percent increase in the first period and 65 percent increase in the second. The shift in Guatemalan land use represents a 153 percent expansion in export crop land to 1976–78 but only a 20 percent gain in food crop land. Similarly in Nicaragua, though food crop land increased by 92 percent, export crop land rose by an amazing 219 percent, for a relative shift of 66 percent. In El Salvador during the same period, the changes were less sharp; food crop land grew 35 percent while export crop land went up 71 percent, a relative shift of 27 percent.

The timing of this shift in land use varies among the countries, a fact that

TABLE 3.5
*Change in the Allocation of Land to Export Crops
Relative to Food Crops, 1948–52 to 1981–83*[1]

Country	From 1948–52 to 1976–78	1981–83	From 1961–65 to 1976–78	1981–83
Costa Rica	69	52	80	43
El Salvador	27	13	–20	–29
Guatemala	109	65	29	2
Honduras	0	31	0	31
Nicaragua	66	29	4	–20
Central America	53	37	11	0

NOTE: 1. Figures are for the percentage change in the ratio of
agricultural land devoted to the harvest of export crops (bananas,
coffee, cotton, sorghum, sugar) relative to that of food crops (beans,
corn, and rice; and wheat in Guatemala).
SOURCE: Calculated from Table 3.4.

becomes clear with a comparison of the two starting periods in Table 3.5
and with a look back to Table 3.4. The relative increase in the proportion
of land allocated to export crops ended first in El Salvador; accordingly,
the ratios for comparisons with the 1961–65 beginning period there are
negative. These ratios are also minimal or negative for Nicaragua, where
the proportion of export crop land declined from the mid-1960s to the
early 1970s but then increased through 1976–79, bringing the figure just
past that of the early 1960s. Similarly, the shift of land to export crops
relative to food crops peaked in Costa Rica in the early 1970s and in
Guatemala late in the same decade. This evidence suggests that constraints
on the rapid rise in land devoted to export crops may now have been
reached in Central America (with the possible exception of Honduras), at
least temporarily.

These constraints have been most substantial in Nicaragua, Guatemala,
and El Salvador; in each country, the amount of export crop land actually
declined from 1976–78 to 1981–83 (by 23, 8, and 6 percent, respectively); in
Costa Rica export crop land rose slightly (2 percent), but less than food crop
land. Critical factors in explaining this reversal in the trend in land use
patterns include the armed conflicts that expanded in the first three countries
between these two periods and the subsequent changes in agrarian policy in
Nicaragua and El Salvador. The relationship between political constraints
and land use patterns also runs in the opposite direction, however. As will be
shown in Part II, the postwar agrarian transformation was a primary cause of
the armed conflicts and therefore of the subsequent policy changes. That is to
say, the transformation associated with the expansion of export agriculture
generated new forces that have acted to constrain its further expansion.

Clearly, international constraints were at work as well. Market limits were reached in the 1970s for all of Central America's major agricultural exports; the future seemed to promise at best only slowly growing international markets and uncertain prices. Cotton illustrates the point well. Because it is the most speculative of the commercial crops, the amount of land planted in cotton has fluctuated widely over the years. The fundamental determinant of this pattern, of course, has been the perception of probable profits. In 1981–83, for example, unadjusted cotton prices were no better than they had been in 1979 (IDB, 1984:464); but real 1979 prices were only three-quarters of what they had been in 1970–74 (Kessing 1981:32). By contrast, the costs of the imported inputs necessary for mechanized cotton growing continued to rise relentlessly (United States, Department of Agriculture Foreign Agricultural Services [USDA] 1981:2). Furthermore, land that could easily be converted to the new export crops already had been converted by the 1970s; this undoubtedly is a primary reason why Table 3.4 shows only a minor difference in the amount of export crop land between 1971–73 and 1981–83. With world prices higher, less productive or more remote land probably would have been converted to export production as well, but such incentives have been lacking in recent years.

In light of the above discussion, the exception of Honduras to these patterns can be shown to be only apparent. The latest developing country in the region, Honduras did not initiate its coffee boom until over half a century after the rest. The postwar transformation was similarly slow in coming to Honduras. While export crop land increased between 1948–52 and 1961–65 in Nicaragua by 139 percent and in Guatemala by 96 percent, the increase in Honduras was under 4 percent. Furthermore, peasants in Honduras were better able to defend their interests once export expansion began, at least for a time, for reasons that will be explored in chapter 6. Although export crop land increased from the early 1960s to the mid-1970s, the ratio of export to food crop land therefore remained stable. It is not until the latest period (and after the passing of the apex of peasant power) that the allocation of land to export crop production relative to food crop production registered the kind of increase typical of the other countries in the years before.

In summary, the rapid conversion of land to export crop production is a dynamic that has occurred consistently throughout the region, often surpassing the growth in land allocated to basic food crop production. Eventually, however, this pattern of changing land usage almost reversed because of combined political and economic constraints. El Salvador and Nicaragua were the first to manifest both trends, followed by Costa Rica and then Guatemala. Honduras was later than the rest in developing the pattern, and in fact the first stage apparently has yet to run its course in that country.

CENTRAL AMERICA AND THE
INTERNATIONALIZATION OF AGRICULTURE

The postwar expansion of Central American export agriculture is the latest in a sequence of stages that have reinforced the region's linkage to the international economic system. Trade in agricultural commodities was part of pre-Conquest economic life. Spanish colonialism internationalized this trade, carrying it beyond Middle America to the Iberian peninsula and eventually to other parts of Europe. The development of the coffee and banana trades in the nineteenth and early twentieth centuries further tied Central America to the international system. Although this linkage was crucial to the interests of economic elites and governments, most of the region's people worked apart from this international connection, in subsistence agriculture. (Nevertheless, as chapter 2 described, the lives of previous generations had been substantially affected by the original transformations).

The postwar expansion of agricultural exports furthered the region's integration into the international system as a larger share of the population became more dependent on the success of agricultural exports and/or the availability of agricultural imports, from wheat to fertilizer. With the increase in cotton, sugar, and beef exports and the further expansion of coffee cultivation, a substantial segment of the population is now dependent on the response of foreign markets. This dependency is not limited to commercial farmers and their employees; peasants in Honduran agrarian reform settlements and on their individual plots in the Guatemalan highlands now produce fruits and vegetables that are consumed in the United States. Meanwhile, increasing numbers of farmers, small as well as large, make at least some use of imported fertilizer, seeds, or expertise.

Concurrent with the increasing ratio devoted to export production has been the growing reliance on food imports, consumed largely in urban areas. Their availability also affects price levels of farm goods. Central America's integration into the emerging world food system has been furthered by the foreign-based multinational corporations that are often involved in the importation of agricultural inputs and commodities and in the processing and marketing of agricultural production. The internationalization of Central American agriculture, then, includes not only the expanded scope of the international connection (the relative share of land, workers, and consumers involved), but also the region's penetration by international actors, from development agency advisors to multinational agribusiness.

From the perspective of traditional notions of comparative advantage, the internationalization of Central American agriculture is regarded as a positive development. Through the production and export of certain commodities of which it enjoys a comparative advantage over other countries,

Central America is able to maximize its trading potential and, accordingly, promote its economic development.[11] Increasing export earnings can mean more funds for investment—both private investment of profits and public investment of monies from taxes on exports and income. Finally, a growing export sector can foster the development of new businesses through backward linkages (producers of goods and services consumed in production) and forward linkages (processing and marketing of the export crops). As a result, expanding export production also can provide more employment and income for rural workers.

The doctrine of comparative advantage has long had its dissenters, especially in Latin America. Their arguments tend to focus on two issues brought to the fore particularly by the Argentine economist Raúl Prebisch and other scholars associated with the Economic Commission for Latin America of the United Nations. This position claims, first, that the prices received by Central America for its agricultural exports have declined relative to the cost of the manufactured goods it imports from its industrialized trading partners. There is much evidence to support this claim for Central America (as reported in this chapter), but its more general application is still the subject of substantial controversy.[12] The second claim of this position is easier to demonstrate. The prices of primary commodities are very unstable, and as they rise and fall dramatically, so too do export earnings. Such instability is especially traumatic for countries, such as those of Central America, that are dependent on the export of only a few primary commodities. Great price instability hinders rational economic planning by both private individuals and governments, and substantial economic (and therefore social and political) havoc can be created when prices fall. It is not surprising, then, that export diversification has been a major goal in Central America.

CENTRAL AMERICAN EXPORT EXPANSION: AN ASSESSMENT

Some of the positive results of the regionwide effort at export diversification and expansion can be seen in the following tables. An indication of the importance of coffee is provided by part A of Table 3.6. On the eve of World War I, coffee constituted at least 80 percent of the exports of El Salvador and Guatemala and almost two-thirds of those of Nicaragua. Coffee had comprised 88 percent of Costa Rica's exports as recently as 1892 (Cardoso 1977:189), but the 1914 figure demonstrates the considerable impact on that nation of the banana trade. The continuing need to diminish reliance on coffee exports is shown by the figures for 1937; just prior to World War II, coffee still constituted 91 percent of El Salvador's exports, 66 percent of Guatemala's, 53 percent of Costa Rica's, and 44 percent of Nicaragua's. As can be seen from part B of the table, by the late 1970s the dependence on coffee had been cut about in half in each country with the exception of Honduras. The declining importance of bananas, traditionally the other primary export, is also indicated in part B. The starting point of these data, the early 1960s, is too recent to portray the corresponding increase in the importance of cotton and instead part B shows the trend after its peak. However, the table generally does register the growing importance of beef

TABLE 3.6
Structure of Exports

A. Coffee Exports as a Percentage of Total Exports

Year	Costa Rica	El Salvador	Guatemala	Honduras	Nicaragua
1914	35	80	85	—	63
1930	59	88	—	—	45
1937	53	91	66	—	44
1954	41	88	71	26	46
1958	55	73	72	15	38
1966	39	48	44	14	17
1971	26	41	35	13	16
1977[1]	31	53	39	28	25
1982	27	58	31	24	30

NOTE: 1. Annual average for 1975–79.
SOURCES: 1914: Woodward 1976:160; 1930, 1937: International Institute of Agriculture 1947; 1954, 1958: Herring 1964:825; 1966, 1971: Payer 1975:156–157; 1977, 1982: IDB 1980–81:447; 1984:465.

B. Share of the Five Major Exports of Total Exports, 1960–64 and 1975–79

Product	Costa Rica		El Salvador		Guatemala		Honduras		Nicaragua	
	A	B	A	B	A	B	A	B	A	B
Bananas	26	24	—	—	8	2	45	24	1	1
Beef	4	6	—	1	2	2	3	6	6	10
Coffee	49	29	57	47	58	30	16	28	24	25
Cotton	—	1	20	10	13	12	2	2	33	24
Sugar	4	5	2	3	3	10	—	1	5	6
Total	83	63	79	64	84	56	66	61	69	66

A = 1960–64.
B = 1975–79.
SOURCE: Condensed from Weeks 1985:76–77.

and sugar exports. Finally, this evidence indicates that Guatemala, Costa Rica, and El Salvador have had success in reducing their overall dependence on the export of the five leading agricultural commodities, unlike the other two countries. It must be noted, though, that Honduras and Nicaragua were less dependent on the five in the first place.

Placing these trends in a larger context, Table 3.7 provides indicators of economic, agricultural, and export growth for the two decades following 1960. This evidence shows successful expansion of the gross national product and of value added by agriculture for each of the countries. The increase is less impressive when it is remembered that population growth rates for the region are quite high, ranging from 3 to 3.5 percent annually during this period. The growth in exports was even more substantial, particularly in Costa Rica (8.2 percent annual average), Honduras (7.6 percent), and Nicaragua (7.1 percent). But export expansion in the 1970s was not as successful as it had been in the previous decade: all of the countries registered a decline in their annual average of export growth for the 1970s compared to the previous decade, especially Guatemala which dropped from an 8.1 percent rate to 3 percent (Weeks 1985:67).

The expansion of exports was in any case something of a mixed blessing; as Table 3.7 indicates, exports as a percentage of gross domestic product (GDP) increased markedly in each country during the sixties and seventies. This trend is at odds with the experience of Latin America as a whole (which had a 13 percent decline), and Weeks (1985:51–52) takes it to be an indication of the continuing underdevelopment of Central America. The evidence suggests that the agro-export development model has increased the region's

TABLE 3.7
Economic and Export Growth, 1960 to 1979

Country	GNP[1]	Agriculture[1]	Exports[1]	Exports: GDP[2]
Costa Rica	6.3	2.8	8.2	87
El Salvador	5.9	3.5	6.0	25
Guatemala	5.6	4.6	5.6	43
Honduras	5.5	4.0	7.6	48
Nicaragua	6.3	5.3	7.1	40
Central America	6.2[3]	4.2[3]	6.7	44

NOTES: 1. Average annual percentage increase; for agriculture, figure is growth rate of value added.
2. Percentage increase for export earnings as a share of gross domestic product from 1960 to 1980, except for Nicaragua and Central America, which are to 1975, and El Salvador, which is to 1979 (Source: IDB 1981).
3. To 1978 for GNP, 1977 for agriculture.
SOURCE: Condensed from Weeks 1985:52, 62, 64, 67.

dependence on its exports—and therefore its vulnerability to the international economic system—more than it has promoted the growth of the internal economy. The greatest increase in vulnerability occurred in Costa Rica, which also has the highest ratio of exports to GDP, 37.8 percent. It is followed by Nicaragua,where the ratio had increased to 33.7 percent by 1975. In 1980 the comparable figures for Honduras and Guatemala were 30.1 and 20.9 percent respectively, while El Salvador stood at 25.5 percent the year before. By comparison, for all of Latin America and the Caribbean, the average ratio of exports to GDP declined from 13.4 percent in 1960 to 11.6 percent in 1980 (Weeks 1985:52).

An example of some of the tradeoffs that have occurred is provided by the cattle industry in Costa Rica. The expansion of beef exports has been a major developmental objective in that nation since the 1950s; accordingly, a substantial share of agricultural credits has gone to stimulate its growth, as documented earlier in this chapter. Yet in the 1970s, the amount of credit the cattle industry received from the national banking system was more than the amount earned by beef exports (which accounted for close to one-half of beef production). In certain years in both the early and late 1970s, the credits received were about three times the amount earned by beef exports (Place 1981:69).

Over recent decades Costa Rica and its neighbors have received sizable loans from international agencies to promote the expansion of exports, as well as for other developmental objectives. The growth of the Central American economies, however, has not been proportional to the foreign debts that have been incurred, as Table 3.8 clearly demonstrates. According to the evidence in part A, the foreign debt has increased at a more rapid rate than have exports since at least 1960. Nicaragua entered the 1970s with its foreign debt larger than its annual export earnings; by the later part of the decade both Costa Rica and Honduras crossed this threshold, joined in the early 1980s by El Salvador and Guatemala.

The relationship between foreign debt and export earnings had deteriorated sharply; in the quarter-century since 1960, the change in Nicaragua was by a factor of fifteen, in Honduras and El Salvador by nine, in Costa Rica by eight, and in Guatemala by four. Most ot this deterioration has occurred in the last few years, as can be seen in part B of the table. In just six years the foreign debt increased by about 160 percent in each country except Nicaragua, where the growth was 258 percent. At the same time, export earnings dropped in the conflict-torn nations of El Salvador and Nicaragua and grew only minimally for the rest during these years of recession and declining terms of trade. The consequences are shown in the table's third column: the foreign debt–exports earnings relationship rose dramatically in all the countries, catastrophically in Nicaragua. As a result of this trend, just the service

TABLE 3.8
Indicators of External Public Debt Burden

A. External Public Debt Outstanding as Percentage
of Export Earnings, 1960–84

Country	1960	1970	1978	1980	1982	1984[1]
Costa Rica	64	98	187	253	412	430
El Salvador	28	55	76	87	213	239
Guatemala	44	61	88	69	140	176
Honduras	37	80	155	203	328	336
Nicaragua	73	124	181	474	826	1084

B. Percentage Changes in Debt Burden Indicators, 1978–84

Country	Debt	Exports Value	Debt: Exports	Service Payments: Exports
Costa Rica	154	11	130	43
El Salvador	169	–11	214	467
Guatemala	167	33	100	405
Honduras	158	19	117	97
Nicaragua	258	–40	499	71

NOTE: 1. End date is annual average for 1982–84.
SOURCES: Calculated from IDB 1982, 1986. Data on 1960 and
1970 exports from UN 1985.

payments made on the foreign debt can consume much of any year's export earnings. A meaningful comparison between countries and across years is difficult, though, because of the possibility of negotiating payment postponements. Nonetheless, as the last column of part B indicates, annual service payments as a percentage of export earnings have risen substantially throughout the region.

The Central American countries, then, are now locked into a situation where a high and increasing percentage of their export earnings must be used to pay their foreign debts. As a result, a new imperative for export expansion has been created: exports must be expanded to pay foreign creditors. Ironically, as the example of Costa Rican cattle suggests, at least some of that debt was created by loans used to stimulate earlier rounds of export expansion— an expansion that has not always paid its own way. The final irony is that the guidelines governing loans from the United States insured that they did benefit U.S. interests, which provided the goods and services purchased by the loans (see, for example, Dosal 1985).

CONCLUSION

Many features of the postwar agrarian transformation in Central America are well summarized by two terms: *commercialization* and *internationalization*. The traditional dualistic system of subsistence peasantry and inefficient haciendas (joined more recently by banana plantations) has been replaced by a highly differentiated agrarian structure in which even the most remote peasants are touched by the monetarized commercial system. This transformation has been promoted by new commercial opportunities both in growing urban areas and overseas. Export markets have been especially important to development-minded elites, who have continued into the present era to seek their objectives through the expansion of agricultural trade. One result has been the further linkage of Central America to the international system. The developmental objective has been elusive, however. While individuals have prospered, the region's dependence on exports has increased. Furthermore, a new imperative for trade expansion has been created; as foreign debts have climbed, so too must exports, just to stay even.

This assessment of the agro-export development model in Central America is still incomplete, however, because its impact on rural society has yet to be examined. The historical overview of the previous chapter and the work of other scholars suggest that the implementation of the model in societies such as those of Central America will undermine the economic security of much of the rural population. The claim to be examined is that many people's access to land, food, and employment will have been reduced by the implementation of this model, and that the creation of necessary alternatives for a rapidly growing population will have been inhibited. The purpose of the following chapter is to evaluate the postwar experience with rapid agricultural export expansion in the perspective of this hypothesis.

NOTES

1. For a detailed discussion of the development of the cotton and beef industries in Central America, see Williams (1986), which was not published until this work was largely completed. Readers of that fine study will find that our efforts are complimentary, with little duplication beyond this chapter. Among the case studies of individual countries that parallel at least parts of this chapter, see Grindle (1986) for Brazil, Colombia, and Mexico; Galli (1981) for Colombia; Caballero (1984) for Peru; and Feder (1981) and Sanderson (1986) for Mexico.

2. Background on Honduras during this period may be found in Blutstein et al. (1971), Checchi (1959), Posas (1979), and Posas and del Cid (1981).

3. For background on Nicaragua during this period see OAS (1966), Deere and Marchette (1981), IBRD (1953), Laird (1974), Lethander (1968), and Núñez Solo (1981).

4. Of course, it must be remembered that almost all the figures provided in this book

should be regarded as approximate, given the difficulties of collecting reliable data in poor countries, especially for the earlier time periods.

5. Major sources for this section include Adams (1970), Belli (1970), Browning (1971), Deere and Marchette (1981), DeWitt (1977), Harness and Pugh (1970), IBRD (1953), Laird (1974), Lethander (1968), Place (1981), Quiros (1973), and Satterthwaite (1971).

6. Useful in preparing this section were Allen, Dodge, and Schmitz (1983), *Foreign Agriculture* (1960), Guess (1979), Metrinko (1978), Myers (1981), Parsons (1965), Roux (1978), Shane (1980), Spielmann (1972), and USDA (various issues).

7. Although the United States has encouraged Central American export growth, it also pursues policies that restrict that growth, such as beef and sugar import quotas and cotton dumping to lower world prices. For further discussions, see Brooks (1967) and Pastor (1982).

8. All sources used for this section are cited in the text.

9. For a discussion and criticism of this approach, see Newfarmer (1983).

10. Several agricultural agreements have been signed between the governments of Honduras and Japan in recent years; see, for example, *La Tribuna* (1983:40).

11. For a more sophisticated handling of the concept of comparative advantage, see Chenery (1979).

12. Among the many discussions, including those of further bibliographical sources, see de Janvry (1981:158–162); Ffrench-Davis and Tironi (1982:49–125); Gordon-Ashworth (1984); Lofchie and Commins (1982); Meier (1984:502–505); Payer (1975); Streeten (1974); and United Nations Economic Commission for Latin America (UNECLA) (1950).

CHAPTER 4

Agrarian Transformation and Rural Economic Security

After three decades of export expansion and commercialization in the agricultural sector following World War II, most of Central America's rural population remained very poor. In fact, the number of rural people with insufficient access to food, employment, and land had increased dramatically by the mid-1980s. Many public officials and international advisors continue to recommend further expansion of agricultural exports as the best solution to this continuing tragedy; others point to the obvious role played by the area's rapidly growing population. Although descriptive accounts have been offered of the connection between the expansion of commercial, and expecially export, agriculture in the postwar period and increasing rural misery, it was not until the publication in 1979 of William Durham's *Scarcity and Survival in Central America* that the issue received its first careful, systematic analysis for this region.

In his landmark study, Durham (1979:21–51) demonstrates that the pressing problems of land and food scarcity in El Salvador are not primarily the result of a high population growth rate. Rather, the scarcities are primarily the consequence of the concentration of land ownership that has occurred with expanding production of crops for the export market. In 1971, for example, 21.8 percent of the agriculturally active population of El Salvador had access to no land, while 29 percent more had access to only one hectare (2.47 acres) or less. Durham's analysis indicates that for this slight majority of the agricultural sector, "it was not so much the rapid growth of the population after 1892 as the simultaneous trend toward land concentration that created the scarcity of land" they faced (p. 48). The underlying cause of this concentration was the development of new opportunities for export crops, first coffee and then cotton and sugar. As land ownership was consolidated and land switched to export production, basic food production suffered; while per-capita food production declined in El Salvador from 1950 to 1970, the amount of land per capita devoted to export crops actually increased.

Following the lead of Durham and pursuing the historical patterns identified in chapter 2, this chapter will analyze the impact of the expansion of commercial agriculture on the rural population of Central America in the postwar period. Through an integration of descriptive accounts with an analysis of empirical data, the impact of this transformation on the following aspects of rural economic security will be discussed: access to land, food, employment, and income; and environmental quality.[1] The chapter will end with a discussion of the merits of the agro-export development model in countries with gross disparities in the distribution of key resources.

ACCESS TO LAND

Central America entered the contemporary period with land distributions that were grossly unequal. Most of the rural population lived on small subsistence plots, while most of the private land was owned by a small percentage of the landholders. Pressure on land supply already existed in El Salvador and in the most densely settled portions of the other countries. Because much of the region's land is not suitable for cultivation and because population has grown at rapid rates, it can be assumed that eventually population growth alone would progressively erode access to land for rural people. But this has not been the only force with which peasants have had to contend.

As commercial agricultural possibilities expanded in the postwar period, peasants found themselves in competition with more powerful groups. Sometimes the competition has been financial; as the commercial boom in agriculture developed, land values increased. New profit-making possibilities attracted affluent urban groups to speculative agriculture, thereby increasing the demand for land and, again, inflating land values. As values have increased, poor rural people have found themselves priced out of the market. On occasion, the competition has been settled by force as peasants have been dispossessed of land whose use they had enjoyed. This usurpation in turn has led to land invasions and occupations by angry peasants and, as a result, violence among peasants, large landholders, and sometimes the state.[2]

Traditionally, small landholders in Central America have had an insecure claim to the land that they worked, whether they were sharecroppers, renters, or "owners." An agricultural census in Honduras in the mid-1960s, for example, found that the probability of producer ownership steadily increased with farm size; only 14 percent of the smallest farmers (under 1.4 hectares) owned their land, while 94 percent of the largest (over 609 hectares) were owners (Fonck 1972:30–31). More recently, an AID report in 1982 found that three-quarters of Honduran farmers still had insecure tenancy (USAID 1982:1).

In one tenure pattern typical of traditional agricultural systems in Latin America, peasants lived and worked on land that belonged to a large landowner, using it in return for a contribution of their labor or a share of their production. This arrangement between families may have gone back for generations, but it has been swept aside in many cases by the spread of modern commercial agriculture. The peasants have been turned out to make way for more intensive cotton or sugar growing or cattle grazing. A primary location of this transformation has been the Pacific lowlands. In his description of the change in this part of El Salvador from subsistence tenant farming mixed with low-density cattle grazing to mechanized cotton cultivation, Browning (1971:236) noted the cancellation of tenant relationships and the eviction of squatters. If they remained in the area, the only income-earning opportunity for the dispossessed came during the short cotton-picking season. They were reduced to living in straw huts built on the public right-of-way along roads and riverbeds.

A similar fate has befallen many renters. Surveys in both Honduras and Nicaragua in the 1960s found that most rental contracts were unwritten and usually covered less than one year (Fonck 1972:31; Lethander 1968:185). Although such relationships might have been stable in the past, as commercial alternatives opened to owners, renters often were pushed aside. Sometimes contracts were not renewed; on other occasions, rental prices were escalated too rapidly for peasants to afford (Parsons 1976:11–15). One technique that has been applied throughout the region has been to rent out uncleared land at a nominal price for a short duration. At the end of the contract, the land, now cleared by the renter, is converted to cattle grazing. No longer needed, the former renter must move on to find new land.

The major source of conflict, however, has been the use of land where access rights are in dispute. Despite the impact of the Liberal reforms of the nineteenth century, public lands remained in all of the countries, especially Honduras. Furthermore, ownership of land in previously remote areas is frequently unclear. Peasants have often enjoyed use of such lands for years, even generations, without challenge. The expansion of export markets in the contemporary period, however, has made these lands attractive to elites, and it is here that peasant and elite interests have collided directly.

This conflict has been most intense, and best documented, in Guatemala. Lands isolated from the well-populated highlands and from good coffee-growing areas had long been an important frontier region for land-poor peasants. This was true, for example, of the Pacific lowlands, which were of little interest to elites until after World War II. As previously described (in chapter 3), new export possibilities (cotton), insect and disease control, and improved transportation opened the area to commercial use. Peasants were pushed aside in what has been called a "massive displacement" (Quiros Guardia 1973:87) as vast land holdings came to monopolize the area. Today the highest degree of land concentration in Guatemala is found in the Pacific lowlands; by 1964 the largest 3.7 percent of farms in that region occupied an incredible 80.3 percent of the land (Graber 1980:20). Although not in such an extreme degree, the same pattern can be found in Nicaragua; there too land concentration is greatest in the Pacific region, where 1.6 percent of the farms held 55.8 percent of the land in the mid-1960s (Taylor 1969:19).

More recently, the pattern has been replicated in the northern parts of Guatemala, especially in those areas close to the Northern Transversal Strip, where a road is being built from the Caribbean to the Mexican border across the neck of the country. This area was well settled by Indians prior to the Conquest but then depopulated by the introduction of malaria and other tropical diseases. As land pressures increased in the highlands centuries later, Indians returned, especially in recent decades. As long as elites perceived this area to be remote and unattractive, Indians could settle freely on public lands, lands thought to be public, and private lands with or without the (absentee) owner's consent. Peasant access to this land began to be challenged by the late 1960s, however, as road construction and the possibilities of mineral wealth now made the area of interest to elites (Carter 1969:309; Lassey et al. 1969:6–42).

One of the first large-scale manifestations of this conflict occurred in 1978 in the town of Panzós when over one hundred Kekchi Indians, including at least twenty-five women and five children, were massacred by soldiers. Families of many of the Indians in this area had worked their land for the previous forty to one hundred years, but without legal title. In recent years, though, entire communities of Indian peasants have been displaced by developers attracted by discoveries of oil and nickel deposits and by the booming real-estate market along the road (International Work Group for Indigenous Affairs [IWGIA] 1978:11; Aguilera Peralta 1979). A statement issued by priests and nuns from the Diocese of La Verapaz (which includes Panzós) claimed that in their attempts to gain more land, landowners would "resort to semilegal manoeuvres and all sorts of pressures, without excluding violence" (IWGIA 1978:45). Peasants in the area had been working to obtain legal titles, but without success. On May 29, 1978, some seven hundred peasants from a number of outlying communities traveled to Panzós, some in protest, others to learn of documents that they had been told had arrived from the capital concerning their efforts to work through government channels to protect their interests. In response to a very minor provocation, soldiers apparently thought they were being attacked by the peasants. The statement by the La Verapaz religious workers describes the result:

> Soldiers ... started to blaze away; some of them climbed onto the town hall building and shot from there on the crowd of men, women and children. At the same time, there were trigger-happy individuals at different spots, some even from private houses, who joined the general shooting, firing at those who tried to run away in different directions. . . .
> The utterly terrified peasants, trying to escape in turmoil, found death in the park, in the streets, in the neighboring cornfields, and some who got seized by panic flung themselves into the river and drowned before reaching the other side. (IGWIA 1978:47)

The Northern Transversal Strip had been officially designated for colonization by landless Indians. By 1979 it was reported that "much of the best land has already fallen into the hands of wealthy farmers and army officers" (Riding 1979:A2). In fact, former presidents General Kjell Laugerud and General Romeo Lucas García were reported to possess large estates in the area, which came to be known as "the zone of the generals" (Riding 1979:A2). To the north and even less developed, but facing similar pressures, is El Petén. Both it and the strip are seen as especially valuable for cattle grazing. In the mid-1970s, 60 percent of the country's cattle were grazed in the south, but because of competition from export crops and pesticide contamination from cotton spraying, forecasts were that the north would be the major cattle region by 1990 (Hemphill 1976:3).

Although the violence has not been as pervasive or as excessive in the other countries of the region, similar dynamics have occurred elsewhere as well. No less an authority than the second Somoza president, Luis, attested to the dispossession of peasants in Nicaragua. He told an agrarian reform symposium in 1965 that rapid agricultural development since 1955 caused

> a violent displacement of the campesinos who traditionally worked the lands in periods of unemployment. Before my eyes I saw lands cleared and many people leave, permanent workers, sharecroppers, and squatters—by the force of the plow and machinery. (quoted in Taylor 1969:19)

Similarly in Honduras, observers have described the impact of the spread of commercial agriculture on the peasantry as an "enclosure movement" (e.g., Parsons 1976:11–15). This characterization is particularly apt for that country, which, uniquely in the region, entered the contemporary period with much of its land public—in 1974, still about one-third of all land. Although Honduras has a low population density, good agricultural land is increasingly scarce there. Consequently, as land values have increased in recent decades, peasant access to public lands has been contested by other interests who have been willing to use physical force. As will be elaborated in Part II, there is a direct relationship between the widespread violence in recent years in rural Central America and the intensified competition for land between peasants and large growers, a result of the spread of commercial agriculture.

Peasants' efforts to defend their interests—whether through peaceful petition, land invasions and occupations, or the creation of peasant organizations—have often been perceived by elite groups as a challenge to their priorities. This perception strengthens intensely when radical guerrilla movements advocating structural transformations in behalf of the poor appear in rural areas. The result in El Salvador, Guatemala, and Nicaragua has been repression directed at the rural population—a repression that reached extraordinary levels in the early 1980s in the two first-named countries.

An indication of the extreme disparity in access to land in the region is provided by Tables 4.1 and 4.2. Table 4.1 gives the findings of all of the region's official land ownership surveys. The most recent results show that in the 1970s in El Salvador, the largest 1.5 percent of holdings had 49.5 percent of the land; in Guatemala, 2.6 percent of holdings had 65.5 percent; in Honduras, 4.2 percent of holdings had 56 percent; in Nicaragua, 1.8 percent of holdings had 46.8 percent; and even in Costa Rica, 9.1 of holdings had 67.2 percent of the land.

These figures are not directly comparable among countries because they come from different years and because the size categories used in the surveys vary. Table 4.2 standardizes the data so as to allow intercountry comparisons and also to facilitate comparisons within individual countries over time. It presents a coefficient of inequality for both the smallest and the largest farms during the latest agricultural census (sometime in the 1970s).[3]

Looking first at the small farms, for both time periods they had only about 4 percent of an equal share of land in Guatemala, Honduras, and Nicaragua. Although their share improved marginally over time in the first two countries, it declined in Nicaragua, which thus had the worst underdistribution of land in the 1970s. Costa Rica also registered a decline sufficient to place it behind El Salvador in the 1970s. The latter had the biggest increase in the share of land in the smallest category, a still very small 9.8 percent of an equal share. In each country, new land had been brought into cultivation by small farmers in the period covered here, land either previously too marginal to be attractive or in frontier regions. Nonetheless, most of these gains by

TABLE 4.1
Land Distribution by Farm Size Categories, 1950s to 1970s

Country Size (Hectares)	Percentage of All Farms 1950s	1960s	1970s	Percentage of Land 1950s	1960s	1970s
Costa Rica	(1955)	(1963)	(1973)	(1955)	(1963)	(1973)
1 –< 10	51.0	49.8	47.8	5.1	4.7	3.8
10 –< 20	15.1	15.0	14.0	5.3	5.1	3.9
20 –< 100	28.0	28.2	29.1	28.3	27.8	25.1
100 –< 1000	5.5	6.6	8.6	31.6	36.6	42.0
1000+	0.4	0.4	0.5	29.7	25.8	25.2
El Salvador		(1961)	(1971)		(1961)	(1971)
< 1	—	47.2	48.8	—	3.9	4.8
1 –< 10	—	44.2	43.9	—	18.0	22.5
10 –< 50	—	6.7	5.8	—	20.6	23.2
50 –< 200	—	1.5	1.2	—	19.8	21.1
200+	—	0.5	0.3	—	37.7	28.4
Guatemala	(1950)	(1964)	(1979)	(1950)	(1964)	(1979)
< .7	21.3	20.4	31.4	.8	1.0	1.3
.7–< 3.5	54.9	54.6	47.0	8.2	10.6	9.2
3.5–< 7	12.2	12.5	9.7	5.3	7.0	5.7
7 –< 44.8	9.5	10.4	9.3	13.5	18.9	18.7
44.8–< 450	1.9	1.9	2.3	21.9	26.5	30.7
450 –< 900	0.2	0.1	0.2	9.5	10.0	12.8
900+	0.1	0.1	0.1	40.8	26.0	21.6
Honduras	(1952)		(1974)	(1952)		(1974)
< 1	10	—	17	0.4	—	0.8
1 –< 5	47	—	47	8	—	8
5 –< 10	18	—	15	8	—	8
10 –< 50	21	—	18	27	—	28
50 –< 100	3	—	2	11	—	12
100 –< 500	2	—	2	18	—	22
500 –< 1000	0.2	—	0.1	8	—	7
1000+	0.1	—	0.1	20	—	15
Nicaragua		(1963)	(1971)		(1963)	(1971)
< .7	—	2.1	5.8	—	—	—
.7–< 3.5	—	33.7	25.9	—	1.6	1.0
3.5–< 7	—	15.6	12.1	—	2.0	1.2
7 –< 35	—	28.1	31.7	—	12.0	11.1
35 –< 77	—	10.2	12.3	—	12.5	11.7
77 –< 350	—	8.9	10.3	—	30.8	28.1
350 –< 777	—	0.9	1.1	—	11.3	11.0
777+	—	0.6	0.7	—	29.7	35.8

SOURCES: Costa Rica: Carvajal 1979b:2; El Salvador: OAS 1975:53; Guatemala: Hough et al. 1983:71; Honduras: Ruhl 1984:50; Nicaragua: Warnken 1975:47, 49.

TABLE 4.2
*Coefficients of Inequality in the Distribution of Land,
1950s/1960s and 1970s[1]*

Country	Smallest Farms		Largest Farms	
	1950s/1960s	1970s	1950s/1960s	1970s
Costa Rica	.1	.079	74.3	50.4
El Salvador	.08	.098	75.4	94.6
Guatemala	.037	.041	167.7	114.7
Honduras	.04	.047	93.3	110.0
Nicaragua	.04	.032	49.5	51.1

NOTE: 1. Coefficients were obtained by dividing percent of all land by percent of all farms in both the smallest and largest farm categories from Table 4.1 (to provide closer equivalence, the two smallest Nicaraguan categories are used and the two largest for Guatemala and Honduras). A coefficient of 1.0 for all size categories would represent an equal distribution of land. A figure less than 1.0 indicates underdistribution; over 1.0 means overdistribution. Guatemala and Honduras use last two size categories; Nicaragua, first two. For example, Costa Rica's ".1" in 1950s/1960s means the smallest farm had one-tenth of an equal share of the land, and the "74.3" in the third column means the largest farms had 74.3 times an equal share.
SOURCE: Calculated from Table 4.1.

smallholders are not registered in these data as they were offset by population growth and dispossession.

Limited access to land, combined with rapid population growth, has meant a declining person:land ratio and a growing landless population. In Guatemala, for example, arable land per capita was 1.7 hectares in 1950, .92 in 1973, and .79 in 1980 (Hough et al. 1983:73). In the western highlands, the most intensely farmed region of the country, per capita land for the rural population was 1.35 hectares in 1950 and 1.03 in 1964, with projections of .81 for 1980 and .61 for 2000 (Merrill 1974:23). The problem is regionwide; the percentages of rural families with 4 hectares of land or less in 1970 were as follows: El Salvador, 86.7; Guatemala, 83.9; Costa Rica, 72.6; Honduras, 65.8; and Nicaragua, 59.5 (Weeks 1985:112). Such figures are not fully comparable because of productivity differences between the countries; generally, subsistence requires more land in the last two countries and less in Costa Rica.

Complete landlessness has developed during recent decades as a particularly severe problem for the rural population. Percentages of landless rural families in 1970 were as follows: Nicaragua, 33.8; Honduras, 31.4; Guatemala, 26.6; Costa Rica, 26.3; and El Salvador, 26.1 (Weeks 1985:112; also see Lassen 1980:125–157). These rates, however, include workers in banana plantations, which are unevenly distributed across the countries. Compared to other farmers, banana workers are envied for their job security and incomes (Seligson 1980a:99). Clearly, agricultural wage earners with security and incomes beyond the subsistence level must be differentiated from peasants who lack security and income as well as land, and it is to this latter group that the term *landless* will be understood to apply. Ruhl (1984:48) subtracts about 4 percent from the total Honduran landless population for this reason, and a comparable reduction should be applied to the Costa Rican figure.

Once this adjustment is made, landlessness in the early 1970s is seen to be most serious in Nicaragua, followed by the other countries at roughly the same point, with the exception of Costa Rica. During the 1970s, however, the landless population rose most swiftly in El Salvador. A United Nations study estimated that 11.8 percent of rural Salvadoran families were landless in 1961; the corresponding figure for 1971 was 29.1 percent. By 1975 the landless proportion had increased to 40.9 percent, with only 3.7 percent of rural families having holdings above 5 hectares (Burke 1976:476). In 1981 there were reports that landlessness in El Salvador had reached an incredible 60 percent of the rural population (Simon and Stephens 1982:5).

For the largest farms summarized in Table 4.2, the country groupings change somewhat: Guatemala and Honduras remain the most unequal group, but Nicaragua and El Salvador shift places from the comparison of the smallest holdings. For the three countries with the worst overdistribution of land in the largest farms, the disproportionate share of these estates by the 1970s was around one hundred times that of an equal distribution. Even in Costa Rica and Nicaragua, the shares were more than fifty times that of an equal distribution. The most substantial trend toward decrease in overdistri-bution occurred in Guatemala (though it still had the greatest inequality), followed by Costa Rica. However, increases in this measure of land concen-tration occurred in El Salvador and Honduras, and marginally in Nicaragua. What is remarkable here is that in three of the countries, the share of land in the largest farms actually increased, as measured by official censuses. Observers in each country have pointed out that in recent years, owners have subdivided large holdings and registered them in the names of various family members as a precaution in the face of threatened land reform (especially the expropriation of underused land on large estates). It should also be noted that the underreporting of large estates is a recurrent problem (Hough et al. 1983:19).

Access to land also has a qualitative dimension. A peasant family that has been forced off of 5 hectares of fertile land and has moved to 7 hectares of eroded hillside with little fertility has improved its position in the data discussed above; in reality, of course, its living standard will deteriorate with its ability to produce. Numerous reports point out that the most fertile land is controlled by the largest holdings, the farmers with the smallest holdings being left with the less valuable land. Yet the small farmers use their land intensively, usually for food crops, while many of the large holdings are still underutilized and devoted primarily to export crop production and cattle grazing. Data from El Salvador in the 1970s make the point well. Farms with under 1 hectare cultivated 80.9 percent of the land, while farms over 200 hectares were on the average only 26.8 percent cultivated (Durham 1979:52).

In summary, Central America entered the contemporary period with gross inequalities in access to land because of the agrarian transformations of the Conquest, the colonial period, and the Liberal reform era. In the decades following World War II, this already serious inequality was worsened by both rapid population growth and further land concentration, as the powerful outbid the poor or dispossessed the weak of land in order to take advantage of new commercial opportunities, especially for export commodities.

Increasing numbers of rural families have found themselves with a diminishing land supply or, most seriously, with no land at all. Their loss is both psychological and material. The continuation of a land-based lifestyle is a strong value for farming families, not only in peasant communities in later-developing countries but also among commercial family farmers in other countries such as the United States. When pushed off of the land, the farming family has lost a lifestyle that is usually intensely preferred, from which a meaningful and stable identity and worldview were derived, and that connected it to earlier generations. The loss is also material, of course. Land provides security: even the smallest holding has room for a home, for some subsistence crops, and perhaps for growing firewood. As the size of that holding shrinks, its ability to produce subsistence diminishes as well. The great majority of the region's rural people no longer have enough land to sustain a family.

ACCESS TO FOOD

The damaging impact of the conversion of land to coffee growing in the past century was noted by many observers. In Guatemala, for example, the first report of the newly organized Department of Agriculture pointed out in 1899 that

> Guatemala has found it necessary to import corn and other foodstuffs, whereas before coffee production became so extensive articles of prime necessity were produced in adequate amounts, and at low prices, within the country itself. (quoted in Mosk 1955:17)

As coffee cultivation continued to spread during the next decades, food production suffered; annual corn production from 1919 to 1929 was no better than it had been in 1899 (Jones 1966:189). Similarly in El Salvador in the 1920s, a new wave in the conversion of food crop land to coffee drove food prices up rapidly; between 1922 and 1926 corn prices doubled and bean prices escalated 225 percent (Durham 1979:36).

The expansion of export crop production is directly related to food scarcity, and therefore to malnutrition, in at least four ways. First, land was often converted from food to export production. Sometimes small farmers undertook this conversion, but generally it was the work of larger landowners, who might dispossess peasants in the process. Second, during the postwar period new land was opened up for cultivation—67 percent more land up to 1976–78 for the crops examined in this study. Much of this land could have been devoted to the production of food for the growing population, but instead, 63 percent of it went to export crops, while a substantial amount of additional land (not included in the present data) was converted to cattle grazing. Third, peasants desiring to buy their own land have had to face not just a decreasing supply but also its inevitable concomitant, higher prices, which they often cannot pay. Finally, there are the vast holdings the banana companies obtained earlier in the century, largely without disturbing landholding patterns. As good land became scarce in the last several decades, these holdings were "plainly needed by, but inaccessible to, a rural population that had quadrupled since 1900" in Honduras (Durham 1979:177) and increased by comparable amounts elsewhere. United Fruit's Costa Rican holdings in 1950, for example, constituted not only 4 percent of the country's entire territory, but also almost double the amount of land planted in the three basic food crops. Banana company holdings in Honduras in 1971 were estimated still to be around two hundred thousand hectares, which was about one-half of the total area planted at that time in the three basic food crops. Furthermore, the land controlled by the banana companies is usually among the most fertile in the region, yet over the years much of it has been left uncultivated; in Honduras in 1960, only 17.7 percent of that land was under cultivation while another 11.1 percent was devoted to cattle pasture (Carias and Slutzky 1971:275).

Food Supply Trends

The data provided in the next series of tables show that Central American food production has been harmed, in some cases significantly, by the expansion of export agriculture. Table 4.3 gives the per capita domestic production of the basic food crops for each country (beans, corn, and rice, plus wheat for

TABLE 4.3

Change in Per Capita Domestically Produced Food Supply, 1948–52 to 1981–83

Country	Per Capita Production[1]				Percentage Change 1948–52 to 1976–78	1948–52 to 1981–83
	1948–52	1961–65	1976–78	1981–83		
Costa Rica	143	113	128	127	–10	–11
El Salvador	131	88	121	105	– 8	–20
Guatemala	182	164	138	164	–24	–10
Honduras	170	175	137	145	–19	–15
Nicaragua	158	146	137	163	–13	3
Central America	160	140	133	142	–17	–11

NOTE: 1. Per capita domestic production of basic food crops (beans, corn, and rice, plus wheat for Guatemala); reported in kilograms per capita. Per capita production cannot be compared meaningfully between countries.

SOURCE: Calculated from UNFAO, various years.

Guatemala). Looking first at the period 1948–52 to 1976–78, one notes substantially the same situation in all five nations: per capita production declined, especially in Guatemala and Honduras. Furthermore, domestic per capita food production is at its lowest point after two and a half decades of agricultural development in three of the countries, Guatemala, Honduras, and Nicaragua. This bottom point was reached by El Salvador in 1961–65 and by Costa Rica (where the average diet is the least dependent on the basic crops among the countries in the region) in the early 1970s.

When the troubled period of the late 1970s and early 1980s is included, the trends change somewhat for all the nations except Costa Rica. A decline in domestic food production is still registered in every country with the exception of Nicaragua, where the policy commitments of the new revolutionary leadership undoubtedly reversed the trend. A huge expansion of corn production in Guatemala reduced the magnitude of that nation's postwar decline. In contrast, food production in El Salvador changed little from 1976–78 to 1981–83, increasing much less than the population; as a result, the magnitude of El Salvador's decline was substantially greater for the later end date, most likely reflecting the upheaval of its civil war.

In recent years, public officials in each of the countries have given attention to the need to become more self-reliant in food production. The importance of reducing food imports has been stressed in the face of each nation's escalating foreign debt. Success in this endeavor depends on a number of factors besides the commitment of public officials, such as world prices and the relative profitability of food and export crops. This latter factor seems to have been related to the increase in corn production in Guatemala noted above and to the increase in Salvadoran per capita domestic food production after the mid-1960s. Because the Salvadoran data reported here could be interpreted as somewhat at odds with Durham's (1979) analysis for that country, a closer look at the evidence is warranted.

The two sets of data are not in contradiction; they cover different time periods, though, so conclusions based on the trends they describe could vary. Significantly, where they overlap (1948–71), the trends correspond. Putting the two sets of data together therefore gives a more complete view of Salvadoran developments. Durham's (1979:22–33) overall findings are that per capita food production generally stayed constant until the 1950s, when it dropped at about the same time that per capita land in basic food crops declined while that in export crops increased. His data also indicate that the decline in per capita food production halted in the early 1960s and then reversed; by 1968–71, production was back up to the level of 1957. Similar trends occurred in both indicators of farmland use. Durham discussed these changes in the context of the "cotton crash" of 1965–67 that resulted from soil exhaustion, insect damage, and poor world prices; cotton plantings never again reached their high-water mark of the previous decade. In the following two decades, land planted in corn increased by 18 and 29 percent respectively, though much of it was marginal land. More important, a significant effort was undertaken to increase corn yields with the technical and financial assistance of international advisors (Davis 1973; Davis and Weisenborn 1981; and T. S. Walker 1981). As a consequence, corn yields increased in El Salvador from 1961–65 to 1978–79 by 70 percent, almost double the rate for Central America as a whole. Corn yields by 1979 were almost double those of Honduras and Nicaragua. These fluctuations in the per capita production of basic food crops are summarized in Table 4.3; what should be stressed is that production declined in El Salvador by almost 20 percent across the three decades.[4]

A more accurate estimate of the region's supply of basic food, but for a far shorter period of time, is possible using data supplied to the U.S. Department of Agriculture by its regional attachés. Because the number of years covered is so small (two to five), the major value of Table 4.4 is the comparison it allows between per capita food production and more complete measures of food supply, which can then be used to assess the validity of the less complete data appearing in the previous table. The first column of Table 4.4 gives the mean annual per capita basic food production for a few years in the late 1970s, the same indicator as that used in Table 4.3. The next column reports the mean annual domestic food supply per capita, which takes into account not only production but also exports, livestock feed use, and stocks on hand at the beginning of the year for the same food crops as well as for

TABLE 4.4
Indicators of Net Supply of Basic Food Crops, Late 1970s

Country	Mean Domestic Production per Capita[1]	Mean Domestic Supply per Capita[2]	Percentage Difference (1–2)	Mean Total Supply per Capita[3]	Imports: Percentage of Use[4]
Costa Rica	85.3	59.8	−30	122	41
El Salvador	118.8	122	2.7	156.6	20
Guatemala	153	147.4	− 3.7	170.8	14
Honduras	122.8	112.2	− 8.6	143.2	19
Nicaragua	100.5	122.5	22	167	24

NOTES: 1. Domestic production per capita represents mean annual production of beans, corn, and rice (plus wheat for Guatemala).
  2. Domestic supply per capita represents mean annual production plus sorghum production and stocks on hand, minus exports and livestock use.
  3. Total supply per capita represents mean annual domestic supply plus imports of beans, corn, rice, sorghum, and wheat.
  4. Imports as percentage of use represents mean annual percentage of five food crops consumed by both humans and livestock that was imported.
  SOURCE: Calculated from USDA *Attaché Reports*: Costa Rica, Oct. 10, 1979, Nov. 29, 1981; El Salvador, Nov. 15, 1979, Nov. 30, 1980; Guatemala, July 26, 1978, Aug. 28, 1981; Honduras, Sept. 11, 1978, Sept. 12, 1980, Aug. 31, 1981; Nicaragua, Oct. 27, 1980, Oct. 14, 1981.

sorghum. Although traditionally grown for livestock use, sorghum in recent years has come to be an important staple, primarily in Honduras (where it comprises up to one-half of food production) and El Salvador (where it is up to one-sixth of production).

The most significant score on this table is given in the third column, which show the percentage difference between the first two columns. In each case, with the exception of Nicaragua, the more complete measure is either less than or only marginally greater than the domestic production figure. It seems safe to assume that the same proportion would hold for the longer time span covered in Table 4.3. The Nicaraguan exception does not diminish this conclusion because the data for that country in Table 4.4 cover only the tumultuous years of 1979 and 1980. Although the data source is incomplete, it appears that domestic supply was substantially higher than production (relative to the other countries) because of large stocks of food on hand at the beginning of each year, in part the result of a decline in livestock feed use.

As domestic food production has dropped behind population growth rates, the countries of the region have been forced to import greater quantities of food to meet expanding needs. Indications of this effort are portrayed in the final two columns of Table 4.4, which include imports of crops also produced domestically, plus wheat. All of the countries now import a substantial percentage of their basic grains and beans; therefore the total supply per capita, which includes these imports, is substantially above the other two measures. This difference is important for the urban population, but the impact it has on the lives of rural people, especially those living in isolated areas, is unclear. It might be economically rational at the aggregate level to convert land to export crops commanding higher prices than basic food crops, which are then imported to cover the resulting food deficit, but it would be rational at the individual level only if everyone were reached by those imports and only if the balance held true for each person. The unfortunate reality is that what a rural family would be able to produce for itself if it had access to land, it might not have the income to purchase in the marketplace, especially if it has been displaced from land then converted to export crops.

A good illustration of this point is provided by Boyer's (1982:226–234) field research in the southern highlands of Honduras. Among the families he studied, two-thirds commonly could not produce enough food to meet their needs. Boyer estimates the minimal amount of land (with a three-year fallow cycle) needed to provide a family with an adequate diet to be about 7.2 hectares in that area; but the mean land access of his subjects was only about 2.6 hectares. Meanwhile, from 1976–78 to 1981–83 the ratio of export crop land to food crop land in Honduras increased from 58 to 76 percent (see Table 4.1).

Beef Supply Trends

Food crop land has been lost during recent decades not only to export crops but also to cattle raising. If this conversion resulted in enhanced domestic meat supply, then its impact on rural food supply might be neutral or even positive. This has not been the case, however. Table 4.5 makes this point clearly for the years between 1961–65 and 1980–81. The evidence indicates that beef raising in Central America increased so substantially that production per capita increased except in El Salvador (and Nicaragua after the revolution). Much of this production, however, was meant for the export market. When exports are taken into account, the per capita supply of beef declined in every country except Nicaragua until 1976–78. When the end date is extended to 1980–81, Costa Rica and Guatemala both show increases in per capita supply, while Nicaragua shows a decline. Furthermore, domestic beef prices have been internationalized: in 1949 beef prices in Costa Rica were about 25 percent of those in New York City, but by 1978 they had climbed to 77 percent of New York prices (Place 1981:147–148).

A closer look at the evidence discloses a pattern that applies to each of the countries with the partial exception of El Salvador. It is clear that beef production in Central America has increased since 1960 because of the

TABLE 4.5
Changes in Per Capita Beef Production and Supply,
1961–65 to 1980–81[1]

Country	Production to 1976–78	to 1980–81	Production per Capita to 1976–78	to 1980–81	Supply per Capita[1] to 1976–78	to 1980–81
Costa Rica	97	138	30	44	–21	6
El Salvador	52	45	– 7	–20	–22	–23
Guatemala	95	144	23	40	– 6	11
Honduras	107	113	34	21	– 5	–30
Nicaragua	118	64	35	– 9	43	– 3
Central America	97	105	25	16	– 2	– 6

NOTE: 1. Supply is based on production minus exports.
SOURCE: Calculated from UNFAO, UN, various years.

stimulus of the export market and international financial assistance, as discussed in the previous chapter. During the first phase of this expansion, exports climbed rapidly, outpacing production; consequently, the domestic beef supply declined. Because much of the cattle grazing occurs on land previously devoted to food crops, the impact of these developments on domestic food supply has been severe. Compounding the problem for many peasants is the fact that they did not themselves make this switch in production; instead, they were dispossessed by cattle ranchers.

During this stage, the decline in domestic beef supply has often been steep: in Costa Rica, it was down by 23 percent (to 1972–74); in El Salvador, by 22 percent (to 1976–78); in Guatemala, by 10 percent (to 1969–71); in Honduras, by 30 percent (to 1980–81); and in Nicaragua, by 12 percent (to 1972–74). Among the major exporters, Honduras was the last to initiate this phase, and it is the only country where the trend continues. It has climbed up to behind Costa Rica to become the fourth-largest Latin American beef exporter to the United States. In 1980–81, Honduras exported 51 percent of its total beef production, the highest percentage registered by any country in the region. El Salvador also came late to beef exporting, an effort that substantially ended with its civil war. It is the one country where insufficient production relative to population increase also accounts for the decline in domestic beef supply.

In the second phase of the expansion of cattle raising, production continues to increase, now more rapidly than exports, thereby halting the decline in domestic beef supply. In this phase there has been more variation among the countries in the relationship between production and exports, with several factors accounting for the differences. As discussed earlier, beef exporting in recent years has encountered serious difficulties, from quota ceilings and price problems in the United States to pesticide contamination at home. On the positive side, economic growth has created a growing middle sector in urban areas, thus expanding the domestic market for beef. Local demand would appear to be more important than exports as a stimulus for expanding beef production in Costa Rica and Guatemala in the early 1980s; but export expansion remains more important in Honduras, as it was in the other countries a few years before.

The Scope of Malnutrition

If the people of Central America had access to sufficient food to provide adequate diets, then the harmful effects of agricultural export expansion on food supply would be of little concern. Unfortunately, malnutrition is one of the most prominent manifestations of the region's poverty; the nutritional impact of major socioeconomic changes must accordingly be a primary criterion in their evaluation. Adequate data for a close examination are not available, but the evidence that does exist demonstrates continuing high levels of malnutrition and even a deterioration in the nutritional status of some groups.

In *The Production Yearbook*, the Food and Agricultural Organization annually reports data on average daily calorie and protein consumption. The *Yearbook* shows increases for all of the Central American countries.[5] However, these indicators measure *apparent* consumption: they are based on total food supply, including imports; that is, they are similar to the data in Table 4.4 on "total supply," and therefore they are subject to the same qualifications. More accurately, then, the FAO figures show an improvement in the region's per capita total food supply but, in themselves, tell us nothing about either trends in distribution or malnutrition. Costs Rica makes the point well. In 1972 it produced three times its protein requirements and almost twice its caloric requirements (Carvajal 1979b:73); yet, as the data below will show, there is still substantial malnutrition in that country. As Carvajal (1979b) points out, "the constraints on these nutrients getting to the people lie in their distribution system and proceeds from their sales" (p. 74).

There are studies that report on the magnitude of malnutrition in Central America, though data on trends over time are lacking. Some of this evidence is summarized in Table 4.6. The first column estimates the percentage of the total population that consumes less than the FAO's recommended number of calories daily for each country. The second column shows the percentage of the total population that consumes less than 90 percent of the recommended

TABLE 4.6
Indicators of Malnutrition, in Percentages of Population

Country	Percentage of Population Consuming Less than Recommended Calories[1]		Child Malnutrition[2]		
	<100% of Calories	<90% of Calories	Total	Moderate to Severe	Increase, 1965–75
Costa Rica	34	20	57.4	13.7	−10
El Salvador	72	61	74.5	26.0	46
Guatemala	69	48	81.4	32.4	18
Honduras	60	60	72.5	32.2	29
Nicaragua	—	—	56.8	15.0	51

NOTES: 1. Percentage of total population estimated in 1973 to consume less than recommended calories daily (column one) and less than 90 percent of recommended calories daily (column two).

2. Protein-calorie malnutrition in children under five, both percentage of all children and percentage of all children with moderate or severe malnutrition (both columns are for various years, 1971–75). Increase in percentage of all children with calorie-deficient diet, 1965–75.

SOURCES: For total population, Reutlinger and Alderman 1980:407–409. For children, IDB 1978:138–141. (Increase was calculated from data in IDB's table because increase reported in table seems to be in error.)

standard. For both indicators, malnutrition is the worst in El Salvador, with Guatemala and Honduras alternating as the second worst. Predictably, Costa Rica's performance is much better than for the rest (data are not available for Nicaragua); nonetheless, its malnutrition rates are still substantial, with one-third of the population existing below the recommended caloric intake level. In fact, a 1975 study found malnutrition in some regions of Costa Rica affecting as much as 43.2 to 62.5 percent of the population (Carvajal 1979b:71).

Perhaps the most prominent feature of these data is the evidence they provide that in three of the countries (El Salvador, Guatemala, and Honduras), virtually half the population, or more, consumes less than 90 percent of the recommended daily calories. Actually, many people consume far less than this. An FAO study of Guatemala in 1970 estimated that average daily calorie consumption for the poorest half of the population was only 61 percent of the recommended amount. On the other hand, the consumption of the highest income groups was excessive: medium income people (the next 30 percent of the population) took in 108 percent of the recommended amount; high income people (the next 15 percent) 133 percent; and very high income people (the top 5 percent) consumed 193 percent of the recommended calories (USDA 1981).[6]

The remaining three columns of Table 4.6 report three indicators of malnutrition for children under the age of five. Although the malnourished of all ages are more susceptible to diseases than others and less capable of recovery, this vulnerability is the greatest among small children, and malnutrition is associated with high rates of mortality among the young. Furthermore, protein deficiency is of greater consequence for the young: if deprivation is too severe in the first years, it can result in diminished brain development. The percentages of protein-calorie deficiency for children under five in Central America in the early 1970s were incredibly high, ranging from the high 50s for Costa Rica and Nicaragua to the low 70s for Honduras and El Salvador to 81.4 percent in Guatemala. When the children with only mild malnutrition are removed, the countries' rankings are the same except that Honduras falls to the level of Guatemala, with almost one-third of all children under the age of five suffering from moderate to severe rates (mainly the former) of protein-calorie malnutrition. Tragically, as the final column shows, the occurrence of undernutrition among Central American children increased during 1965–75, a decade in which the region's gross national product increased annually by a rate of 4.9 percent.

The obvious connection between childhood malnutrition in rural areas and the family's lack of sufficient land has been documented by several studies (Brown 1983:18; Carvajal 1979a:227; Valverde et al. 1977:6). Children's nutritional status can also be a function of the type of agricultural system in which families live. The worst instances of moderate to severe malnutrition in El Salvador in 1976 were found in the coffee and the subsistence regions, but for different reasons (Valverde et al. 1980). In the subsistence regions, inadequate fertile land and the lack of other income-generating opportunities accounted for diets unable to meet basic needs. In the coffee-growing regions, however, land is fertile, and the cash crop produces substantial incomes for the landowners. The inadequate diets of the 13 percent of the Salvadoran population that lived on this land and produced the crop, then, were a function of the form of social organization within the region and the resulting distribution of the income that is largely generated by the coffee workers.

The continuing high rates of malnutrition in Central America are in part a result of the region's rapidly increasing population. But the deterioration of the per capita domestic food supply documented in this chapter has occurred simultaneously with a major transformation in agrarian society. The spread of commercial agriculture and the rapid expansion of the share of land devoted to agricultural commodities aimed at foreign markets are fundamental causes of the continuing misery of many of the rural people in Central America. Now they must find new means of providing for their needs. Under existing socioeconomic structures, however, alternatives have been difficult to discover.

ACCESS TO
EMPLOYMENT AND INCOME

Peasants have been urged by public officials and technical advisors to
diversify their production into cash crops both to enhance their living standards and to contribute to the economic development of their countries.
Generally, this is good advice for farmers with enough land to follow it, and
they have responded increasingly. But this strategy is relevant only to a small
and diminishing percentage of the rural population. With the rates of landlessness and near-landlessness escalating, the goal of improving rural incomes
must be discussed in the context of access to more land and/or to other
income-producing opportunities. Pending a redirection of the trend toward
reduced land access (a subject of Part II), the availability of other income-
producing opportunities is the major hope for many rural people.

One option, of course, is to leave the countryside altogether and migrate
to the cities. Increasing numbers of former peasants have made just this
choice. The percentage of the total population living in urban areas has
grown in each country; in Guatemala, for example, it went from 25 in 1950
to 40 in 1980. Indeed, Guatemala City is expected to hold about 30 percent of
the country's entire population by the year 2000. For many migrants,
however, migration alters the context of the problem but does not solve it.
Between 1964 and 1973, the number of urban jobs in Guatemala increased at
only one-half the rate of growth of the urban population (United States
Agency for International Development, Office of Housing 1980:4).[7]

For the landless and near-landless who have remained in rural areas, the
situation generally has deteriorated; for many, it has become desperate.
Relative to need, few significant employment opportunities have been created
in rural Central America in recent decades, with the exception of jobs on the
large, commercial, export-oriented farms. These have done more to worsen
the unemployment problem than to ameliorate it, however, because the
conversion to export crops created much of the landlessness in the first place.
Furthermore, the major export crops of the postwar period require less labor
than others. This is particularly true of cotton growing, which is heavily
mechanized and which at its peak covered about 10 percent of the region's
cropland but provided permanent employment to less than .6 percent of the
agricultural labor force (Quiros Guardia 1973:102). Similarly, cattle raising
is seven to twenty times less labor intensive than are other forms of agriculture (Ashe 1978:15). It is the small farm that makes the best use of Central
America's abundant labor supply, yet the great bulk of the region's land is
owned by a small percentage of large holders. In Costa Rica, for example,
small farms generate three to four times more employment than do large ones
and are usually just as productive (Ashe 1978:13).

   This system of export production in concentrated landholdings is incapable of utilizing the existing labor supply effectively, especially in Guatemala and El Salvador. Consequently, rural un- and underemployment have climbed in recent years. In Guatemala in the early 1970s, the World Bank (1978:15) estimated, rural unemployment reached 42 percent. It was estimated in the early 1980s that three-quarters of the landless had no permanent employment (Hough et al. 1983:77). Studies of Guatemala during this period accordingly found "a general deterioration of the social and economic conditions of its peasant population," especially the Indians (Davis and Hodson 1982:46).

   Even before the 1970s, full-time employment potential was estimated to exist for only 43 percent of El Salvador's rural population (Nathan Associates 1969:59s). A 1976 International Labour Organization study found El Salvador's underutilization of its agricultural population (47 percent underemployed) to be the greatest in all of Latin America (Daines 1977:30; also see OAS 1975). Rural unemployment in each of the countries has been cyclical. In Nicaragua in the mid-1970s, for example, the rural work force was fully employed for four months of the year; unemployment rates for the rest of the year varied from a monthly low of 13 percent to a high of 42 percent, with an average rate of 24 percent for those eight months (Peek 1983:284; also see Núñez Solo 1981:70–73).

   The major income-earning opportunity for this growing surplus of unemployed and underemployed peasants is seasonal work on the large export-producing estates. Some live close enough to do this work with minimal disruption to their family life, but many others, especially in Guatemala, must leave their homes and migrate to the estates temporarily. The most substantial migratory pattern in the region is the flow of Indians from the western highlands to the large farms in the Pacific lowlands. This pattern, it will be recalled, goes back centuries. Labor was coerced from highland Indians by the conquerors in the sixteenth century for the cacao and indigo plantations. Continuing labor scarcities led the political system to sanction the coercion of the labor necessary to develop the coffee sector in the nineteenth and twentieth centuries. Such laws were repealed in the 1940s; now the coercion comes from the impersonal workings of the economic system.

   Deteriorating living standards in the western highlands (from declining person:land ratios, soil exhaustion and erosion from overuse, and few opportunities for migration to new lands) have created a surplus labor pool that provides the necessary labor for the coastal plantations. By 1975 some 60 percent of the economically active rural population of the highlands migrated to work on the plantations (Cardona 1978:36–37),[8] making it the world's largest migratory labor force as a percentage of total population (Paige

1975:361). By the end of the decade, some estimated that around six hundred thousand peasants were part of this seasonal migration (Washington Office on Latin America [WOLA] 1983:3). Yet the income earned in this work is meager, while the transportation, living, and working conditions are often subhuman, according to an International Labour Organization report (Plant 1978:85; also see Burgos-Debray 1984:21–22). Prescient Indians displaced by the expropriation of communal lands by coffee growers over a century ago sent the following message to the president of Guatemala in 1864:

> Everyone is well aware of the ploys used by the coffee growers to seize almost all our land. . . . We cannot help but deplore the fact that these coffee growing gentlemen want to treat us like the European colonists treated the Indians or natives in the country we know today as the great Republic of North America. . . . Could it be that they want to use this factor and historic precedent against us . . . that they want to take our only element of vitality from us, throw us out of our homes and off our land and turn us and future generations into a nomadic and wandering people. . . ? (quoted in Cambranes 1985:74–75)

Income distribution figures for each of the Central American countries make it clear that there is a direct relationship between access to land and rural families' incomes. In 1973 in El Salvador, for example, rural families with landholdings of over 50 hectares constituted only 1 percent of the population but received 30 percent of all rural income. Meanwhile, the 9 percent of the families with adequate farm holdings (between 5 and 50 hectares) received 8.75 times the income of families with 1 to 5 hectares, 16.6 times the income of those with less than 1 hectare of land, and 20.6 times the income of the landless. Data for Guatemala would be similar,[9] but it should be noted that income inequality has not been this great in Costa Rica (Seligson 1980a:90) nor in Honduras (Torres 1979:16–17). Prerevolutionary Nicaragua fell somewhere between the two sets of countries (Núñez Solo 1981:50).

To assess more accurately the relationship between rural stratification and income, one must differentiate categories among both the landless and the landed. Seligson (1980a:90–99) divides the Costa Rican landless into four types. The first two have steady employment but substantial differences in incomes and living conditions. Plantation workers (mainly banana workers) are the envy of the rest of the landless, who rank these unionized laborers in status just after titled landowners. Employees of haciendas (mainly coffee workers), however, make only one-third the income of the plantation workers and usually suffer terrible living conditions as well. But they do have security, unlike the remaining two types of landless peasants, day laborers and migrants.

Modern cotton farms are not important in Costa Rica and are not included in Seligson's study. Other evidence (Valverde et al. 1980) would suggest that life for permanent workers on such farms is better than it is for coffee workers, although certainly less desirable than that of the banana workers. Temporary workers (day laborers and migrants) not only lack employment security but also often toil under inhumane conditions. The plight of the worker in the cotton fields of prerevolutionary Nicaragua, for example, has been summarized this way:

> Harvest workers were stuffed into barracks shelves with roughly the room per person of an Atlantic slave ship; fed rice and beans only if they picked 100 pounds or more of cotton per day; deprived of any semblance of privacy or sanitary facilities; exposed to the unrestricted use of pesticides; and driven to back-breaking labor in the 110 [degree] heat of the Pacific coast by man-killing piece rates. Malaria, dysentery, and diarrheal disease were endemic; intestinal parasites, almost universal. (Paige 1985:106)

Important distinctions can be made among rural people with landholdings not just in terms of the quantity of land they possess but also in the relative security of their access. The most secure but least numerous are owners with legal titles. They are followed by landholders without such titles (who constitute the majority in Honduras, for example, though not in Costa Rica), tenants, and then squatters.

The impact of the spread of commercial agriculture on rural incomes, then, varies among social groups. Those who have managed to hold on to sufficient land have undoubtedly benefited from new income-producing opportunities (for example, see Brintnall 1979:111–114). Others who have been able to obtain permanent employment on modern commercial farms may have improved their position as well, but peasants who have been pushed into the growing pool of the landless and near-landless and who survive as day laborers or migrant laborers are more likely to have experienced a decline in income as well as a loss of security. For the countries where the trend toward export agriculture has gone the furthest—Guatemala and El Salvador, followed by Nicaragua—many studies conclude that living standards have deteriorated for much of the rural population. Despite the losses experienced by many individuals, however, there are data indicating a lessening of rural income inequality in recent decades in both Costa Rica (Fields 1980:241) and Honduras (Molina Chocano and Reina 1983:77). The implications of these trends will be discussed in the concluding section of this chapter.

ENVIRONMENTAL DEGRADATION

Rapid population growth and the expansion of export agriculture have accounted for substantial damage to the natural environment in Central America. Both forces have caused deforestation and soil erosion and exhaustion. Both have diminished the land's ability to support the future's even larger population.[10]

Because of both population growth and commercial growers' encroachments on peasants' land, land scarcity has been a major contributor to erosion and to the exhaustion of soil fertility. Peasants have been forced to overwork their land, for example reducing or eliminating the crucial fallow cycle of traditional growing practices. They have also been pushed onto steeper hillsides which, once cultivated, are soon eroded by torrential rainfalls. The rains carry the soil into reservoirs, silting them up and ending their usefulness earlier than projected (Hoy 1984).

Commercialization, especially the rapid conversion of land to cotton growing, has also had a direct impact on soil exhaustion and erosion. Browning's (1971) comparison of coffee and cotton growers is most telling in this respect. As he points out,

> whereas coffee farmers realized that sound techniques of cultivation based on applied research were a necessity for the long-term future of the crop, the cotton farmers cleared and cultivated the coastal plain in an attempt to gain maximum and immediate profits with little thought of the long-term effects of their activities. (pp. 240–241)

The conversion of land to cotton growing in Guatemala is discussed by Adams (1970:375–378) in the same terms; he found "short-term investment for quick profits" leading to the "systematic destruction of the land." Similar damage to the soil of the Nicaraguan Pacific lowlands was described by a study mission from the International Bank for Reconstruction and Development in the first years of the cotton boom (IBRD 1953:29).

A major victim of the expansion of agricultural land has been the region's forests and woodlands. Much of the forest cover had already been eliminated in the highlands before the contemporary period and in the Pacific coastal region before the 1960s. Since 1960 deforestation has accelerated. Between 1961 and 1978, almost 40 percent of the remaining forests were cleared; at the same rates, some estimate, virtually all forest will have been eliminated by 1990 (Myers 1981:5). This destruction has been the greatest, in both percentage and absolute area, in Guatemala, which lost almost one-half of its remaining forests in less than two decades. Honduras's denudation has been almost as large, and in fact unofficial sources report a loss of up to 72 percent there (Myers 1981:5). In an important sense, however, the greatest despoil-ment occurred in El Salvador; although its absolute loss was the smallest in the region, it was stripped of all its remaining forest.

Some of the forests lost have been those on mountain slopes cleared by peasants in their search for land. Probably the major cause of denudation since 1960, however, has been the expansion of beef raising for export markets. Forests have been felled in formerly frontier regions to make way for cattle, with much of the timber left to rot on the ground; up to 86 percent of it was wasted in this manner in Costa Rica between 1955 and 1973 (Ashe 1978:37; also see Guess [1979] and Place [1981]). Since the mid-1970s, though, Costa Rica at least has begun to give attention to this destruction, to consider conservation measures, and to develop national parks (Myers 1981:8). Nonetheless, for every hectare reforested in Costa Rica in 1982, 12 were deforested (*La Nación* 1982:6A).

An additional dimension of deforestation is its effect on the region's energy supply. Wood fuel is the major source of energy in Honduras, El Salvador, and Guatemala, and in 1979 wood provided about 47 percent of all energy consumed in the isthmus as a whole, especially in cooking. Dimin-ishing forests, then, also mean a shrinking supply of this major energy source and, consequently, higher firewood prices in both rural and urban areas. Forestry by small farmers is the most important source of fuelwood, though it is not the major cause of deforestation (Jones 1984:8). As peasants lose access to land, they are probably losing access to their major source of fuel as well. Despite the central importance of small farmers' forestry to the well-being of much of the region's population, until recently virtually all forestry research has been concerned with construction-quality timber, much of which is aimed at the export market.

A final environmental problem has been the indiscriminate use of pes-ticides, most especially by cotton growers. One report (cited by Weir and Shapiro 1981:12) documents more than fourteen thousand poisonings and forty deaths from pesticides in the Pacific lowlands between 1972 and 1975 alone. Because of excessive use of pesticides, people in Guatemala and Nicaragua during this period were thirty-one times as likely to have DDT in their blood as people in the United States (Weir and Shapiro 1981:12–13; Collins 1986:161–166). Careless pesticide use has also led to the evolution of pesticide-resistant species of malaria-carrying mosquitoes, especially in Nicaragua (Holland 1973:37).

CONCLUSION:
AGRO-EXPORT DEVELOPMENT IN
UNEQUAL RURAL SOCIETIES

The evidence presented in this chapter clearly substantiates the claim that the
implementation of the agro-export development model in Central America in
the postwar period has substantially undermined the economic security of
many of the region's rural people. The quantitative data available support the
numerous descriptive accounts that portray the conversion of land to export
crops as enriching the few, while a much more sizable proportion of the
population has suffered from diminishing land access, food supply, and
employment opportunities. The harmful effects of the expansion of agricultural export production under conditions of gross inequality have occurred throughout the region and in each of the individual countries, though
there are variations in the experiences of individual countries.

The postwar agrarian transformation in Central America carries an
impact strikingly similar to those felt in earlier eras when rural society was
transformed by the expansion of export agriculture. Like the cacao, indigo,
and coffee transformations, the boom in agricultural exports in the contemporary period was ignited by elites who were able to use foreign markets to
enrich themselves and to bring in badly needed revenues to underwrite the
region's development. In each case, some prosperity and progress were
created, but primarily in urban centers. In rural areas, the implementation of
the agro-export development model has often diminished the quality of life
for peasants. For example, Place (1981) concludes on the basis of her field
research in Costa Rica's Guanacaste Province that

> rapid economic growth in Guanacaste during the past several decades has
> apparently not improved the quality of life of many *campesinos*. Every "old-
> timer" that I interviewed told the same story: each claimed that 20 or 30 years
> ago people used to live better, although they had little money. There was plenty of
> land available on which to grow crops, there was abundant game to hunt and
> more domestic animal products were available. Diet was apparently more varied
> and food was more abundant. *Campesinos* were basically self-sufficient and
> could support a family with relatively little effort. Today, they have no access to
> land because affluent investors have moved in and taken over, and . . . [public
> lands] have disappeared. They have to buy food now, but wages are insufficient
> to cover a family's needs. (p. 177)

The response of rural people to the disruption in their lives and the deterioration of their living standard is crucial to an understanding of the crisis in
contemporary Central America. Before that discussion is taken up in Part II, it

remains to examine the implications of this chapter for the agro-export development model.

Certainly there is much to commend in an argument that in order to improve living conditions, the countries of Central America need to diversify and expand exports, including agricultural exports (USAID 1984:1). A strong rationale exists at the theoretical level for the viability of the agro-export development model (Goldberg 1981; Hillman 1981). But the consequences of the modernization of Third World agriculture argue for caution. As noted in chapter 1, agricultural modernization in later-developing countries has tended to reinforce social inequalities, especially and most seriously in those whose social structures were already significantly unequal.

The nature of existing social structures is critical to the impact of export-led development models (Adams and Behrman 1982; Johnston and Clark 1982:254–256; Timmer 1982:37–39). An examination of the perceived contemporary success stories (countries such as South Korea and Taiwan, which have combined economic growth with income distributions more equitable than those in most nations) makes it clear that the social context is as important as the model. On the basis of her extensive research, Adelman (1980) makes the point explicit:

> The successful countries all followed a process in which the asset that was going to be the major asset of production at each stage of development was redistributed before rather than after its productivity was improved. This asset was redistributed either in terms of direct ownership or in terms of institutional access to its productive utilization. Only after redistribution were policies undertaken to improve the productivity of the major asset. (pp. 442–443)[11]

More specifically, the agricultural commodities stage of these countries' export-led development experience *followed* a substantial redistribution of the land. This prior structural change allowed rapid economic growth with relative equity, a direct contrast to the recent Central American experience. Such successes no more vindicate a general export-led development model as viable for all societies than the failure of the Honduran banana enclave to ignite the development of that country can be taken to teach the opposite lesson.

The socially conditioned impact of the agro-export development model is confirmed by other evidence from Central America as well. Generally, the region serves as a negative example that reinforces Adelman's point, though the case of Costa Rica is somewhat of an exception. That country's historical development contrasts with those of its neighbors. Into the twentieth century, it retained a strong rural middle class which, together with the relative absence of a neofeudal class of large landowners, allowed it to develop a vibrant political democracy after World War II. Accordingly, Costa Rican development policy has been implemented with a more explicit welfare component in a less unequal social structure than those of neighboring countries. One six-nation study of a diverse set of Third World countries found Costa Rica and Taiwan unique in having successfully combined rapid economic growth with declining inequality (the other countries studied were Brazil, India, the Philippines, and Sri Lanka). Interpreting these results, the author concludes that perhaps "a distributionally oriented development program that integrates the poor into the mainstream of the economy may cause a higher growth rate, other things being equal" (Fields 1980:241; also see Seligson and Muller, 1985).

It must be stressed, however, that claims for Costa Rica's uniqueness can be carried too far. The usual pattern in the evidence surveyed in this chapter was for Costa Rica to manifest the same trends as the other countries of the region but usually at a lesser rate. Substantial increases in both population and the share of land devoted to cattle raising have created serious land pressures, while the world economic crisis of the early 1980s crippled the economy, eroded financial security, and aggravated social tensions. To the extent that Costa Rica shares the agrarian structures of the region, then, it also suffers from the resulting problems.

NOTES

1. For a similar analysis for Latin America as a whole, see Grindle (1986:111–131).
2. One good description of this process is Posas (1981a), which discusses the Honduran North Coast region.
3. A Gini index for land concentration was not used here because, as a single score, it misses the different patterns that exist for inequality among smallest and largest holdings.
4. These fluctuations in per capita basic food production are missed by Mooney (1984:63), who looks at only one decade, 1969–70 to 1978–79, a time of rising per capita production. For evidence on the impact of the civil war on basic food production, see United States Department of State (1984:276–278).
5. See the related discussion in Wilkie and Moreno-Ibáñeze (1984).
6. The complete citation is USDA Foreign Agricultural Service, "Guatemala—Agricultural Situation." Guatemala:USDA, 1981.
7. Some see this situation as a blessing. The following paragraphs appeared in a 1963 guide for U.S. businesspeople:

LABOR POOL WITHOUT BOTTOM!

To the prospective plant operator, the availability of labor in El Salvador is one of the most favorable factors to be found. The industrialist is assured of one of the most plentiful labor supplies in the Hemisphere. . . .

. . . It is evident that there will be many applicants for every industrial job created here. (quoted in Conway 1963:19–20)

8. Migration is the greatest from the most remote of the highland provinces. Smith (1978, 1984a, 1984b) suggests that this is because land scarcity problems are more recent in those areas, and therefore economic alternatives have not been developed there. In the more central areas, by contrast, such problems are long standing, and adaptation has been possible over time.

9. Income distribution for the whole population is outrageously skewed for both countries. A 1974 survey of metropolitan San Salvador found that the top 10 percent of the population received more of the total income than did the remaining 90 percent (Karush 1978:72). A similar feat was almost accomplished in 1968 by the top tenth of all Guatemalans; their share of the national income was 47.5 percent. Just the top 5 percent received 35.2 percent of all income (Graber 1980:15).

10. For a discussion of well-developed conservation methods among Guatemalan Indians in an area of high population density, see Veblen (1978).

11. For background on South Korea, see Adelman and Robinson (1978); on Taiwan, see Clark (1985) and Puchala and Stavely (1979). On both as well as other newly industrializing countries, see Corbo, Krueger, and Ossa (1986).

PART II
Political Conflict

CHAPTER 5

Guatemala:
From Reform to a
Reign of Terror

The postwar period began with much promise in Guatemala. Through large popular demonstrations in 1944, the country cast off the tyranny of right-wing dictatorship with the overthrow of Jorge Ubico. Relatively fair and free elections were held for the first times in 1945 and 1950. In contrast to the traditional system, which served and protected narrow, elite interests, the popular governments initiated reform programs, including an ambitious agrarian reform. The reform period was aborted in 1954, however, through a destabilization campaign and an armed invasion by a small exile army, both sponsored by the United States.

Guatemala has been dominated by the military since 1954, usually with a military officer serving as president. For a variety of reasons, ranging from personal, institutional, and class interests to ideological orientations, many in the military have perceived popular mobilization as a threat. When provoked, the military has relied on repression, with each round more widespread and indiscriminate than the one before. The repression after the "liberation" of 1954 was followed by a regional reign of terror in the late 1960s and early 1970s. By the end of the seventies, the entire country was engulfed in a reign of state terrorism that continued into the present decade. According to the British Parliamentary Group on Human Rights (United States, House, 1985a:63); the death toll after thirty-one years of military rule had climbed to over one hundred thousand killed and thirty-eight thousand disappeared; another million were internal refugees (Bowen 1985:106). This in a country whose population during these three decades grew from 3.5 to 7.5 million people.

Although all sectors of society have suffered from the terror, the majority of the victims have been peasants. As this chapter will demonstrate, the system of control established in rural areas during the colonial period and reinforced by the liberal reforms of the last century has been threatened in the postwar period by the mobilization of the peasantry and by the appearance of guerrilla movements committed to radical change. Especially disturbing to elites were the activation of Indians in the western highlands (still about one-half of the population) and the forging of ties between Indians and the revolutionary forces.

The agrarian changes discussed in Part I opened up new possibilities for some rural people but led to deteriorating living conditions for many others. Encouraged by such new actors from outside as church people and development workers, peasants organized to assert and defend their interests. Although military counterinsurgency campaigns have justified themselves as combating the "communist menace," the demobilization of the peasantry, and especially the Indians, has been a primary objective of the military and its civilian supporters in the postwar period.

THE REFORM YEARS:
1944–1954

The most important public policy of the progressive administrations of 1944–54 was the agrarian reform program initiated in 1952. The constitution adopted in 1945 prohibited the *latifundia* (neofeudal estates with much unused land) and the extension of those already in existence, but land redistribution did not reach the top of the political agenda until the election of Jacobo Arbenz, who assumed office in March 1951. The agrarian reform law, which passed the Guatemalan Congress by an overwhelming margin in 1952, was intended, as it stated, to "eradicate feudal property in the rural areas" and to "develop capitalist methods of agricultural production."[1] This law and its implementation generated much controversy within Guatemala, especially concerning the issues of the lack of judicial oversight and autonomy, the concentration of power in the hands of the president, the amount to be paid in compensation, the impartiality of the reform bureaucracy, and the role of Communists and other radicals in encouraging peasants to initiate expropriation proceedings. Nonetheless, in its brief lifetime the program had substantial success. The total area distributed equaled about 20 percent of the nation's arable land, and the program reached close to 24 percent of the population (Aybar de Soto 1978:181, 210). Furthermore, production of basic food staples increased, allowing imports to be reduced.

The approximately 1.8 million acres distributed under the program represented three types of holdings: public lands, domestically owned *latifundia*, and United Fruit Company lands. Guatemala had a substantial amount of public land that could be distributed because of the confiscation during World War II of farms owned by German nationals, who held many of the most productive of the large coffee estates. These now-public lands constituted a little over 18 percent of those distributed under the program.[2]

Of the 1.5 million privately owned acres both expropriated and distributed by the program, most were unused land on large, domestically owned estates. The law exempted from expropriation farms under 223 acres as well as those between 233 and 670 acres that had at least two-thirds of their area under cultivation. Clearly, the purposes of the law were simultaneously to bring into production the vast expanses of unused fertile land and to provide individual plots to landless peasants. As a result, the reform failed to generate much enthusiasm or support among Guatemala's large Indian community, which would have preferred a communal reform restoring lands lost to the expansion of coffee growing in earlier periods (Wasserstrom 1975:474).

Some of the most glaring examples of unused land belonged to the United Fruit Company, long a dominating and controversial presence in Guatemala. In 1953 and 1954 a total of about 70 percent of the company's 550,000 acres of holdings were expropriated. Despite the massive loss this seizure represented to the company, its production activities were not directly threatened. Most of its land—between 74 (Aybar de Soto 1978:200) and 85 percent (Schlesinger and Kinzer 1983:75)—lay fallow. Only about 4 percent of its holdings were at the time used for growing bananas, so even granted that the company required reserves of four times that amount to rotate cultivation in the event of disease, clearly it was left after the expropriations with adequate holdings for its banana-growing activities. But even though its productive potential was not directly threatened, the dominant position that United Fruit had enjoyed over both its work force and the government of Guatemala certainly were.

The fruit company was also distressed over the form and amount of compensation that it was offered. The law provided for compensation in twenty-five-year bonds based on property values as declared for tax purposes (always understated). The government offered about $1.2 million in compensation; the company demanded $16.5 million as the land's fair value. In response to these various challenges to its hegemony, United Fruit expanded its already considerable efforts to convince the United States government and public that vital U.S. interests were seriously endangered in Guatemala.

United Fruit had felt threatened at least since 1947, when a labor code favorable to workers was passed in order to actualize the promises of the 1945 constitution. The code initially limited the right to organize rural unions to agricultural enterprises employing at least five hundred people. Not only did United Fruit now have to contend with lawful labor unions, but it also was bitter about what it perceived to be the discriminatory scope of the code. The size restriction was removed the following year, however, generating more domestic opposition to the reform program. There were other reforms, too, that addressed the historic imbalance of power in rural areas. The vagrancy law was abolished in 1945, and a ceiling on land rents was established by the Law of Forced Rental in 1949 at 10 percent of yield, reduced in 1951 to 5 percent.

More generally and more fundamentally, the established powers were threatened by the spreading politicization and mobilization of the rural population. This social change was the result of three major factors, though there were substantial variations from village to village.[3] First, beginning in 1945 local officials were to be elected. Many villages came to be led by elected Indians rather than appointed Ladinos, bringing "dignity and responsibility to the Indians in place of the traditional subservience and dependency" (Siegal, quoted in Davis 1983a:8). The elections catalyzed a fair amount of political activity in many villages and led to the penetration of the countryside by the major national political parties. In a number of cases, progressive Ladinos encouraged Indian political participation because, as a minority within the local Ladino community, they would otherwise be outvoted (Adams 1957).

Second, the reforms themselves mobilized rural people. Through the rights guaranteed by the constitution and the new labor code and respected by the government, peasants began to organize leagues and unions. The National Confederation of Peasants of Guatemala (CNCG) was formed in 1950 and held its first national meeting the next year; by 1954 it claimed some four hundred thousand members. The formation of unions sometimes led to strikes; for example, those at national estates in 1950 spread to large private estates and resulted in wage increases. Most important, the reform law called for the formation of local agrarian committees that were to initiate expropriation proceedings, when appropriate, in response to peasants' requests. The committees consisted of two representatives appointed by government officials and three from local peasant leagues or unions. The grassroots nature of the program encouraged the mobilization of rural people, both to initiate expropriations and to form peasant organizations. By late 1953 almost fifteen hundred of these committees had formed.

Finally, for the first time outside forces penetrated rural society with the intention of assisting peasants to organize in behalf of their own interests. These organizers were especially important in explaining the agrarian reform, assisting in the formation of agrarian committees, and encouraging the initiation of expropriation proceedings. Because these organizers were radicals and often Communists, the threat that they and their activities represented to established interests was substantial. Indeed, the National Confederation of Peasants of Guatemala itself was under Communist influence (Blasier 1976:155).[4] Although Arbenz envisioned an agrarian reform that would modernize agricultural production without alienating middle-sector groups, leftist politicians and labor organizers hoped to radicalize the reform in order to transform the agrarian class structure (Wasserstrom 1975:454–457). In particular, they encouraged—and sometimes led—illegal land seizures, especially in Escuintla, where peasants were well organized. As the number of seizures increased into 1954 (sometimes with violence, such as the hanging in January of two landowners), opponents of Arbenz believed that his administration lacked both the will and capability to maintain rural order. Although the various agrarian policies of the reform period were relatively moderate by today's standards and did not directly threaten fundamental economic interests of the elite, the system of domination from which elites profited was endangered as peasants began to claim some of their potential power.

The change in the countryside during this period was substantial. As pointed out in chapter 1, patronage relationships are a primary embodiment of peasant subordination in the traditional social structure. Outside organizers often help to break down this domination by offering alternative sources of economic assistance and protection as well as by advocating competing value systems. This transformation in Guatemala during the period 1944–54 has been well described by anthropologist Richard Adams (1970):

> Indians and Ladinos found that it was possible to seek out other authorities and sources of power than those familiar in the unitary patronal system. Whereas before, the *patrón* or the elders had the last word, it was increasingly assumed that not only were they no longer the final authority, but they also could be ignored almost at will. The operation of these new organizations demonstrated that *campesinos* could expect some satisfaction without retribution from the local landowner or the local council of elders. (p. 191; see also p. 205)

The growing numbers of peasant organizations illustrate this change: in 1948 twenty-three peasant *sindicatos* (unions) and five peasant *uniones* (leagues) had been legally recognized; in 1954 the respective numbers were 345 and 320 (Murphy 1970:445–447).

The Arbenz government was overthrown in June 1954 by a destabilization campaign and an armed invasion, both organized and financed by the United States (Immerman 1982; Schlesinger and Kinzer 1983). Central to the animosity of the Eisenhower administration toward the Guatemalan government was the impact of the agrarian reform program on the United Fruit Company. Nonetheless, it is well established and widely accepted (e.g., Blasier 1976; Bowen 1983; Krasner 1978) that the United States intervention was not motivated directly by a desire to protect the economic interests of United Fruit but rather by the fact that the Guatemalan attack on United Fruit reinforced Washington's unwarranted perception that "international Communism" was successfully establishing a beachhead in the Western hemisphere—a perception that United Fruit invested considerable efforts in promoting (Schlesinger and Kinzer 1983).

RURAL CONTRADICTIONS SHARPEN: 1954–1980

Following Guatemala's "liberation," as it was called, urban and rural masses were demobilized through repression. Within a month over four thousand radicals were jailed, and many labor leaders and peasants were killed (Handy 1984:186–187). The leading union confederations, such as the National Confederation of Peasants of Guatemala, were abolished, many local unions were declared illegal, and the remainder were sharply restricted in their activities. The right to vote was restricted, disenfranchising over one-half of the electorate. This demobilization of the peasantry proved to be successful only temporarily, however.

Counterrevolutionary Agrarian Reform

The "liberation" program reversed the accomplishments of the agrarian reform. Virtually all of the reform recipients were removed from their recently gained land, by force if necessary, and it was returned to its original owners. The primary beneficiary of this campaign was the United Fruit Company, which received back all of its expropriated lands. Furthermore, a number of the national farms were privatized; thirty-nine were distributed to private owners in holdings averaging over 7700 acres each (Hough et al. 1983:29). A few years later, in 1960, President Miguel Ydígoras announced that two of the remaining national estates would be divided among deserving members of the military—probably meaning officers who had sided with him against a coup attempt eleven days earlier (Adams 1968–69:109, n. 3).

In the context of counterreform in 1954, both the new president of Guatemala, Carlos Castillo Armas, and the United States government needed to develop an alternative solution to the country's agrarian problems. Their answer was the Guatemalan Rural Development Program.[5] The U.S. Congress had given the Eisenhower administration "a blank check to make Guatemala 'a showplace for democracy'" (McCamant 1968:32). Between 1954 and 1959, the United States spent just under $14 million for rural development in Guatemala, primarily for the resettlement of peasants in nineteen colonization projects located mainly along the Pacific slope. Altogether, Guatemala in 1955 received more than 21 percent of all grant aid to Latin America (Bowen 1985:91).

Much of the land for the colonization projects (over a hundred thousand acres) was donated by the United Fruit Company. When its lands were returned after the overthrow of Arbenz, they came back with many squatters living on them. The understanding was that in return for United Fruit's donation of land, the government would clear out the squatters on the company's remaining holdings.[6] By 1963 the U.S.–backed project had settled 4887 families, while a separate effort distributed 16,722 small plots to landless peasants. Meanwhile, between 1950 and 1962 the number of landless farm families had increased to one hundred and forty thousand (Hildebrand 1969:59).

The model employed in the development projects was imported from the United States; its objective was "to create independent middle class farm owners and operators" (Hildebrand 1969:36). A 1970 AID evaluation concluded, not surprisingly, that the impact of such colonization projects on the "land tenure structure has been negligible, if any" (Gayoso 1970:5). Nonetheless, in the late 1970s the United States once again became involved in a resettlement program, this time in the western corner of the Northern Transversal Strip, which runs across the neck of the country. Here AID provided $5.6 million to finance a pilot resettlement project involving four thousand families. Because of land grabbing by elites in the region, however, one foreign analyst was quoted in 1979 as claiming that "by the time the experiment is completed, there'll be no land left to distribute." Indeed, it was reported that "much of the best land ha[d] already fallen into the hands of wealthy farmers and army officers" (Riding 1979:A2).

Overall, very few of the landless or land-poor peasants of Guatemala have been served by the land distribution programs of the post-1954 governments. Even when permanently employed plantation workers are excluded from analysis, a recent study prepared for the USAID mission to Guatemala found, only 8.9 percent of the needy benefited in 1955–64, 3.5 percent in 1965–73, and 5.7 percent in 1974–81 (Hough et al., 1983:32–35). However, half of the parcels distributed have been larger than 25 hectares, the bulk of them over 100 hectares, especially under the 1970–74 administration of Arana Osorio (Hough et al. 1983:98; Gayoso 1970).

Rural Repression

Given the deterioration of the position of much of the peasantry detailed in Part I, it is not surprising that radical guerrilla organizations appeared hoping to mobilize the peasantry in behalf of a radical restructuring of Guatemalan society. The first such organizations, led by military officers who had failed in an attempted coup in November 1960, centered their activities in the eastern mountains. Regrouping, they never numbered more than several hundred fighters and eventually divided into two different organizations. Although they attempted to mobilize Indians, the group remained almost totally Ladino in composition. Their efforts were frustrated both by the legacy of centuries of well-grounded Indian distrust of Ladinos and by the fact that ethnic tension had been intensified in the East by the politics of the reform period.

The military allowed civilians to take control of the government with the elections of 1966, in which Julio Méndez Montenegro was the victor. It is widely acknowledged that in return, the civilian government consented to give the military a free hand to conduct its counterinsurgency campaign. The military, and the paramilitary death squads allied with it, eliminated not only the guerrillas but also thousands of innocent peasants, especially in the department of Zacapa, apparently believing in the deterrent effect of widespread, systematic terror. Between three and eight thousand noncombatants are estimated to have been killed betweeen 1966 and 1968.[7] United States military assistance was important to the counterinsurgency effort, supplying training, advice, and helicopters and other equipment. The attitude of the U.S. military mission was clear. The situation was described in *Time* (1968):

> To aid in the drive, the army also hired and armed local bands of "civilian collaborators" licensed to kill peasants whom they considered guerrillas or "potential" guerrillas. There were those who doubted the wisdom of encouraging such measures in violence-prone Guatemala, but . . . the head of the U.S. military mission was not among them. "That's the way this country is," he said. "The Communists are using everything they have, including terror. And it must be met." (p. 23)[8]

Altogether from 1950 to 1979, the United States supplied Guatemala with over $60 million in military assistance and trained over thirty-three hundred Guatemalan military officers at U.S. military facilities (Trudeau 1984:61; McClintock, 1985b).

Violence escalated in urban areas during 1966–68 as well, from both leftists and, especially, right-wing death squads. The paramilitary groups were not independent organizations but were rather, according to Amnesty

International (1981a:24–25), "providing cover for military and police activities" and "preserv[ing] some semblance of democratic government." The violence diminished somewhat in 1968 when, in the wake of the daylight kidnaping of the archbishop of Guatemala City, the defense minister and Colonel Carlos Arana Osorio, the head of the military's counterinsurgency campaign, were sent to diplomatic posts overseas. However, in 1970 Arana, "the butcher of Zacapa," was elected president. The repression escalated once again, especially in the eastern mountains and Guatemala City. With Arana in control of state power, a "regime of terror and violence may said to have been institutionalized" (Johnson 1972:17). Once again popular mobilization was repressed, this time ferociously; "official violence was now used to stamp out any form of peasant or labor protest" (AI 1981a:26). The Committee of Relatives of Disappeared Persons estimated that there were some fifteen thousand cases of disappearance between 1970 and 1975, at least 75 percent of them attributable directly to government security forces (AI 1981a:26).

Despite considerable violence committed against its leaders and membership, the Christian Democratic party was able to run such an effective campaign for the presidency in 1974 that the military's candidate was able to "win" only through fraud. During the first year of General Kjell Laugerud's administration, official violence declined, but following the earthquake that devastated the western part of the country in February 1976, rural repression began once again. Its scope expanded yearly until a reign of state terrorism pervaded the country, especially the western highlands. As in the earlier operations in the eastern mountains, the immediate target was leftist guerrillas. The military's indiscriminate counterinsurgency campaign, however, was directed not just at denying the revolutionaries a supportive popular base but also at destroying any autonomous popular organizations in the countryside. In contrast to the previous decade, by the late 1970s a substantial degree of popular mobilization had occurred; accordingly, the military engaged in much more widespread violence in order to secure its objectives.

Peasant Mobilization

The sources of peasant mobilization and organization in the 1970s were many. Among the most important were the activities of Church workers, especially those involved with Catholic Action; the efforts of progressive political parties; development efforts initiated by workers from outside; the continuing deterioration of the peasantry's economic condition; government repression; and the resurgence of radical guerrilla movements.

Catholic Action was begun in 1946 by Archbishop Mariano Rossell

Arellano as a conservative reaction to the changes made during the reform period. As the archbishop stated it, "Our small Catholic Action was one of the greatest comforts in those hours of enormous distress in the presence of Marxist advance that invaded everything" (quoted in Warren 1978:89). The intention was to bolster the Catholic faith of Indian communities, but the important long-term effect was to undermine for many Indians their attachment to village religious traditions and their submission to traditionalist elders. This "liberation" made them available for later mobilization by change-oriented outside forces. Freed from traditional beliefs, which often gave supernatural and individualistic explanations for suffering, the new converts were now more open to the perception of material and collective causes and solutions to problems.

Life in Indian villages had been grounded in religious beliefs and practices that combined Catholicism with pre-Columbian religion. As this synthesis evolved, the authority of Indian religious leaders was reinforced, partly as a defensive reaction against the waves of Ladino attacks on Indian communities over the centuries and partly because Ladinos countenanced it since Indian deference to the religious hierarchies reinforced the overall system of social control (Carmack 1983:244; Warren 1978:89). A major purpose of Catholic Action was to further the Christian conversion of Indians by attacking and undermining indigenous "superstitions." But as Indians rejected traditional religious beliefs, they also freed themselves from the conservative authority of traditional religious leaders and societies (i.e., the cofradías). This process of conversion was often experienced as one of "liberation" (Falla 1978:519–525). In many communities the cleavage between traditionalists and the new converts (catechists) became one of the most important lines of conflict.[9]

If the catechists rejected some of their native customs, they did not repudiate their Indian heritage; instead, they "affirm[ed] Indian ethnic pride in the face of Ladino racism, economic exploitation, and political control" (Davis 1983b:8; see also Brintnall 1979; Burgos-Debray 1984; and Warren 1978). Studies found that Catholic Action fostered in the new converts, usually younger Indians, a group consciousness that connected them to neighboring villages (Handy 1984:241) and that encouraged them to see "themselves as 'apostles' carrying the new 'social gospel' of the Catholic Church to their less fortunate Indian brothers and sisters" (Davis 1983b:8). Consequently, the conversion process promoted by Catholic Action attacked not only the traditional Indian hierarchy but also the system of social control benefiting Ladinos.

This point is well illustrated in a highland Indian's answer to a Ladino's comment that the fading of native customs was "very sad": "Yes, it is sad . . . for you!" (Brintnall 1979:141). While traditionalists worried about maintaining good ties with their Ladino *patrones*, the catechists tended "to see such relationships as repressive and exploitive, blocking the progress of Indians and the leveling of the two ethnic groups" (Warren 1978:135). They also rejected deferential, submissive behavior towards Ladinos, even feeling free to express hostility toward them openly (Brintnall 1979:175). Freed from traditional restrictions and magical explanations for their deprivation and inferior status, the converts were often leaders of new peasant organizations. The first fifty members of a peasant league in El Quiché discussed by Falla (1978:485–489), for example, all were Catholic Action converts.

Historically, few Indian communities have been served by priests; in the early 1950s, for example, there were only three priests in all of the department of El Quiché and only 194 active priests in the entire country (Falla 1978:440). In order to promote Catholic Action and to meet the challenge of Protestant missionaries, foreign priests were welcomed to Guatemala. By 1963 El Quiché had twenty-five priests, and the country had 415 by the late 1960s, only 15 percent of them native born (Falla 1978:451; Handy 1984:239).

The concerns of many of these priests went beyond religious conversion, however. In the northern portion of the Indian department of Huehuetenango, Maryknolls from North America had established a presence in most villages by the early 1960s and had converted thousands of Indians. But their efforts were also addressed to rural development and included founding schools, clinics, and credit cooperatives. In response to government inaction in face of the serious land pressures in the highlands, the religious workers initiated their own colonization project in the late 1960s in the underpopulated Ixcán region of the far north of the department (and the country). Encouraging Indians to become colonists rather than continue to migrate seasonally to the Pacific plantations, they helped with infrastructure construction and the creation of a broad rural development movement across northern Guatemala. Most significantly, the foreign Church workers gave serious attention to the development of indigenous leaders, not only to carry out these projects but also to take the reformist social message into the most remote Indian villages (Chernow 1979; Davis 1983a:3–5).

The missionaries were not alone in their efforts. Among the outside organizing forces were new, progressive political parties. The most important of these was the Christian Democratic Party, which had close ties to Catholic Action. Organizers established local affiliates of the national party, encouraged supporters to run for local offices, and helped to establish peasant leagues and cooperatives. Furthermore, the Christian Democrats were critical in some areas to Indians' achievement of political power on the local level (see, for example, Brintnall 1979:158–160).

Rural development projects were also initiated by foreign governments

110

and private organizations. Beginning in the late 1960s, the United States AID mission to Guatemala began "placing high priority" (Davidson 1976a:1) on rural development; a $23 million rural development sector loan approved in 1970 for cooperative development and basic food crop production was seen as marking "the first time substantial resources were being directed at the Highlands" (Davidson 1976a:1). The Arana administration was skeptical of the value of such "socialist" institutions as cooperatives, but it was willing to allow AID to undertake the project as long as the cooperatives did not lead to "the development of a potential 'pressure group' that would become 'broadly representational' in nature and begin to apply political pressure on the government" (Davidson 1976b:14). The AID contractor consciously tried to keep the cooperatives nonpolitical; however, this attempt generated conflict with the existing cooperative movement. It consisted largely of Christian Democrats in opposition to the existing government, many of whom "bitterly criticized" the cooperatives as an imposed foreign model. Some viewed the AID project as an attempt to destroy the existing cooperative movement (Davidson 1976b:15, 23–24).

Within a few years many of these tensions were reduced. The AID project grew more sensitive about competing with existing cooperatives, more Guatemalans were moved into leadership positions, and the Christian Democratic Cooperative federation began receiving some AID funding. Furthermore, during the early years of General Laugerud's administration (1974–78), the government's attitude toward cooperatives changed to one of cautious encouragement. By fall 1975 about 20 percent of highland Indians participated in some form of cooperatives (Handy 1984:240). Following the earthquake of February 1976, which killed over twenty-three thousand people, especially in the highlands, another two hundred private and public foreign organizations initiated activities in the country (Gondolf 1981). Shortly thereafter, Guatemala had 510 cooperatives, including 57 percent of them in the highlands, with a combined membership of more than 132,000 people (Davis 1983c:162).

Although these rural development efforts brought new credit opportunities, technical assistance, marketing possibilities, schools, literacy projects, and health clinics, they were not able to keep up with the deteriorating economic situation experienced by many Indians, especially those in the western highlands.[10] As detailed in Part I, the eviction of peasants from their land, together with the steady increase in population, intensified already serious pressures on the land. Arable land per capita declined from 1.7 hectares in 1950 to .92 hectares in 1973 to .79 hectares in 1980. Consistently since the 1950 census, 88 percent of the farms in Guatemala have been under 7 hectares, the estimated size necessary to support a family adequately. Landlessness among rural families was estimated in 1970 at 26.6 percent. By

1975 about 60 percent of the economically active rural population of the highlands had to migrate to plantations to find work, making this the most migratory labor force in the world (Paige 1975:361).

During the 1970s competition developed for land in underpopulated lowland regions, which became increasingly important as an alternative to the ever more densely populated highlands. Across the northern expanse of the country, Indians were dispossessed of land by military officers and domestic and foreign economic elites, who coveted the region for its cattle-ranching and mineral possibilities. In order to obtain it, they once again turned repression against the peasantry. A counterinsurgency campaign began in northern El Quiché a month after the earthquake. Nominally aimed at a small guerrilla band, it was soon targeted against the cooperative movement; within the next year and a half, close to two hundred cooperative members in the region disappeared. Similar repression occurred in northern Huehuetenango. It was during this period that one of the most activist of the Maryknoll priests died in a mysterious plane crash (Chernow 1979; Davis 1983a:5–6). It will be recalled that the infamous massacre at Panzós, discussed in the last chapter, was directed against Indians who were protesting the appropriation of their lands in the northeastern part of the country.

Freed from deference to traditional conservative authority structures, encouraged by outside social change advocates, confronting a deteriorating economic situation, and now faced once again with government repression, increasing numbers of Indians began to organize for economic and political action. Indian candidates were again winning municipal elections, and in the mid-1970s two were elected to the national congress. In 1978 the Committee for Peasant Unity (CUC) was founded, the first organization to bring together Indian subsistence and migrant farmers with poor Ladino farmworkers. It quickly affiliated with the two-year-old, urban-based National Committee of Trade Union Unity (CNUS). In its first public appearance, at the May 1 Labor Day parade, the CUC presented the largest public demonstration of Indians the country had seen (Black 1983b:6–7; Burgos-Debray 1984; Davis 1983c:165).

The strength of the CUC and its threat to elite interests were demonstrated by a series of strikes in 1980. A strike of seventy thousand sugar cane workers and forty thousand cotton pickers was called in February to protest working conditions and the abysmally low minimum wage.[11] Although it did not meet their demand for a five-dollar-a-day minimum wage, the government was forced to raise the daily minimum from $1.12 to $3.20. Another CUC strike in September took ten thousand coffee pickers off of the job during the crucial days of the harvest period (Black 1983b:7–8; Davis 1983c:165). Further organizing successes were precluded, however, by the government's escalating violence against union leaders and members. During

1980 alone, about one hundred ten union leaders as well as over three hundred peasant leaders were killed (Bowen 1985:104).

What was most notable about Indian political activities, though, was the support many gave to the new guerrilla movements and the high proportion of active involvement in the revolutionary struggle.[12] There is much diversity in material conditions among Indian communities (Handy 1984:250) and within them (Brintnall 1979:165–169); accordingly, the degree of receptivity to the guerrilla armies varied as well. Nonetheless, involvement was sufficiently widespread by the early 1980s to place Guatemala in the initial stages of a "modern 'peasant war'" (Davis 1983c:159).

A remnant of the guerrilla organizations of the 1960s made its first appearance in the western highlands in January 1972 as the Guerrilla Army of the Poor (EGP). Dedicated to winning the support and involvement of the Indian peasantry, it undertook the slow process of education and mobilization. Its first military action was the public murder in 1975 of a local landlord notorious for oppressing his labor force. It was in response to this killing that the army initiated its counterinsurgency campaign in northern El Quiché. As the repression increased, so did Indians' support for and involvement in both the EGP and a second guerrilla group, the Organization of the People in Arms (ORPA). Begun in 1971, the ORPA emerged publicly in 1979 in the southern portion of the highlands. Support was so substantial that by 1982 it could operate freely throughout the area.

The system of control over the Indian population established in the colonial period and tightened through the centuries was coming apart. The history of many Indian communities featured periods of rebellion (Carmack 1983), but now the mobilization was regionwide. It began as Indians' peaceful effort to assert and defend their interests through both the cooperative movements and the political process, but as these efforts were repressed, increasing numbers of Indians gave their support to the guerrilla armies. Undoubtedly greatest of all threats to elites was the active involvement of numerous Indians themselves in the revolutionary struggle. In response to these various forms of mass politicization and mobilization and in order to reinstitute control, the Guatemalan military undertook a systematic campaign of state terrorism that exceeded even its own past levels of barbarity.

SYSTEMATIC STATE TERRORISM: 1980–1984

On January 16, 1980, one hundred peasants from the northern region of El Quiché completed their long journey to Guatemala City to request the appointment of a special commission to investigate military repression in their area. They were from the communities where the counterinsurgency had begun in 1976, and in recent months the harassment, torture, rape, and murder of noncombatant Indians had intensified. Some of the Indians, along with a few supporters, occupied the Spanish embassy on January 31 to publicize their grievances. They selected this embassy because most of the priests active in their area, some of whom had recently been deported by the government, were from Spain. Against the wishes of the ambassador, the police attacked, killing all but one of the demonstrators and two former Guatemalan officials who were in the embassy talking with the peasants. A letter that the protesters had given to the ambassador explained that they had undertaken the long journey to the capital and faced the risks of the occupation in order to enlist the support of "honorable people," who would, they hoped,

> tell the truth about the criminal repression suffered by the peasants of Guatemala. . . . To a long history of kidnapings, torture, assassinations, theft, rapes and burnings of buildings and crops, the National Army has added the massacre at Chajúl [one of the villages in their region]. . . . We have come to the capital to denounce this injustice, this evil, this cowardice of the National Army, but we also come because we are persecuted and threatened by forces of repression. (quoted in Handy 1984:247)

Tragically, their efforts were futile. The scope of the rural violence increased until it surpassed that in urban areas, which had escalated since the controlled election of General Romeo Lucas García in 1978 (Americas Watch Committee [AWC] 1982). Opponents and possible opponents of the regime disappeared by the hundreds—politicians, labor leaders, journalists, professors, students, and church workers. A fiction was maintained that this was the work of autonomous paramilitary groups, but an Amnesty International report (1981b) established that the selection of victims and the deployment of the murderers "can be pin-pointed to secret offices in an annex of Guatemala's National Palace, under the direct control of the President of the Republic" (p. 3).[13]

General Lucas had at one time been the commander of the counterinsurgency effort in El Quiché, and under his presidency the rural violence intensified. At first, leaders were assassinated or disappeared in small numbers. Increasingly through 1980 and 1981, key villages were attacked, often with dozens of casualties, in an effort to deprive the guerrillas of a supportive population. Instead, this intermittent but brutal repression often strengthened their Indian support. A scorched-earth policy was instituted in late 1981; "thousands of troops swept across an area, killing suspected leaders, burning fields, and attempting to drive a wedge between the peasantry and the guerrillas" (Davis 1983c:167). Forced out of the old villages, the surviving population had to flee to the mountains or relocate in new ones controlled by the military. This change in military strategy coincided with the president's brother's assumption of the role of defense minister. Trained by the French, Benedicto Lucas employed a strategy apparently inspired by the French experiences in Vietnam and Algeria (Bowen 1985:116–123; Handy 1984:256–257).

The scope of the violence directed against the Indians and those who worked with them is indicated by the following small sample of the incidents Davis and Hodson (1982) compiled and verified by crosschecking with other independent sources.

December 7 [1979] Soldiers stationed at the army base in Jaboncillo, Chajul, make daily incursions into the town, ransacking houses, raping women and stealing money. They kidnap, torture and interrogate 12 persons at the army base. Residents flee to the hills to escape from the soldiers. . . .

February 1 [1980] Men in civilian dress kidnap Gregorio Yuja Xona, the only Indian survivor of the Spanish Embassy massacre, from a Guatemalan City hospital where he was being guarded by government forces. He is later found tortured and assassinated. . . .

September 6 [1980] The army attacks the village of Chajul. Early in the day, Father Tomás Ramírez is taken to a cornfield and shot in the head.[14] At noon, helicopters drop four bombs on the convent, killing eight people. Soldiers go into the streets and kill everyone they meet. They enter a house and kill an 11-year-old boy. In the evening, they round by 65 peasants, interrogate and beat them, and kill 36. Many villagers flee to the mountains. Those who remain, mostly widows and children, have little to eat and no firewood to keep them warm. . . .

February [1981] Soldiers invade several villages in San Juan Comalapa, Chimaltenango. Residents initially resist the soldiers after they grab an infant from its mother and kick it to death. Their resistance is broken, and the soldiers kill 168 peasants in the villages of Patzaj and Panimacac. . . .

September 19–20 [1981] The army launches a major offensive against the villages of Xeococ, Buena Vista, Pascaal, Vegas Santo Domingo, Pachicá, and Pichec in Baja Verapaz. Villages are bombed and people are machinegunned as they try to escape. In Vegas Santo Domingo, the soldiers line the people up in a row, cut off their arms and legs and kick them into a grave. Residents claim that 200 people, including entire families, are killed. (pp. 47–52)

In March 1982 the official candidate, General Anibal Guevara, won the presidency in a clearly fraudulent election. He was denied the opportunity to assume office, though, by a coup undertaken the following month by junior military officers. By this point, the Lucas regime commanded little support at home or abroad. Corruption was rampant, while the economy was collapsing; the war against the rural guerrillas was going poorly; the urban violence was too excessive even for most opponents of the left. As Lucas's candidate and as the former defense minister and architect of the failing counterinsurgency campaign, Guevara was unacceptable to too many influential people.

The Reagan administration had pressured Lucas to hold fair elections: it wanted to assist the Guatemalan military in its "fight against Communism" but was restrained by Congress from doing so because of the Lucas government's atrocities. The U.S. administration hoped that elections could lead to a legitimate, moderate government, which it would then be allowed to provide with military assistance.[15] As Acting Assistant Secretary of State John A. Bushnell testified before the Senate in May 1981, "I think given the extent of the insurgency and the strong communist worldwide support for it, the administration is disposed to support Guatemala" (Associated Press [AP], 1981). In congressional testimony two months later, the administration ignored the Guatemalan government's responsibility for the killings, blaming the violence on "the willful efforts by both right and left to polarize the country" (United States, House 1981c:5).[16]

Placed at the head of the new junta in 1982 was retired General José Efraín Ríos Montt, brought out of obscurity to serve. The defrauded candidate of the Christian Democratic victory in 1974, a committed evangelical Christian, and a man with a reputation for personal integrity, he had also served as Arana's chief of staff in 1973 and had left Guatemala in 1974, a rich man with large estates in the northern regions of the country (Black 1983b:16–17). Under Ríos Montt, the violence did largely end in the cities. The Reagan administration hoped that this change would be sufficient to win the grant of military aid, but Congress continued to balk.

Following his visit to Guatemala in December 1982, Reagan declared that Ríos Montt had been getting "a bum rap" and was "totally dedicated to democracy in Guatemala" (Cannon 1982:A17). The U.S. administration did provide Ríos Montt with some support through executive action: the State Department announced in October 1982 that the United States would no longer block international development bank loans to Guatemala. Even during Reagan's first year in office, Guatemala had been able to purchase jeeps and helicopter parts because such equipment had been removed from a control list that restricted their sale to gross violators of human rights. The administration went further in 1983, removing the five-year-old embargo on arms sales to Guatemala (Black 1983b:27–32; Trudeau and Schoultz 1986:44–45).

Some semblance of order had been returned to urban areas, and the Reagan administration also claimed that the rural campaign had been cleaned up (Black 1983b:28). In fact, the reign of terror in the countryside intensified under Ríos Montt. Among the primary findings of an Americas Watch Committee (1983) mission to the Guatemalan refugee camps in southern Mexico were:

1. The Guatemalan government's counterinsurgency program, begun in early 1982, has been continued and expanded by the Ríos Montt government and remains in effect at this time.
2. A principal feature of this campaign is the systematic murder of Indian non-combatants (men, women and children) of any village, farm or cooperative, that the army regards as possibly supportive of the guerrilla insurgents or that otherwise resists army directives.
3. Although civilian men of all ages have been shot in large numbers by the Guatemalan army, women and children are particular victims; women are routinely raped before being killed; children are smashed against walls, choked, burned alive or murdered by machete or bayonet. . . .
5. Incidental to its murder of civilians, the army frequently destroys churches, schools, livestock, crops, food supplies and seeds belonging to suspect villages, cooperatives or private farms. An apparent purpose, and clear effect is to deprive entire villages and farm communities of the food necessary for survival. . . .
8. The Guatemalan armed forces make extensive and conspicuous use of helicopters, mortars and incendiary bombs in attacking rural villages, in destroying and burning crops, and in harassing refugees seeking to escape and routinely use helicopters for surveillance of refugee camps in Mexico. . . .
10. It is widely known within the refugee community, and among displaced Indians in Guatemala, that the principal supplier of such helicopters—and the principal supporter of the Ríos Montt government—is the United States. (pp. 6–7)

As the Americas Watch Committee (1983) report, "Creating a Desolation and Calling it Peace" noted, "The enormity of the horrors being perpetrated by the Guatemalan Army may make it difficult to grasp the cruelty and impact of the Army's actions" (p. 21). But the authors go on to relate the following vignette "that may make comprehensible what is taking place":

Late in the heat-choked smoky evening that we spent in the Chajul refugee camp, we sat on a wooden bench with three refugee farmers, all middle-aged, who had heard about our visit earlier in the day. One man turned to us in the darkness and said, "You know, I had heard stories from others in my village that the army was murdering women and children in other towns, but frankly I did not believe those accounts since the murders seemed so brutal and without reason. But then the army killed my son and his children and my daughter and her children, and now I believe all of these stories." (p. 21)

RECONSTRUCTING RURAL SOCIETY: 1984 TO THE PRESENT

Following the decimation of the indigenous population in the first decades after the Conquest, the remaining Indians were resettled in centralized villages in the 1540s. Sometimes they were brought from outlying areas to more central locations; in other cases new villages were created. This resettlement facilitated the Europeans' creation of a system of social control that was to their benefit, allowing them better to manage the threat of rebellion, utilize Indian labor, and alter indigenous religious practices. Over four centuries later, in the early 1980s, the Indians of Guatemala were violently subjugated again. Violent conquest was again accompanied by the reconstruction of rural society, this time in order to insure the long-term elimination of the threats of radical insurgencies and autonomous Indian movements. The major components of this reconstruction were the penetration of the countryside by the military apparatus, the resettlement of the population in model villages located within new development zones, and the implementation of reeducation programs.[17]

Wishing to maintain the control it had won in the highlands through its indiscriminate violence in the early 1980s, the military reorganized its structure in 1982. The country was redivided from nine into twenty-two military zones, corresponding to department lines, with a major base to be located in each one. Although this move expanded the permanent military presence in rural areas, the military itself did not have sufficient resources or personnel to penetrate much of the countryside, especially remote mountain areas. Crucial to the task was the creation of civil defense patrols in the highlands.

Initiated on a small scale in 1981, the civil patrols grew rapidly until their numbers reached seven to nine hundred thousand within a few years, usually through coerced participation. The patrols nominally exist to protect villagers from "subversives," but it is their other functions that have proven most valuable to the military. The military cannot maintain a constant presence everywhere throughout the highlands, though from its new regional bases it can respond rapidly where it is needed. Once they have been trained to a functional level, the civil patrols serve as paramilitary surrogates by maintaining a military presence (important tangibly as well as symbolically)

and collecting information. They are also used to augment the numbers of
regular military units in action and to search for and return Indians who have
fled the violence into the mountains. Finally, the patrols are used as a
socialization instrument. Participants are not only involved in various activities aimed at instilling patriotism and identification with the military but also
implicated in the military's atrocities, as the following account makes clear.

> Stories, or perhaps more accurately they should be called confessions, were
> repeatedly related about how during sweeping operations the men were forced to
> torture and kill suspected insurgent sympathizers. ... In order to prove their
> loyalty, and manhood, the army requires them to torture and kill, "passive
> guerrillas." ...
> The idea seems to be that, once these people become involved in the crimes,
> they become accomplices and allies in the government counterinsurgency
> campaign. ... On December 22, 1982, all the men from Chiul, El Quiché, for-
> cibly led by the local army commander, surrounded the neighboring village of
> Parraxut. After separating the inhabitants by sex and age, the officer ordered the
> villagers from Chiul to massacre all the men. Those who refused were executed by
> the soldiers. Next, all the women who refused to be raped were killed; the follow-
> ing morning the rest met the same fate. ...
> Gradually, as the conditioning process makes "real men" of the civil patrol
> members, the proportion of regular army troops accompanying them on sweeps
> and other functions is reduced, while the process of instilling discipline continues.
> (White 1984:111–112)

The military acknowledges that 440 villages were destroyed during the
counterinsurgency of the early 1980s (Black 1985:16). During recent years
up to one million Guatemalans have been displaced from their homes—close
to one-seventh of the population. Their resettlement has given the military a
further opportunity to extend its control of the countryside. Seven "Development Poles" (zones) have been created in the northeastern areas that provided
the greatest support to the guerrillas. Within each pole, model villages have
been built, usually on the sites of the more centrally located destroyed villages.
Here the Indians are resettled after being rounded up by military and civil
patrols in the mountains to which they had fled. Members of different Indian
groups have often been placed in the same village as a deliberate effort to
erode ethnic identities. The villagers do the construction work under the
supervision of the military and its civilian technicians; in return, they receive
food and eventually a home. By early 1986 construction had been initiated or
finished in twenty-four of the more than fifty planned model villages, with
about fifty thousand Indians resettled.
    Whether living in model or other villages, Indians are coerced into
joining the Civil Defense Patrols and laboring on military-initiated projects.

To refuse is to run the risk of being labeled a subversive, which invariably brings death. Furthermore, the possibilities of supporting a family have diminished for many, as the deteriorating economic situation of the 1970s has been aggravated by the dislocations of the 1980s. The military has considerable food to distribute, thanks to a substantial international relief effort (directed toward the highlands) whose implementation it largely controls (Barry 1986:39–78). In return for food, the Indians are expected to work at such projects as constructing model villages and roads.

Although both efforts are justified as serving the needs of the local population, it is mostly the military's concern for control that is actually served. The roads are a good example. The Agency for International Development, which provides much of the financing, defends them as meeting developmental objectives, but many observers in the region see other purposes: "You'll see right away that there is always a military outpost at the end of all the roads in the Altiplano. The roads are for the security of the country" (Guatemalan agronomist, quoted in Barry 1986:58).

From Ríos Montt's program of "beans and bullets" to his successor's platform of "work, shelter, and food," the Guatemalan military has been concerned with winning the hearts and minds of the rural population. In part this is to be done by providing goods and services such as the food, work, and housing mentioned above. In part, too, it is to be accomplished by indoctrination. Indians are constantly reminded that the guerrillas were unable to deliver on their promise of a better life and are told repeatedly that the attacks on their communities were actually carried out by the guerrillas. Within the model villages, much attention is given to patriotic symbols and activities, such as the raising and lowering of the flag and the singing of patriotic songs. At school, children learn "respect for the flag, respect for the authorities, and how not to be deceived by the communist delinquents" (quoted in Barry 1986:35).

CONCLUSION

Guatemala exemplifies the essence of the causes and the extreme of the consequences of the crisis in contemporary rural Central America. The system of elite domination established in Guatemala over the centuries to coerce land and labor from the peasantry is rivaled only by El Salvador's famed oligarchy. The first effort to reform this system ended with the overthrow of Arbenz in 1954. The reforms were overthrown as well, and the newly mobilized popular forces were repressed into passivity. Before the democratic period, Guatemala had been ruled by personal dictatorships; after 1954 the power was in the hands of the military. Its coercive capacity expanded in the following decades with substantial assistance from the United States, which remained vigilant about a "communist" threat to Guatemala. When small guerrilla forces appeared in the 1960s, the military demonstrated its willingness to kill indiscriminately and on a massive scale.

Nevertheless, the domination of Guatemala by the military and by prospering economic elites did not remain unchallenged. Popular mobilization continued through the 1970s at ever-increasing levels. Some of the popular groups had shared in the benefits of the country's economic growth and were seeking reforms characteristic of the aspirations of emerging middle sectors worldwide. Many others, especially Indian peasants, were motivated by deteriorating economic security as they lost their access to land, in short supply because of population growth and the landgrabbing of elites. The mobilization of both middle-sector and peasant groups was facilitated by the efforts of other political actors, who entered rural areas in new numbers during the 1970s. Priests, development workers, political party organizers, labor activists, and revolutionary guerrillas offered their encouragement and their assistance to help peasants build better lives for themselves.

In order to combat the new round of guerrilla activities, the military applied its strategy from the 1960s: eliminate not just suspected guerrillas but also potentially supportive populations. The first years of this repression only intensified and widened opposition to the military and the system. The structures of domination were coming apart. To hold them together and to reinstitute control where it had eroded would require tremendous coercion—a step that the military was willing to take.[18] By the early 1980s state terrorism was instituted on a systematic level. Tens of thousands of Guatemalans, especially Indian peasants, were murdered. At least for the time being, the system was maintained.

On the surface, the political system changed during the mid-1980s. Elections were held in 1984 for a constituent assembly, and a relatively fair and free presidential election took place in 1985. Not only was a civilian elected, but he was Vinício Cerezo, the candidate of the Christian Democratic Party and a well-known reformer. The military was compelled to allow this "democratization," especially because of the continuing economic crisis. The real gross domestic product declined by almost 5 percent from 1980 to 1984 and was expected to fall again in 1985 (IDB 1986:394). The nation's economic problems made elites vulnerable to international pressures: external assistance was conditional upon an improvement in the country's international image. As the transition to civilian government proceeded, assistance resumed, including military aid.[19] Cerezo hoped to utilize this opening to consolidate a democratic system in Guatemala, but he had to move cautiously, acknowledging that he actually held little power. Consequently, he refused to propose land reform or to investigate past military human-rights abuses (Ford 1986). While he occupied the executive office, the military continued to occupy the countryside. The Guatemalan agrarian system has been built and maintained by coercion. From 1954 to the late 1960s to the early 1980s, increasingly widespread repression was required to maintain the system in the face of popular mobilization. In the mid-1980s, the military and its allied economic elites were still in control because of their willingness to wield that repression.

NOTES

1. For further information on the reform, see Aybar de Soto (1978); also see Blasier (1976), Handy (1984), Martz (1956), Monteforte Toledo (1972), Schlesinger and Kinzer (1983), Wasserstrom (1975), and Whetten (1961).

2. For further background on these farms and the controversy over what to do with them, see Monteforte Toledo (1972:219–222). At least one scholar maintains that their confiscation was forced by the U.S. government (Schmid, n.d.).

3. Handy (1984:125–126) gives a good summary of these variations. For a more in-depth discussion of rural politics during the reform period, see Wasserstrom (1975).

4. The Communist issue is well discussed by Blasier (1976:154–158). Pearson (1969:350–373) cites a CNCG membership in 1954 of 256,000—a figure he still sees as inflated. The CNCG was organized by noncommunist progressives, originally in face of hostility from the Communist Party, which was largely unsuccessful in similar organizational attempts.

5. For further information on agrarian reform in the post-1954 period, see Adams (1970), Handy (1984), Hildebrand (1969), Minkel (1967), Pearson (1963a, 1963b), and Whetten (1961).

6. Despite the counterrevolution, United Fruit was never able to return to its previous dominant position in Guatemala. An antitrust suit filed by the U.S. Justice Department within a week of Arbenz's overthrow eventually led to judgments that forced the company to divest some of its banana-producing and -marketing operations and that forbade it to expand its banana operations. Later, Del Monte cleverly preempted a United Fruit Company takeover attempt by entering the banana business itself. In 1972, ironically, it purchased United Fruit's Guatemala operations. (On Del Monte's operations in Guatemala, see Burbach and Flynn 1980:207–210.)

7. For discussions of this period see Amnesty International [AI] (1981a), Booth (1980), Bowen (1985), Gott (1971), Johnson (1972, 1973), and McClintock (1985b).

8. The quote is from Colonel John D. Webber; his assassination is the subject of the story.

9. For further information see Adams (1970:278–317), Brintnall (1979:117–169), Colby and vanden Berghe (1969:102–103), Ebel (1964:100), Falla (1978:446–459), and Warren (1978:87–169).

10. Of course, there also are Indians who have profited from the economic changes of the postwar period. Brintnall (1979:111–115), for example, describes highland Indians who have dug irrigation ditches to grow garlic as a cash crop. Interestingly, these more affluent Indians were among the most likely to reject the authority of their traditionalist elders and convert to orthodox Catholicism.

11. For contrasting Indian peasant views of the strike (and broader issues), see Burgos-Debray (1984:227–235) and Sexton (1985:148–151); the first is the testimony of an organizer; the second, that of a labor contractor.

12. For discussions of the guerrilla movements of the 1970s and 1980s, see Black (1983a, 1983b), Handy (1984:244–250), Paige (1983), and Payeras (1983). In addition to the two organizations discussed in the text, there were three other, less important guerrilla organizations, the Rebel Armed Forces (FAR), the Guatemalan Workers' Party (PGT), and the Revolutionary Movement of the People (MRP–Ixim).

13. President Lucas's brother, General Benedicto Lucas García, is reported to have admitted that the government was responsible for at least 70 percent of the murders and disappearances during that administration (Nairn and Simon 1986:14).

14. Sixteen Catholic priests were murdered in Guatemala from 1976 through 1984 (United States, House 1985a:78).

15. In the face of the human rights legislation of the mid-1970s and the commitment of the Carter administration to the promotion of human rights, a split developed between the United States and Guatemala from 1978 to 1980. It should be noted, however, that economic assistance to Guatemala continued during this period, as did the delivery of military aid already in the pipeline (Schoultz 1983:188–189). Guatemalan officials rejoiced when Reagan defeated Carter in 1980 because it was widely expected that the new president would sharply alter policy toward their country.

16. The Reagan administration spoke in 1981 of a new approach directed toward establishing communications with the Guatemalan government to bring it out of its "siege or . . . bunker mentality." It was hoped that this stance would give the Guatemalans the "self-confidence [they] needed" to end "terrorism and violence" without violating human rights (United States, House 1981c:10–13).

17. Major sources for this section were Barry (1986), Black (1985), Handy (1984), and White (1984). The rural political system was also reorganized along corporatist lines in order to tighten central government and military control of the countryside. For a description of how this system functioned prior to the return to civilian government in 1985, see White (1984:121–122).

18. The military's scorched-earth policies were opposed by some field commanders. The Central American militaries are not unified institutions but are permeated by divisions based on service, generational, personalistic, and ideological lines.

19. The U.S. Congress agreed to appropriate the following sums for fiscal year 1985: for development aid, $40.1 million; for cash transfers, $12.5 million; and for military training, $300,000. For the next fiscal year, the Reagan administration requested $10.3 million for military aid but $7 million less for development aid (Trudeau and Schoultz 1986:45).

CHAPTER 6

Costa Rica and Honduras: The Limitations of Reform

Land tenure relations in Costa Rica and Honduras before World War II were notably different from those in the rest of the region. As has been discussed, the peasants of these two countries had not experienced the same demands for their land and their labor as had their counterparts elsewhere in the region. By midcentury, though, the situation began to change. Land pressures and conflicts increased as population growth and the expansion of commercial farming, especially for the export market, created land scarcities that resulted in agrarian conflict. In response, both Costa Rica and Honduras have undertaken since the early 1960s programs to reform land tenure relations, sometimes with the United States as a participant. The two countries have created similar types of programs, including colonization, adjudication of land disputes, redistribution of property, and titling of landholdings. But each nation also manifests some unique patterns. In particular, agrarian politics in Honduras in the last few decades have been considerably more complex than those in Costa Rica, and therefore more attention will be devoted to Honduras here.

This chapter's analysis of agrarian policy in contemporary Costa Rica and Honduras will demonstrate both the accomplishments and the limitations of reformism in situations of dire need. Many rural people have benefited from the reform programs, and rural dissatisfaction has been kept lower than it otherwise would have been. However, as a result of rapid population growth and the expansion of commercial agriculture, landlessness and rural unemployment are worse now than before the reforms were initiated. Because of the way political power is distributed and the limitations

of the prevailing ideologies, the reforms in both countries have been too mild
to respond adequately to the basic needs of many rural people.

THE INITIATION OF
AGRARIAN REFORM

Costa Rica

The foundation of Costa Rica's agrarian reform program was passed into law
in 1961. This action was primarily a reflection of domestic politics; indeed,
serious governmental deliberation on agrarian reform had occurred in that
country since the middle 1950s. Concern continued to grow as the
population exploded at an alarming rate. Land pressures in the countryside
led to increasing numbers of peasants taking matters into their own hands by
occupying unused property, thereby heightening rural tensions (Hall
1985:210; Riismandel 1972:203–207). In addition, the successful passage of
agrarian measures was facilitated by Eisenhower's endorsement in 1960 of
such reforms, Kennedy's more fervent support the following year, and especially, the promise inherent in the Alliance for Progress of help from the United
States to finance their implementation (Rowles 1985:131–132, 198–199). It
also is possible that AID officials spoke favorably of the proposal to Costa
Rican officials (Riismandel 1972:206–207).

The Costa Rican law, authorizes the expropriation of unused private
lands, but the redistribution of private property has never been an important
aspect of the country's reform process. In fact, many of the legislators voting
for the measure did not expect that it would be fully implemented, valuing it
instead for symbolic purposes (Rowles 1985:216). The law requires full
compensation for expropriated land; supreme court decisions in 1967 and
1969 mandated, respectively, that payment must be in cash, if so desired, and
that it must be at full market value. Under such tight constraints, implementation of the law was restricted until 1970 to a series of colonization projects,
which settled only 1272 peasant families on 87,500 acres in often unsuccessful colonies, and to a very limited titling of land held by squatters who could
prove legitimate possession (Seligson 1980a:126–131, 1984:31).

Although only 14 percent of United Fruit's almost five hundred thousand
acres in Costa Rica was cultivated during the 1950s (Salazar 1962:140–141),
the multinational's huge holdings have never been seriously threatened by the
law. One of the colonies started in the mid-1960s, Bataan, was on 25,900
acres of land purchased from United Fruit for $549,414. The land was a

former banana plantation, and the price included substantial infrastructure (Riismandel 1972:224–225). But further purchases or expropriations were largely precluded by the conservative nature of the law and, later, the supreme court decisions.

Honduras

Agrarian reform first came to Honduras in the early 1960s in response to both external stimuli, through the Alliance for Progress (Fonck 1972:28–29), and internal pressures, described below. The most liberal Honduran president up to that point, Ramón Villeda Morales, established the National Agrarian Institute (INA) in 1961. The following year he gained congressional approval for an agrarian reform law that was aimed particularly at the fruit companies' uncultivated land, though it applied to all idle lands not fulfilling their social function (*International Labor Review* [ILR] 1963). Villeda was one of the Latin leaders most in line with the Kennedy administration's progressive preferences, but his agrarian reform law was quite unpopular with the U.S. ambassador and leading U.S. legislators, not to mention the fruit companies. Ambassador Charles Burrows recalls that he told the Honduran president, "This is not a good law. It's going to cause you all kinds of trouble, and I think you ought to take a very, very close look at it" (Burrows 1969:14). Meanwhile, U.S. senators put pressure on the Kennedy administration to protect the interests of the fruit companies and to uphold the principle of adequate compensation, which meant, in the words of Senator Wayne Morse, payment in "hard, cold American dollars" (United States, Congress 1962:21614–620).

Standard Fruit indicated that it could live with the law, but United Fruit had no intention of doing so. It stopped its planting program, throwing many Hondurans out of work. At the same time, Villeda took a long-scheduled trip to the United States. Before returning to Honduras, he met with United Fruit officials, with whom he had a "very satisfactory conversation." He promised them a revised law that would be, in Burrows's (1969) words, "livable for private interests" (pp. 16–17). Before Villeda's trip, Burrows (1962) had written to the State Department,

> I am sure that The Fruit Company is in an excellent position and can probably get much of what it wants from the Honduran government in terms of agrarian law revision, replacement of INA personnel or anything else. Please pass this on where it will do the most good. (p. 2)

The revision was delivered, and the INA director was removed (Posas 1979:126).

On October 3, 1963, the eve of national elections scheduled to select his successor, Villeda was overthrown by a military coup. Although Burrows (1969:35–36) claims that the coup was unrelated to the agrarian reform, the fact that the probable victor in the election was the head of Villeda's party and would continue with his general reform program was undoubtedly a primary cause of the coup (Anderson 1982:113; Shaw 1979:139), even though the candidate was ambivalent about the agrarian reform. More generally, large landowners, both domestic and foreign, were alarmed at the growing mobilization of peasants on the north coast (Pearson 1980:302). Posas (1981b:22) argues that these elites supported the coup as a conservative reaction against the awakening of popular forces in the countryside.

The cause of agrarian reform largely disappeared in Honduras from the time of the coup until the late 1960s, just as it disappeared from the U.S. foreign policy agenda. The progressive rhetoric of 1961 reflected the abstract goals of intellectuals close to Kennedy; implementation of the U.S. role in the Alliance for Progress, however, was left to career officials with different perspectives and interests, including a need to be responsive to legislators. Many of the latter agreed with major economic elites that structural reform was unwise and even dangerous (Lowenthal, 1973; Montgomery, 1984; Olson, 1974; Petras and LaPorte, 1973). As one high AID official admitted to a researcher, "We were particularly shocked by Kennedy's endorsement of land reform and the implication that we would push it. None of us had the slightest intention of doing so in our capacities" (quoted in Olson 1974:111).

Furthermore, Central America's land-based elites, still dominant political forces in each of the countries, were not about to permit the implementation of reform measures that seriously threatened their privileged position. Consequently, for the United States, agrarian reform became "technical modernization without structural reform" (Petras and LaPorte 1973:394). Passage of the original agrarian reform legislation in Central America received U.S. encouragement, indirectly as well as directly in some cases, but effective implementation of that legislation disappeared as an objective of U.S. policy.

SETTLING LAND DISPUTES

Disputes between peasants and large landowners increased during the 1960s in each country, both because of rapidly growing rural populations and because of the dispossession of peasants, especially in Honduras, by landowners attracted to new profit-making opportunities. In response, peasants became more active in asserting their interests. By the later part of the decade, they began to enjoy beneficial government arbitration of their land disputes, again especially in Honduras.

Costa Rica

A primary impetus for passage of Costa Rica's agrarian reform law was the problem of squatters; it was estimated that the country had some 16,500 squatter families in the mid-1960s, a number that grew as the decade advanced. The conservative nature of the law, however, constrained any adequate government response through the colonization program, especially under right-of-center governments. Therefore, in the second half of the decade the government relied on the adjudication of land disputes as its major response to the growing problem of rural conflict. When squatters could prove legitimate occupation, they were given legal titles. When they could not, they were offered an opportunity to relocate to one of the colonies, though in some cases the land in dispute was bought by the government for purchase by the squatter. Dealing with manifestations of the problem rather than the problem itself, this approach was not able even to keep up with the growing number of squatters; in 1966–69, only 2093 families were settled with titles.[1]

Unlike neighboring Honduras, Costa Rica has seen relatively little peasant organization result from landlessness and the consequent disputes over land use. As recently as 1973, only 2 percent of small holders were members of peasant unions, as were only 9 percent of rural laborers, primarily banana workers (Barahona Riera 1980:135). In contrast to those workers, who developed strong (and radical) unions following their first strike in 1934, the rest of the peasantry has been more likely to pursue individual solutions to its difficulties. When peasants have formed organizations, they have usually been related to preparations for land invasions. If these committees or leagues last beyond the invasions, they often affiliate with one of the national organizations. The radical National Peasant Council (CNC), formed in 1967, had three hundred affiliated committees by the late 1970s. The Costa Rican Christian Peasant Federation (FECC) was formed the same year and, as its name suggests, has a Christian Democratic orientation. A third organization, the National Federation of Progressive Boards (FNJP), is based on small, local units that unite peasants with rural artisan and commercial interests (Barahona Riera 1980:422–428; Seligson 1980a:64–77, 104–114).

Honduras

Encouraged by the examples of the Cuban Revolution, serious peasant mobilization in Honduras began in the early 1960s in response to land disputes with a

United Fruit Company subsidiary on the north coast (Posas 1981a, 1981b). United Fruit, desiring to expand its activities into new ventures such as African palm and cattle raising, moved to evict peasants from lands that they rented, in some cases for decades. Peasants in southern Honduras had sent delegations to the capital as early as 1955 to defend their lands against encroachment by large landowners; now those in the north took a new step. Peasants from the affected areas organized together in October 1961, forming the Central Committee of Peasant Unity (CCUC), assisted by leaders who had settled in the area after having been fired by United Fruit in the aftermath of an important strike in 1954.[2] After the meeting, they sent a letter to President Villeda that contrasted their landlessness with the vast, often uncultivated holdings of the fruit company and asked him to require that the land fulfill its social function (Posas 1981a:51).

Dissatisfied by the responses from the government and United Fruit, the CCUC initiated in early 1962 a campaign of recovering idle lands, as peasants occupied and began cultivating them. Up to a thousand peasants also marched on the town of El Progreso, the first time peasants in Honduras had demonstrated in such large numbers in their own behalf. United Fruit ran cattle through some of their plantings in order to drive the invaders out; it also received some assistance toward this end from military forces stationed in the area. CCUC leaders went to President Villeda and were able to convince him to enjoin any further efforts to dispossess them, at least through the harvest. When United Fruit refused the resulting request of local authorities to remove its cattle from the disputed lands, the president sent a commission from the agrarian reform agency (INA) to work out a compromise.

The successes of CCUC were short lived. It reorganized as the National Federation of Honduran Peasants (FENACH) in August 1962, but two months later its directors were arrested at a meeting and held incommunicado for nearly five days. They were released in face of their hunger strike and the pressure of their followers, who had gathered outside the building where they were held. After the coup of 1963, FENACH was destroyed; the leaders who were caught were jailed, its offices and archives were demolished, and its membership repressed. A few of the leaders took to the mountains to initiate armed struggle; they included Lorenzo Zelaya, its president and catalyst. A former labor leader at United Fruit and a communist militant, Zelaya was discovered with six comrades and killed in an armed confrontation in April 1965.

During its brief existence, the militant FENACH faced not only repression but also competition. Within two months of FENACH's formation, a new Honduran peasant federation was organized, the National Association of Honduran Peasants (ANACH). This explicitly anticommunist movement received substantial organizational assistance from the United States through the AFL–CIO and its Latin American arm, the Inter-American Regional Organization of Labor (ORIT) (Volk 1981:8–10). The more militant FENACH had an estimated membership of fifteen thousand in August 1962, and ANACH had five thousand members at its formation two months later. The latter's membership was soon expanded by some eight thousand peasants who deserted FENACH in response to the repression directed against it (Kincaid 1985:137). Despite its more moderate and anti-communist stance, ANACH was also immobilized by government repression in the first years following the 1963 coup. In 1966, when a new president of the federation became more assertive, its financial sponsors forced his resignation. Accusing him of being a communist, they threatened to suspend all assistance if he did not resign (Posas 1981a:85–87).

The repressive mid-1960s were a time of rapid expansion of cotton planting and cattle raising in Honduras (White 1977:174); the area harvested in cotton more than doubled between 1964 and 1966 (FAO 1970). Landowners were responding in part to new commercial opportunities but also to the threat of agrarian reform. Idle lands, or those rented to peasants for a long period, might at some point be subject to expropriation or peasant occupation (Posas 1981a:36–45; White 1977:174). Meanwhile, INA received only minimal appropriations during this period. Not only was it indifferent to the plight of the peasantry, some even saw it as a protector of landed interests (Posas 1979:60). Government-backed eviction increased, and the rental of land in areas of commercial expansion became virtually impossible.

Despite intermittent repression, by the end of the 1960s Honduran peasants had organized and were asserting themselves to a degree unparalleled to that point in Central America and perhaps even in all of Latin America (Astorga Lira 1975:17).[3] Catalyzed by the enclosure movement and land pressures discussed in Part I and assisted by workers from the Church and international agencies, peasant mobilization was facilitated by a political opening that began with the appointment of a sympathetic INA director in 1967 and that was enlarged both by the popular opposition to fraudulent municipal elections in March 1968 and by the fallout of the war with El Salvador in July 1969.

Outside agents for change played an important role in this mobilization, just as they have elsewhere in Central America. Similar in importance to Catholic Action in Guatemala was the radio school movement in southern Honduras. Facing Central America's lowest per capita population of priests in the country with the most difficult terrain, the Honduran Catholic Church developed a radio school network as a way of overcoming these obstacles to bring isolated rural communities literacy, education, and religious teaching (White 1977). There were 7250 students in 343 schools in 1962, and the numbers doubled by 1964 (White 1977:237). The program was placed in private hands so that international funding (especially AID) could be obtained; these hands, however, had been inspired by Christian Democrats. As the program matured through the 1960s, it undertook more directly the successive commitments of peasant mobilization, organization, and support of confrontation with elite interests.

In the early 1960s the program addressed the peasants' consciousness; in the words of one leader, "What we were trying to do was to influence the fundamental way of thinking of the campesino, change his individualism and fatalism and to orient him toward the community" (quoted in White 1977:243). This effort was followed by attempts to organize cooperatives, which came to receive greater priority than religious and literacy activities. Similar currents were moving in other parts of the Church; consequently, White (1977) claims, by 1964 there was a strong movement within the Church whose goals were "promoting highly participatory, solidar[it]y community-level action motivated by the communitarian values of Christianity" (p. 245). Furthermore, this movement created a new communications system linking the countryside with modernizing forces and bypassing rural elites (White 1977:401). These activities contributed directly to peasant mobilization, then, by undermining the strength of traditional values and relationships of domination while offering the alternative of more cooperative, assertive values and organizations.

Such efforts by progressive Christians facilitated the formation in southern Honduras of peasant leagues, which grouped together in 1964 as the Christian Social Action Peasant Association (ACADSCH). This movement became FENTCH in 1968 and the National Peasant Union (UNC) in 1970. It was more militant than ANACH, and the competition between the two national peasant organizations for members and affiliates made both more assertive than either probably would have been alone. A third national peasant organization also appeared in 1970, the Federation of Honduran Agrarian Reform Cooperatives (FECORAH), representing peasants settled in reform cooperatives.

As the peasant organizations became more assertive, their major tactic was to stage land occupations. Most of their targets during the early 1960s were unoccupied lands owned by the fruit companies, but later in the decade their objectives were more likely to be land held by domestic interests that peasants claimed was public. Honduras is unique in Central America in that up to one-third of its area was still public as late as 1974 as either national or *ejidal* (community-owned) lands. When land became more scarce and valuable with population growth and commercialization, peasants claimed that large landholders illegitimately enclosed the public lands, often evicting peasants who had been working them. These evictions were the crucial factor

in generating the peasant mobilization of the late 1960s. As White (1977)
points out in his massive study of this development,

> the brutality of many of these evictions proved to be the catalyst in breaking
> down the friendly dependence on helpful patrons and developed a profoundly
> emotional opposition. The evictions were the sudden, sharp deprivation which
> moved campesinos to risk their lives in organizing to counter rural elites and
> protest before government authorities. (pp. 181–182)

Peasants won the appointment of the agronomist Roberto Sandoval as
the director of INA in 1967 by applying pressure, including the threat of a
hunger march. Under Sandoval's leadership, the agency's prevailing clien-
tilistic operations were ruptured as he moved to professionalize it, in part by
bringing in international technocrats. Furthermore, in late 1968 INA began
to adjudicate land conflicts in favor of peasants. Lands proven to be national
or *ejidal* were recovered and turned into communal peasant settlements. If the
land in question was in fact legitimately privately owned, INA often purchased it for peasant settlements. Either way, the results electrified many
peasant communities, accelerating further organization and occupations
(Boyer 1982:104–105; Posas 1981b:26–27; White 1977:600). By the late
1960s the major peasant organizations claimed a combined membership of
some ninety thousand rural families. At the same time government support
for INA increased; its budget was enlarged in late 1968 by the issuance of
bonds and by land sales. The group settlements also were supported by
technical assistance and credits from the National Development Bank.

LAND REDISTRIBUTION

Honduras

With the election of a conservative president in June 1971, however, the
leadership and policy of the INA were to change. The settlement of disputes in
favor of peasants virtually ceased, and those occupying private land were
likely to be arrested. The opposition to reform of large landholders also
solidified during this period. At times violence was employed against squatters. The results were sometimes tragic, as when six peasants were killed at La
Talanquera in Olancho in 1972 (Posas 1979:80). In response, peasants
became more restive, and their hunger march on the capital in December
1972 was partially responsible for the coup that brought the now-populist

military leader Oswaldo López Arellano back to power. Having explicitly aligned himself with popular classes before the coup, he soon issued an emergency land reform measure, Decree law 8.[4] It was followed in January 1975 by an agrarian reform measure, Degree Law 170, which promised to distribute six hundred thousand hectares (almost 1.5 million acres) to 120,000 families in five years.[5]

The realities of political power put an end to the reforms. López was removed from power in April 1975 after it was revealed that United Brands (United Fruit's new name) had paid a $1.25 million bribe to the Honduran government to encourage (successfully) a substantial reduction in a proposed increase in the banana export tax. López's power had already been diminishing, and the previous month he had been replaced as head of the armed forces by Juan Melgar Castro, who then succeeded him as president. Reform-oriented officials were able to hold on to a share of power until the spring of 1977, by which time most had been removed. Sandoval was brought back as the head of INA in October 1975, but his position had been undercut from the beginning by Melgar's appointment of a subdirector whose function was to restrain his boss (Ickis 1983:25), and he left office in March 1977.

The 1975 agrarian reform law established maximum landholding sizes and legitimated the expropriation of idle and underused lands. The law was published two weeks before it went into effect, and its application was delayed for over half a year because of the failure of Melgar's less-than-committed cabinet to approve the necessary implementing regulations. The delays provided large landholders with the time to subdivide property or to begin grazing cattle on it in order to establish use. Their interests were also advantaged by limitations placed on INA's ability to assess in the field the status of land use and by the law's appeals mechanism. INA decisions could be appealed to the National Council which, according to Posas (1979:101), well represented large landholders.

The delay in implementation of the law also provided its opponents with time to act. Most notable were the activities of the Federation of Farmers and Cattlemen (FENAGH), especially in the outlying department of Olancho. Ninety armed men from a FENAGH affiliate seized the regional office of the National Peasant Union on June 19, 1975, in protest against its activities. Then on June 25, six people were killed at a peasant training center in the department capital; and on the same day two foreign priests were murdered, their bodies discovered at the bottom of a well with those of seven other victims. The Catholic bishop was forced to flee the department (Anderson 1982:117–118; *Time* 1975:36). In a departure from procedures elsewhere in Central America, some of the guilty were tried and imprisoned; the commission that investigated the murders declared that they were part of a vast plan directed by FENAGH (Posas and del Cid 1981:211).

In the face of governmental delay and despite occasional violence, peasant mobilization increased throughout 1975, including marches, demonstrations, and a record number of land occupations. In early October the three major peasant organizations united into a front (FUNC) and gave the government until the end of the month to respond to their need for land. When it did not, they responded with massive, simultaneous land takeovers throughout the countryside, returning even when removed by the military. In response to this unprecedented level of popular pressure, which included organized urban interests, the Melgar government finally responded with a plan for the recovery and adjudication of public and idle private lands. Although a substantial amount of land was redistributed, significant opposition to the agrarian reform remained within the government and on the part of economic elites, making implementation of the program very difficult. By early 1977 opponents of reform had clearly won: the last of the progressive military leaders were sent into "diplomatic exile," and in March Sandoval announced his resignation, citing the lack of government support for agrarian reform. During the remaining years of military rule, very little land was distributed, and most of that was through expensive colonization programs, often financed by loans from international donors (Posas 1979:97–111).

When civilian government was restored in early 1982, the new INA director charged, according to one account, that that agency had been plundered "to such a degree that when the Liberal government arrived they found they had an institution that was completely ruined" (*La Prensa* 1982:3). The elected government (1982–86) of Roberto Suazo pledged to satisfy peasants' needs, and the reform pace did quicken under his administration; once again, however, performance fell short of promises. In the first three years of Suazo's term, about 59,000 hectares were distributed (Ruhl 1985:70), far below the original commitment of over 50,000 hectares for 1983 alone (*La Prensa* 1983:4). Not surprisingly, peasant pressure through mass land occupations continued. The peasants' efficacy was retarded, though, by fragmentation; at least fourteen different groups claimed to speak for them in 1984 (Ruhl 1985:75).

Several positive features of the Honduran agrarian reform should be noted. Perhaps most significant is the fact that there has been, in a nonrevolutionary situation, considerable land redistribution and government intervention on the side of peasants in conflicts with larger landholders. Between 1962 and 1980, about thirty-six thousand rural families benefited from the program (see Table 6.1). As Ruhl (1984:55) points out, the number of beneficiaries through the 1970s was equivalent to about 22 percent of the landless and land-poor families in the mid-1970s. Not surprisingly, the reform had important political consequences. Ruhl (1984) notes that it "was very important symbolically because the program demonstrated the contin-

TABLE 6.1
Honduras: Land Distribution under the Reform Process, 1962–84

Period	Families Benefited Total	Families Benefited Annual Average	Land Awarded (hectares) Total	Land Awarded (hectares) Annual Average	Average Grant per Family[1]
1962–66	281	56	1,357	271	4.8
1967–72	5,348	891	34,604	5,767	6.5
1973–74	11,739	5,870	79,552	39,776	6.8
1975–77	12,405	4,135	80,150	26,717	6.5
1978–81	9,174	2,294	38,937	9,734	4.2
1982–84	13,241	4,414	58,770	19,590	4.4
Total	52,188	2,269	293,370	12,755	5.6

NOTE: 1. Land grants were often to groups, not individual families. Therefore this column does not give "average annual size of grant" but instead a measure of per-family size of grants.
SOURCES: Calculated from Morris 1984:101 and from Ruhl 1985:70.

ued flexibility and reform potential of the Honduran government and fostered an 'incrementalist' policy orientation among the peasant organizations" (p. 55; also see Astorga Lira 1975:7).

Despite its achievements, Honduran agrarian reform has fallen far short of both its stated goals and the country's needs. The peak of the reform process was reached in 1973–74, according to all three indicators in Table 6.1: average number of families benefited, average amount of land awarded, and average size of the grants. The pace slackened after the promulgation of the 1975 law. Even at the end of 1980, the number of families benefited and the amount of land awarded were only one-sixth the law's stated goal; in addition, the average size of the grants had declined. Honduras has more landless families now than before the implementation of Degree Law 8 began in late 1972. The grants of the Suazo administration of the 1980s, for example, met less than one-half of the need generated during its tenure (Ruhl 1985:73–74).

The redistribution of land in Honduras was facilitated by the large quantity of national and *ejidal* lands remaining in the country and by the expulsion of Salvadoran settlers in 1969 (one of the precipitating causes of the so-called soccer war between the two countries [Anderson 1981; Durham 1979]). Most of the land distributed was publicly owned. Furthermore, of the private land that was distributed, much was given by the fruit companies voluntarily or obtained through expropriations of holdings in less hospitable climates following the "Bananagate" disclosures that brought down the López government in 1975 (Volk 1981:20–23).

Unfortunately, in many cases the land distributed was in remote areas (USAID 1982:4), insufficient, and of poor quality (Hatch and Lanao Flores 1977:13). Technical and credit assistance was made available to the cooperative farms as part of the reform process, including a $12 million loan initiated by AID in 1974, but the actual assistance received was difficult to obtain and often insufficient (Hatch and Lanao Flores 1977; Tendler 1976). For such reasons, the abandonment rate of reform farms has been high; by one estimate, some 40 percent of the original settlers have left these settlements (USAID) 1982:4). Furthermore, the INA itself has acknowledged that because it concentrated its efforts on the group settlements, the remaining 80 percent of the reform beneficiaries did not receive adequate technical assistance and financial support (*Tiempo* 1983:19a).

Costa Rica

The Costa Rican agrarian reform entered its most active phase during the mid-1970s, centering for the first time on the expropriation of property. This activism was in response both to pressure from below and to the electoral victory of the president who has demonstrated the greatest commitment to the reform.[6] The pace of peasant land invasions intensified in the late 1960s and into the 1970s as a result of increasing land pressures, frustration over the minimal benefits of the reform program, and the encouragement of left-wing urban groups. Rural elites in turn became more likely to call in the police to remove squatters. Indeed, a new rural police force was created in 1969 primarily to prevent land invasions. And the expanding community of foreign growers developed private police forces, which were seen as more reliable than those paid by the public. In the peripheral regions of the country, "a potentially explosive sociopolitical situation" grew (Hall 1985:202; also see Salazar 1979:220–223).

The victor in the 1974 presidential election was Daniel Oduber of the National Liberation party [PLN], the most progressive of Costa Rica's major parties. He had just barely lost the election in 1966, and then in 1970 he lost his party's nomination to its hero of the 1948 "revolution," former president José Figueres. During Figueres's tenure, little was done to advance the cause of agrarian reform despite the deteriorating rural situation. Long identified as a strong supporter of agrarian reform, Oduber as president secured the right for the agrarian reform agency to issue about $12 million in bonds. These were used as compensation for the expropriation of several large holdings, including some of those of the United Fruit subsidiary operating on the southern Pacific coast. The catch, of course, was that the money was soon spent.

The more conservative presidential candidate won in 1978; by the time the PLN returned to power in 1982 (and again in 1986), severe financial crisis limited the country's ability to pursue its model of agrarian reform through full compensation. The economy was on the brink of collapse by 1982 because of rising oil prices, worldwide recession, saturated export markets, and economic mismanagement. Corrections in each of these factors have been responsible for a subsequent partial recovery; especially important has been a substantial increase in United States economic assistance—an increase directly related to President Reagan's geopolitical concerns. Total U.S. assistance in 1983 equaled about 10 percent of Costa Rica's gross domestic product, making it the recipient of the second-highest per capita level of U.S. aid in the world through at least 1985 (Edelman 1985).

Costa Rica redistributed about 413,000 acres of land between 1962 and 1979, approximately 5.4 percent of all land in farms in 1973. The beneficiaries were 5,428 families, three-quarters of whom received their grants between 1975 and 1979. The PLN administration (1982–86) of President Luis Monge did attempt to make good on its campaign slogan of "return to the land." Monge was aided by a new reform law, passed just before he assumed office, that increased the agrarian reform agency's revenues from tax collections. In his first fifteen months, the government acquired ninety farms (only one through expropriation) totaling about 90,000 acres and obtained options for sale to another 50,000 acres. This land was distributed to almost five thousand families (*La Nación* 1984a:16a). However, in 1979 Costa Rica still had over forty-four thousand landless rural families and more than eighteen thousand land-poor families (Seligson 1984:34).

Although the program has failed to keep pace with the growing need, the results for those fortunate enough to have benefited from it should not be overlooked. Reform beneficiaries produce basic food crops with yields above the national averages; are satisfied with the progress they have made; participated at above national rates in both conventional political activities and cooperate activities; and compared to landless peasants, are more trusting in government, more positively oriented toward the future, and more efficacious (Seligson 1980a:136–144, 1984:35–43).

In the 1970s cooperative enterprises were the form of agricultural settlement favored by officials in both Costa Rica and Honduras. Some peasants still received small, individual plots, but officials preferred to settle the landless in cooperative arrangements that varied from communal ownership and work (especially in Costa Rica), to communal ownership with individual plots, to private plots tied together by cooperative credit and marketing organizations. Despite a number of problems the cooperatives have encountered (Hatch and Lanao Flores 1977; Seligson 1980a; Tendler 1976), the members of successful cooperatives are regarded as an elite among the rural masses. Whether on public land, abandoned private farms (Costa Rica), or expropriated property (Honduras), the settlements have also been valued for their greater productive potential.

There has been a close connection, especially in Honduras, between agrarian reform and the commercialization of agriculture (Posas 1979:67–107; Slutzky 1979). These reform projects, such as the huge Bajo Aguán (which by mid-1977 consisted of almost four thousand families organized in eighty cooperatives), have been advantaged over other peasant groups in the provision of credit, technical assistance, and infrastructure development. In a number of cases, the government has required that such settlements devote themselves to export production.[7] Boyer (1982:192–194) cites the example of a reform settlement that attempted, after unpleasant experiences raising cotton and then melons, to return to raising grain and cattle. It was refused credits by the National Development Bank and by other creditors unless it returned to cotton production. Ironically, USAID (1983:6–7) has recently pointed out that the land received by the reform sector "was most often land unsuited for intensive agricultural purposes," while it would be appropriate for livestock grazing.

Finally, it should be noted that multinational agribusinesses also have benefited, usually handling the processing and export of the settlements' crops, often with the Honduran government as the middleman. Cooperatives have received support from international donors, especially the Inter-American Development Bank and the United States. The U.S. even evidenced a preference during the 1970s for group over single-family farms (Tendler 1976:8). As one example, Honduran cooperatives received $12 million in technical and credit assistance from a U.S. loan initiated in 1974.

LAND TITLING

In the 1980s, however, the philosophy of the Honduran and U.S. governments changed from supporting group farms to supporting, as AID (1982) notes, "an agrarian reform based on the principles of private property" (p. 6). This approach offers nothing for the growing number of landless rural families, but it does meaningfully address the real and serious problems of a substantial number of others. Honduran coffee growers, who are seen as "very strong and politically conscious" (USAID 1982:5), in particular have benefited from recent actions.

Most landholders in the two countries lack formal title to their land. In Honduras, AID (1982:1) recently estimated that three-quarters of farmers had insecure tenancy; in Costa Rica, an earlier estimate put the proportions at over half of the farms, and up to 91 percent of those in remote areas (Sáenz and Knight 1971:1, 4, 7).[8] Not only does the lack of title leave peasants vulnerable to dispossession by more powerful interests (a problem especially in Honduras), but it also limits access to bank credits because a formal title is often necessary for collateral. Both insecurity and lack of credit, of course, constrain productivity. For such reasons, in recent years ambitious land titling programs have been undertaken in both countries, their expense largely underwritten by loans from the United States.

The titling program in Costa Rica, which benefited 24,510 families by 1979, had an original goal of covering about 1,630,000 acres. When this land is added to that which was distributed by the government, the total area titled equaled about one-quarter of the amount in farms in 1973. This program was assisted by a $2.7 million loan from the United States in 1970. A later loan of $2.1 million was intended to help more than double the number of beneficiaries and amount of land reached by the program (Seligson 1984:33–35). Although titling programs do not address the fundamental problem of structural inequality and can in fact exacerbate it (by titling unfairly large properties), the Costa Rican program has had its positive benefits. Research demonstrates that title recipients are more likely to receive bank credits and technical assistance and to plant permanent crops—even though most still do not (Seligson 1982:52–53).

In Honduras, the Small Farmer Titling project is based on a $10 million loan and a $2.5 million grant made by the United States in 1982. Its overall goal is seventy thousand titles. Special targets of the program are small and medium-sized coffee growers; of the country's forty-eight thousand coffee producers, about 95 percent have insecure titles to the land they work. These farmers have also gained from a new agrarian reform degree passed in 1981, which exempts coffee lands from the agrarian reform program and abolishes previous restrictions against the granting of titles through the reform process to holdings of under 5 hectares. The intended beneficiaries will gain an important measure of security through this program, especially the less powerful among them; it is estimated that about 57 percent of them work farm units of 10 hectares or less. The recipients also gain better access to credit, which has been especially important in recent years as coffee rust has become a major threat to coffee growing. Control of this disease is possible, but it requires a substantial investment most onerous for small farmers (USAID 1982:1–13). In 1981 the United States initiated a five-year, $9.55 million program in Honduras to help coffee growers, including funds to combat coffee rust.

CONCLUSION

This survey of agrarian policy over the past two and a half decades in Costa Rica and Honduras demonstiates the advantages and weaknesses of reformism in situations of dire need. The recipients of land, titles, and credit and marketing support in the two countries have often enjoyed an improved material position as a result, sometimes substantially improved. The perceived responsiveness of the political system to their needs has in turn generated support for the system and for particular political officials. But at the same time, because structural reform has been beyond the will and capacity of political officials in the two countries and outside of the interest of the United States, the problems of landlessness and near-landlessness are at historic highs. Thus far, the reform programs have been unable to address the structural causes of rural poverty and insecurity.[9]

Agrarian reform has had a mixed history in Honduras. The first attempt at reform, the 1962 law, was in part both inspired by and aborted by external forces—elements of the United States government in both cases, and also the United Fruit Company in the second. Even without those forces, the Honduran government probably did not at that time have the power (or the will) to implement meaningful land redistribution. At the end of the 1960s, however, substantial peasant mobilization altered the configuration of political power. The peasants' dissatisfaction created new pressures on the government and new incentives for political leaders to espouse reformist policies. As a consequence, policies became more favorable to peasant interests, and first the National Agrarian Institute in the late 1960s and early 1970s and then the López Arellano government in 1973–74 altered their orientations. The zenith of populist reformism passed quickly, however, as government leadership changed and the opposition of large landowners solidified. It is also important to recall that little domestically owned private land was redistributed. Peasants have been much less likely to succeed in their attempts to occupy and "recover" idle and underused private lands than in their efforts to claim disputed public lands.

The peasants of Costa Rica have not enjoyed the same organizational strength as their counterparts in Honduras, nor the same political power or policy successes. In part this is due to their numbers; the percentage of the overall economically active Costa Rican population that is employed in agriculture is half that of Honduras (in 1983, 27.7 percent compared to 54.1 percent). Furthermore, the rural standard of living is substantially better in Costa Rica, even for the poor. Most important, Costa Rican peasants did not experience on the same mass scale the land dispossessions suffered by Honduran peasants, a shared experience that was critical to the latter's organized mobilization. Finally, peasant groups in Costa Rica must compete with many more organized interests and face a more institutionalized state, one that is more stable and complex and less personalistic and permeable.

Like its Central American neighbors, Costa Rica does nonetheless maintain a highly skewed structure of land distribution. Individual landless peasants have for decades attempted to rectify this injustice by squatting on idle lands. As the frontier has disappeared, conflicts between squatters and landowners have intensified. Despite the government's various reform efforts, including a renewed commitment to land distribution in the early 1980s, the problem in the countryside has continued to mount. Rural unemployment and landlessness were aggravated in 1985 by United Brands' decision to close its Pacific coast banana operations, claiming that following a long strike it could no longer compete successfully with producers elsewhere (Omang 1985; also see Morsink-Villalobos and Simpson 1980).

In the mid-1980s, both government officials and private observers agreed that the rural problem in Costa Rica was "explosive" (*Libertad* 1985:4; *La Nación* 1983:2a, 1984b:4a; *La República* 1983:21). As one example, in July 1985 about 250 members of peasant families demonstrated in front of the agrarian reform agency, threatening that they would not leave until they received a satisfactory solution to the problem of their continual evictions from the land that they needed (*Libertad* 1985:4). A resolution of the land crisis is most unlikely within the constraints of the existing law, however, because Costa Rica does not have the financial capacity to meet the needs of the rural poor through this approach. But a fundamental alteration of agrarian policy is unlikely in the foreseeable future, given the relative balance of power between peasants and their advocates on one side and larger landowners and other supporters of the prevailing definition of property rights on the other. Accordingly, the land problem promises to remain explosive for some time to come.

In neither country, then, have conditions been conducive to the cause of land redistribution in the first half of the 1980s. Opposition by established interests continues to be successful, undoubtedly reinforced by the atmosphere generated by the war against Nicaragua. The regional economic crisis has tightened already serious financial constraints. Furthermore, redistributive policies and politics based on mass mobilization have always been difficult in Central America, but they are especially problematic now when their legitimacy can be questioned in light of the vigilance elites claim is required in the face of the "communist threat" presented by Nicaragua. No sooner had the Honduran congress passed an antiterrorist law, for example, than peasants found that it was being applied against them. The UNC claimed that in the first week of May 1982, about fifty peasant leaders in the northwest were arrested and accused of being "subversives" (*Tiempo* 1982:5). The repression continued; in the fifteen months beginning in May 1983, 334 members of the UNC were jailed (Kincaid 1985:144). In such a climate, reliance on land titling rather than redistribution is more politically feasible, and undoubtedly more astute. The creation of tens of thousands of more secure farmers builds important centers of support for the regime in a volatile countryside in an unstable region. The switch in policy focus from land redistribution to titling is congruent with the policy orientation of the Reagan administration, both generally and elsewhere in Central America. It certainly is in step with the evolution of the agrarian reform in El Salvador (to be discussed below), where the change in orientation is from redistribution to "land to the tiller."

Part I of this study demonstrated that the number and percentage of landless and land-poor rural families continues to increase in both Costa Rica and Honduras while the per-capita production of basic foods continues to decline. This chapter has shown that pressure by peasants and their urban supporters was substantial enough to redirect public policy partially toward peasants' interests in Honduras in the late 1960s and early 1970s and in Costa Rica in the mid-1970s and mid-1980s. On the whole, however, peasants have been dependent on elites' determination of appropriate policies. In the case of the coffee growers, it can be seen that in the 1980s, some small farmers have been able to gain directly from public policy. Most rural families, however, are instead dependent on the results of the economic development model favored by current policy. The tragic irony is that many careful accounts have found that since 1950, the promotion of commercial export agriculture, along with rapid population growth has been one of the primary causes of their plight in the first place.

NOTES

1. For further discussion, see Hall (1985:202), Riismandel (1972:229), Rowles (1985:212–213), Sáenz and Knight (1971:8), and Seligson (1980a:130–131).

2. Honduran banana workers initiated a prolonged strike in 1954 that had important consequences for agrarian and national politics (Anderson 1981; MacCameron, 1983). For a history of the Honduran labor movement, see Peckenham and Street (1985:89–126).

3. Although there is no readily available and complete discussion of this development, aspects of it are examined in the following works: Kincaid (1985), Morris (1984:45–50, 79–81, 96–100), Pearson (1980:297–32), Pfeil (1977:77–144), Posas (1979:68–76, 1981b), Posas and del Cid (1981:142–152), Ruhl (1984:49–56), Volk (1981:14–23), and White (1977).

4. General López Arellano had become president in 1963 as an air force colonel and had served until 1971.

5. The United States government appears to have had little role in the original steps of the agrarian reform of the 1970s. The drafters of the 1975 law, though, were advised by consultants from the University of Wisconsin at Madison.

6. See, for example, Barahona Riera (1980), Hall (1985:202–204), Rowles (1985:213), and Seligson (1980a:131–135, 1980b:83, 98, 1984:30–31).

7. Nonetheless, when the entire reform sector is considered, basic grains (including sorghum) account for about 80 percent of total production (Ruhl 1985:71).

8. Clarifying land ownership has been problematic. Costa Ricans could homestead up to

30 hectares of public-domain land as late as 1939. Often, though, these same remote, unused lands had been granted by the state years earlier to other individuals for various reasons. A 1942 law allowed such absentee landowners to exchange land settled by homesteaders for other public lands. Sáenz and Knight (1971:II, 32–33) cite one study that claimed that twenty landowners obtained 512,000 hectares of public-domain lands through such exchanges.

9. For a very different view, see the position of Lardizábal (1986), the former president of the Honduran Federation of Farmers and Cattlemen (FENAGH).

CHAPTER 7

El Salvador: From Obstruction to Civil War

Peasant mobilization in El Salvador in the 1970s challenged the system of domination that had allowed a small elite to control most of the land and the profits from its cultivation. This threat was reminiscent of events of half a century earlier. In the 1920s many peasants lost land to coffee growers, who expanded their holdings in tandem with growing markets. The ranks of the landless and unemployed increased further as the Great Depression deepened, causing growers to cut back their operations. Encouraged by leftist organizers from the cities, peasants became more assertive, mounting demonstrations and joining unions. Finally, thousands staged an uprising in 1932. After the rebellion was smashed, close to 1 percent of the country's entire population was massacred. Rural peace was thus restored.

Similar forces have been at the core of the Salvadoran tragedy of recent years, as this chapter will document. Living conditions for many rural people deteriorated in the postwar period as the impact of high population growth rates was aggravated by the loss of land to larger farmers motivated by new commercial opportunities. Breaking out of the "culture of repression"[1] reinforced by the 1932 massacre, many peasants in the 1970s took the risk of joining new organizations that advocated their interests. The elite response was once again obstructionist. A minimal agrarian reform proposal in the mid-1970s was aborted; instead, the powerful relied on repression. Through the rest of the decade, hundreds of people were killed annually; but rather than being a successful means of intimidation, this terrorism incited further popular mobilization, in urban areas as well as in the countryside. By the time of the Sandinista victory in Nicaragua in July 1979, El Salvador was on the verge of a popular revolution.

A coup by junior military officers in October of that year initiated a process that instead led the country into prolonged civil war. A series of rapid changes in government brought a United States–sponsored "centrist" regime to power in early 1980. Vital to the purposes of this regime—and of the U.S.—was an agrarian reform promulgated in March 1980. The objectives and implementation of that reform have been at the core of the controversies concerning the centrist government and United States policy toward El Salvador; accordingly, they will be closely examined in this chapter. Whatever the benefits won by the peasantry, they have come at tremendous cost. Of the over fifty thousand civilian victims the Salvadoran civil war had claimed by 1986, most have been peasants. As in 1932, some of the beneficiaries of the present system have been willing to employ mass murder as an instrument to protect their fundamental interests.

THE OBSTRUCTION OF CHANGE

On May Day of 1930, up to eighty thousand peasants paraded through the streets of San Salvador.[2] At about the same time, the Marxist Regional Federation of Workers of El Salvador claimed to have organized a similar number of agricultural workers. The situation was desperate; male rural unemployment in 1929 was estimated at 40 percent, and it was still climbing the following year (North 1985:35). Thousands of people were attending "popular universities" presented in the countryside by radical students to encourage peasant organization. The administration (1927–31) of Pío Romero Bosque alternated between permissive and repressive responses to this unprecedented mass mobilization. Perhaps most significantly, Romero allowed the country to hold its first fair and free presidential election in 1930. The victor, Arturo Araujo, was an upper-class maverick inspired by the British Labour Party. Any promise of reform was doomed, however. Politically inept, Araujo could not satisfy his multi–class coalition, especially not during the difficult days of the Depression and under the tightest of political constraints. After he had been in office nine months, a coup replaced him with General Maximiliano Hernández Martínez.

Disappointed with the failures and repression of the Araujo administration and now faced with indefinite military rule, radicals decided on a mass uprising as their best alternative. Led by the effective Communist organizer Agustín Farabundo Martí, the conspirators enjoyed substantial success working in Indian communities in the western part of the country, even gaining the support of a number of village chiefs. Unfortunately for their cause, authorities discovered the plot three days before the uprising was to take place and soon had Martí and other leaders under arrest. Nonetheless, the rebellion went on as planned in January 1932. The scope of the uprising was substantial. Bands of up to five hundred people each stormed the towns of Juayuá, Nahuizalco, and Sonsonate, while up to fourteen hundred attacked Ahuachapán and eighteen hundred attacked Tacupa. As the counterattack mounted, some five thousand rebels regrouped at Tacupa and a like number at Sonzacate.

Later, the upper sectors of society would justify the system of domination in El Salvador by their "memory" of the unrestrained barbarity of the Communist-Indian uprising—of widespread murder, torture, rape, looting, and drunkenness. In reality, though the scare must have been substantial and looting was common, Anderson's (1971:136) careful reconstruction estimates about thirty-five civilians killed by the rebels, with other violations of personal integrity minimal. In contrast, the state and private elite forces slaughtered on a massive scale, mostly in revenge after the rebellion had been crushed. A figure of thirty thousand deaths is often cited, but Anderson (1971:135) considers eight to ten thousand more realistic; this number would still constitute close to 1 percent of the population at that time. Especially targeted for death were people who looked Indian in feature or dress and those known or thought to be Communists.[3]

La Matanza (The Massacre), as the event is known, fulfilled its purpose: for the next four decades neither the peasantry nor the left was a force in Salvadoran political life. The military governed the country directly from 1932 until 1979. Along with other security forces, it provided the coercion necessary to keep the agrarian structure intact. Over the following decades the small agro-export oligarchy continued to enjoy the fruits of the majority of the land, even while landlessness and unemployment climbed severely. The key to this system was the continued demobilization of the rural population. The 1907 Agrarian Code's ban on rural unions and strikes was enforced by a National Guard formed in 1912, which large landholders customarily employed to maintain order and prevent protest on their estates (McClintock 1985a:92–98, 124–126). As White (1973:120) observed, "Any 'agitator' among coffee-workers is of course dismissed and if necessary imprisoned or otherwise dealt with."

Maintenance of this culture of repression had become more difficult, however, by the 1960s. The regime's response was the creation of the Democratic Nationalist Organization (ORDEN; i.e., "order"), formed secretly at mid–decade by President Julio Rivera and General José Medrano, chief of the National Guard. This paramilitary organization grew rapidly, eventually "enlisting" up to a hundred thousand peasants and residents of small towns. It linked its members to the military regime through both patronage and socialization into its national security ideology. ORDEN functioned as a large auxiliary to the National Guard for maintaining rural order and as an instrument of repression in which the regime could—hypocritically—deny complicity (Dunkerley 1982:75–76, 115–117; Mc-Clintock 1985a: 204–209; Webre 1979:162–163; White 1973:207). The existence of ORDEN also meant "that political conflict in the countryside could never be a simple case of whole *pueblos* opposing the military," as Dunkerley (1982:76) has pointed out; instead, "the battle would also take place within the communities, with every village becoming a microcosm of the wider civil war" (Dunkerley 1982:76).

The military regime made almost no positive efforts to address agrarian problems. The government purchased some estates through a colonization program initiated in 1932 to make land available to landless peasants. Often little or no technical nor credit support was provided to the settlers, and some of the land was poor in quality. Subsequent reconcentration of holdings was not uncommon. Government land purchases largely ended in 1951. As of 1966 thirty colonies covered 124,000 acres and held a population of around sixty thousand (Minkel 1967:30). By this point, though, the issue of land reform could not be kept off of the policy agenda.

The presidential term of Fidel Sánchez Hernández, from 1967 to 1972, is the analog in the contemporary Salvadoran tragedy to the part played forty years earlier by the Romero Bosque administration. Responding to the economic growth and prosperity of the 1960s, the domestic unity that followed the 1969 war with Honduras, and pressures from the growing urban middle sectors, his tenure was marked by a more tolerant attitude toward discussions of the need for reform and efforts at organizing. Indeed, the administration itself began in 1969 to promise agrarian reform.[4] Although the government's specific intentions were never made clear, its rhetoric helped to legitimate the opposition's discussion of the subject.

The Christian Democratic party (PDC), the most dynamic popular force during this period, soon proposed an agrarian reform program that sought to create a rural middle class through the elimination of both latifundia and *minifundia* (minifarms). After gaining control of the Legislative Assembly, lawmakers favoring reform convened a National Agrarian Reform Congress in early 1970. Although it failed to include peasant interests, the assembly was otherwise broadly representative. Once conservative forces had walked out on its deliberations, it called for an agrarian reform that would include both the "massive expropriation in favor of the common good" of lands not fulfilling their social function and the active participation of the peasantry in the reform process (quoted in Webre 1979:128).

Significant legislative action was precluded, however, by the victory of the government party, the National Conciliation Party (PCN), in the legislative elections of March 1970, most likely the result of renewed tensions with

Honduras. Nonetheless, Sánchez Hernández continued with his reformist rhetoric, much to the dismay of conservatives in the military and the oligarchy. In late 1970 he managed to secure passage of an irrigation and drainage law that established irrigation districts with restricted maximum and minimum property sizes. This was a longstanding proposal vehemently opposed by conservatives because of its qualification of property rights and because it could set a precedent for more substantial agrarian reform. Not surprisingly, implementation of the law was slow.

As the 1972 presidential election approached, the Christian Democrats entered into a coalition with several smaller social democratic parties. They united behind the PDC's most popular leader, José Napoleón Duarte, who had been elected mayor of San Salvador three times. His running mate was Guillermo Ungo of the National Revolutionary Movement (MNR), a close personal friend and the son of one of the founding leaders of the PDC. A major plank in the platform of their National Opposing Union (UNO) was agrarian reform; it called for a legal ceiling on the size of landholdings and the expropriation and redistribution of lands over this limit. The election campaign followed several years of increasing popular organizing. To conservatives it appeared "that leftist agitation was rampant in the country" (Webre 1979:152)—an especially frightening spectacle given events in Chile, where Salvador Allende's Marxist government had just followed that country's first Christian Democratic government into power (Webre 1979:152–153). Consequently, the landed elite and its rightist allies decided to field their own candidate, General Medrano, who had recently been dismissed as commander of the National Guard for allegedly planning a coup.

The military was prepared to protect the system from the threats of reformism and popular mobilization. When Duarte's share of the vote started to gain on that of the government's candidate, radio announcement of the returns was discontinued; when it resumed, Colonel Arturo Molina had won. In response to this obvious fraud a coup was attempted, but it was put down and Duarte was arrested, physically abused, and exiled. The consequences of the fraud were tremendous; in particular, many UNO supporters decided that the electoral process was not a viable instrument for social change under present circumstances in their country. Instead, other strategies would need to be developed.

The desperate need for agrarian reform intensified during the 1970s, but the regime's only response was minor, and even that was aborted (Baloyra 1982:55–63; Berryman 1984:115–117; Montes 1980; Webre 1979:193–195). The government created the Salvadoran Institute of Agrarian Transformation (ISTA) in 1975, and the following year it proposed a reform program in the eastern coastal departments of San Miguel and Usulután. Landowners were given a deadline by which to sell their property, after which it was to be expropriated and distributed to twelve hundred families. The owners of about 150,000 acres were affected, and they were to be fully compensated by funds provided by AID—support that apparently was critical to the formulation of the proposal. Although a major purpose of the reform was to bolster falling popular support for the regime at a time (February 1977) when new elections were approaching, in the end the government was more responsive to the vested interests.

The dispute quickly grew into "one of the most intense confrontations" (Baloyra 1982:55) between different factions of the elite over the future course of Salvadoran agrarian policy. Cutting across military-civilian lines, the debate was essentially between the landed oligarchy and its rightist allies—which adamantly opposed any changes in the agrarian system—and other, more moderate groups, which supported mild reform for developmental or political reasons. The government was able to bring seventy to one hundred thousand rural people (largely ORDEN members) to the capital to support its proposal, but the obligarchy mobilized its many trade associations and utilized its power over the press to force the government to back down amid a campaign of "hysterical anti-communism" (Baloyra 1982:59). A compromise with the landowners was announced, which in effect reduced the program to almost nothing. As the U.S. State Department (1984) noted some years later, "implementation of the reform was blocked by entrenched and politically powerful ownership interests, especially among the cotton growers" (p. 270). The continuing inability of the Salvadoran elite to accommodate even mild reform had been demonstrated once again.

POPULAR MOBILIZATION

The commitment of Salvadoran elites to obstruct meaningful social change was confronted in the 1970s by an unprecedented challenge from popular forces in both urban and rural areas. The economic growth of the 1960s and 1970s increased the size and the aspirations of the urban middle and working classes. Although their growing politicization and radicalization are crucial to a full understanding of the Salvadoran tragedy, that story is tangential to the purposes of this study except for the critical function these urban forces played in promoting peasant mobilization. Meanwhile in the countryside, the rapid spread of commercial agriculture undermined the economic security of much of the peasantry, as elaborated in Part I. Reinforcing this loss of land and employment were the impacts of both a continuing high rate of population growth and the 1969 war with Honduras, which eliminated the neighboring country as a frontier safety valve and returned tens of thousands of settlers to El Salvador.

Some observers have denied that deteriorating economic conditions contributed to popular frustrations in El Salvador in the 1970s and therefore to the civil war that followed (Mooney 1984).[5] It is true that the Salvadoran gross domestic product grew by 5 percent annually from 1968 to 1978, for an annual per capita increase of 1.4 percent, and that per capita production of basic grains increased during this period as well (Mooney 1984:61–63). However, these aggregate figures hide the growing economic insecurity of significant elements of the rural population. As discussed earlier, landlessness among rural families climbed from approximately 12 percent in 1961 to 29 percent in 1971 and to 41 percent in 1975. While the ranks of the landless grew, their incomes declined by 19 percent (more when adjusted for inflation) from 1971 to 1975. When their incomes are measured against the average for all rural groups, they declined by 24 percent for the same years, while the relative share of the largest landowners increased by 23 percent (Montes 1980:132). Meanwhile, rural salaries declined in both absolute and relative terms. When measured in constant units, agricultural wages fluctuated from 1967 to 1973 and then fell by 25 percent to 1976 and by 30 percent to 1978. During the same period, agricultural salaries also lost 23 percent of their value compared to industrial salaries (Montes 1980:115).

The objective conditions for popular mobilization were clearly present by 1973, and they became even more urgent as the decade progressed. But as Montes (1980:220–234, 265–266, 320–333) argues, there was little subjective readiness to organize early in the decade. Soon, though, the emergence of a grassroots reform movement was facilitated by agents from the outside, especially Church workers as well as urban students and politicians.

Although rural unions continued to be illegal, new organizations appeared in the countryside in the 1960s that began to address some of the needs of the peasantry. The two most important were the Salvadoran Communal Union (UCS) and the Christian Federation of Salvadoran Peasants (FECCAS). The American Institute for Free Labor Development (AIFLD, an affiliate of the AFL–CIO) initiated training of peasant leaders in El Salvador in 1962 through an Alliance for Progress program. With assistance from AID, the Christian Democratic party, and the Salvadoran government, this project eventually led to the development of cooperatives and then, in 1968, to the formation of UCS, with an initial membership of four thousand. The formation of FECCAS was catalyzed in 1964 by Christian Democrats. Originally primarily a self-help organization, by the end of the decade it had become more assertive as both peasants and priests grew in their understanding of the challenges they faced (Berryman 1984:100–101; Dunkerley 1982:98–99; Forché and Wheaton 1980:5–6).

As has been demonstrated for Guatemala and Honduras, elements of the Catholic Church played a critical role in the mobilization of peasants. In El Salvador the process often began with the formation of Christian Base Communities, small Bible-study groups in which peasants were encouraged to apply religious lessons about dignity and justice to their own lives. The effect was often revolutionary. As one Maryknoll sister observed,

> When I first arrived in Tamanique, every time a child died the family would say, "It's the will of God." But after the people became involved in the Christian communities, that attitude began to change. And after a year or so I no longer heard people in the communities saying that. After a while they began to say, "The system caused this." (quoted in Montgomery 1982:104)

Participants also elected their own leaders, both lay teachers and preachers; between 1970 and 1976 about fifteen thousand were trained. An early indication of what the Christian Base Communities portended for the landed elite came in 1969 in Suchitoto, a town about 30 miles northeast of San Salvador. Shortly after base communities started in this area of land scarcity, two of the country's wealthiest landowners bought a local hacienda and subdivided it, selling the new units at prices ranging from three to seven times their original cost. Up to three thousand local people demonstrated their outrage in front of the hacienda, demanding lower prices. When this action proved futile, four hundred of them demonstrated in the capital, the first such showing since 1932 not organized by the government (Montgomery 1982:97–117).

Rural organizing in the 1960s and early 1970s was outpaced by similar efforts in urban areas, especially by teachers, students, and industrial workers. Following the disenchantment that resulted from the fraud of the 1972 presidential election and similar duplicity in the 1974 elections, a type of political organization new to El Salvador was created in June 1974. The United Popular Action Front (FAPU) was formed as an autonomous coalition of various popular groups. Representing rural groups were FECCAS and peasants from around Suchitoto. Soon other popular organizations would develop, in part through fragmentation. By the last years of the seventies, they were the most dynamic political force in the country.

During the mid-1970s, then, there were three different kinds of peasant organizations in El Salvador. First, there was ORDEN, a paramilitary force organized by the state to control the countryside. Although its membership was about a hundred thousand peasants, it is usually claimed that all but about 5 to 10 percent had joined only as a means of self-protection (Montgomery 1982:207n). Second, there was UCS, which claimed a membership of eighty thousand by 1976. Given its origins and continuing ties to AIFLD (which provided most of its financial support, the majority of which came in turn from AID),[6] it is not surprising that critics of the UCS from its left have perceived it "as a means of controlling the peasantry by giving its members a piece of the pie" (Montgomery 1982:124; also see Dunkerley 1982:98). It is true that compared to the third type of organization, UCS was more moderate, tied to U.S. interests, bureaucratic in structure with little grassroots participation in leadership selection, and very corrupt, at least during the midseventies. An OAS study in 1977 estimated that almost half of the UCS's members also belonged to ORDEN and indicated that UCS operated as the rural political arm of the government party (WOLA 1979:10). Third, increasing numbers of peasants were mobilized as the 1970s progressed by more radical and autonomous groups such as FECCAS and the popular organizations.

The conflict over the 1976 agrarian reform proposal, then, occurred within the context of the increasing mobilization of peasants, some of whom were participants in grassroots organizations with radical analyses of the structural causes of the peasantry's plight. The rightists' victory over the moderate reformers was relatively easy within the reigning policy-making system, but their determination to maintain the rural status quo now faced an equally determined challenge from popular forces created and/or awakened by the economic changes and political liberalization that had occurred since the early 1960s. The right relied on repression to protect its position. Coming at a time of rapidly deteriorating economic conditions for many rural people, however, the repression of the 1970s had largely the opposite effect, generating even more widespread popular opposition. Finally, the right took recourse in repression on a shockingly broad scale, as it had in 1932, in order to counter the threat from below and the left.

What had been isolated instances of repression in the early 1970s became more frequent by the middle of the decade. Peasants from a local base community were attacked on November 23, 1974 when they occupied idle private land in La Cayetana, San Vicente; six of them were killed, twenty-six were arrested, and thirteen later disappeared. Soon afterward, peasants of the area formed the Union of Rural Workers (UTC), which soon allied with FECCAS. At about this time student activism at the University of El Salvador reached a new peak. A student march in July 1975, protesting the breaking up of an earlier campus demonstration against the extravagant holding of the "Miss Universe" pageant, was fired on by the National Guard. It was estimated that as many as thirty-seven marchers were killed (Berryman 1984:109–111; Webre 1979:188–189). One study of the Molina years suggests that 106 people were murdered or disappeared at government initiative from 1972 to 1977, while the increasingly assertive guerrilla movements on the left killed forty-two security or paramilitary personnel and kidnaped another eight people (cited in Baloyra 1982:190).

Two sets of events in early 1977 indicated what the next two and a half years would be like. First, the regime maintained itself in power by once again committing massive fraud in the presidential election of February 20. Outside observers generally agreed that the slate put forth by the democratic opposition would have won the election had legality prevailed. A week later, a continuing vigil by the democratic forces was attacked by the security forces; up to one hundred people were killed, two hundred wounded, and five hundred arrested (Berryman 1984:121–122). In this fashion the regime was perpetuated. Molina's reformist facade was shed, however, as the new president, General Carlos Romero, was a man of the far right.

The second foreboding event occurred on March 12, 1977, when Father Rutilio Grande was assassinated, along with two peasants accompanying him. Although five other priests were killed during the 1970s, his murder was especially significant. Grande began his pastoral work in 1972 in Augilares, a sugar-growing area close to his birthplace.[7] With a team of co–workers, he sought to facilitate a deepening of the peasants' religious understanding so that they would become active participants in creating, in his words, "a community of brothers and sisters committed to building a new world, with no oppressors or oppressed, according to God's plan" (quoted in Berryman 1984:108). Soon the team had established twenty-seven rural base communities and ten urban ones, with about three hundred leaders selected by the participants themselves. Grande tried to maintain a separation between his religious work and his political activities, but many of those affected by the teachings of his team became active in political organizations, especially FECCAS. As popular mobilization grew, the right came to see church people with liberationist messages as bearing a particular responsibility for this transformation.

During the three months following the electoral fraud of February 1977, two priests were murdered (Grande and then Father Alfonso Navarro a month later), ten were exiled, eight were expelled (five of them tortured first), two were arrested, one was beaten, and another was seized and tortured on two separate occasions. Meanwhile in mid-May, security forces conducted military operations in the region around Aguilares, finally attacking the town itself (Berryman 1984:106–115, 123–127; Montgomery 1982:104–111). This was the context of the first few months after Oscar Romero's selection as archbishop of San Salvador, the country's key religious leader. Misperceived by many as noncontroversial and a "safe" choice, he had been undergoing his own process of consciousness-raising for several years, a transformation accelerated by the death of his friend Father Grande. Archbishop Romero met a similar fate in March 1980, his murder eliminating the most powerful voice for peace in El Salvador.

For the regime to maintain itself and to protect the oligarchy, however, repression would have to increase, because popular mobilization continued to grow in both urban and rural areas. Key examples in the countryside in 1977 included two important land invasions organized by the Popular Revolutionary Bloc (BRP), the largest of the popular organizations; a demand for an increase in the minimum daily wage presented in mid-October by radical peasant unions such as FECCAS–UTC; and the November occupation by rural workers of the Ministry of Labor. For the next two years popular forces kept up a steady pace of such activities, especially strikes, occupations, and demonstrations. Actions by guerrilla organizations grew more frequent as well.

Government repression increased even more rapidly. On November 24, 1977, General Romero announced the Law for the Defense and Guarantee of Public Order, which created a state of emergency, suspending constitutionally protected liberties. The law with this Orwellian name, as Baloyra (1982) notes, "was practically a license to kill" as "government violence reached epidemic proportions" (p. 66). During Romero's twenty-seven months in office, over six hundred Salvadorans were assassinated or disappeared. The most frequent victims of this state terrorism were activists in the popular organizations. Meanwhile, about 132 security and paramilitary personnel were killed by guerrillas, and another sixteen were kidnaped (cited in Baloyra 1982:190).

The growing movement against the Somoza dictatorship in Nicaragua in 1979 intensified the conflict in El Salvador. Romero made his situation even more precarious by alienating his rightist support when he eased the repression in an attempt to reduce tensions with the Carter administration. When Somoza fell in July, his days were clearly numbered. Indeed, three different factions within the military were plotting against him: reformers, the U.S.–oriented center-right, and the rightists. The reformers acted first, deposing Romero in October 1979 and setting up a progressive government with many of the civilian interests that had opposed the regime's candidates in 1972 and 1977.

A "CENTRIST"
MODEL FOR CHANGE

The events of the next few months were complicated and remain controversial. As they are described and evaluated elsewhere and are tangential to the purposes of this study, they will not be discussed here.[8] It will suffice to note that the new government was based on an alliance of the reformers with forces to their right rather than with the popular forces represented by the mass organizations. Nor did the new junta control the security forces, whose repression actually increased in the last months of 1979. Consequently, the October junta was unable to end the repression, initiate meaningful reforms, or placate the increasingly restive left. Given its inherent contradictions, it soon fell, to be replaced by new governments in both January and March 1980. The October government did formulate an agrarian reform under the leadership of the minister of agriculture, Enrique Alvarez (who had held the same position in the Sánchez cabinet almost a decade earlier). The inability of reformers to overcome strong military opposition to this proposal was one of the major factors leading to the departure from the government of the civilian reformers, a number of whom became leaders of opposition forces.[9]

Only two months later, implementation of agrarian reform was initiated under a less progressive government. The involvement of the United States was critical to this turnabout. It had taken Washington some time to decide how to respond to the changed situation after the October coup. By the beginning of 1980, the United States faced in El Salvador governmental instability on the one hand and growing mass mobilization and radicalization on the other. Determined to avoid "another Nicaragua," the Carter administration dispatched a new ambassador to El Salvador to engineer a viable reformist government of the center. At the heart of what Ambassador Robert White later called "a new model for profound ... economic and social change" (United States, House 1981a:6)[10] was agrarian reform, accompanied by the nationalization of the banking and export marketing sectors.[11] This reform was central to U.S. attempts to preempt a popular-leftist victory in El Salvador and to create and perpetuate instead a moderate reformist government.[12]

The key decision makers have not been of one mind, however, either in Washington or in San Salvador. The purposes and the evolution of the reform need to be understood as the outcome of political bargaining, primarily among three major centers of power—the United States government, the Salvadoran military, and the Salvadoran civilian government—as well as with less powerful actors such as peasant organizations. Pro–reform and anti–reform forces in turn have struggled within each of these arenas to determine its role in the fight over the Salvadoran reform. As political fortunes and alliances changed, so did the fate of the reform.

Promulgation of a reform program required a change in the attitude not only of the United States government but also of the Salvadoran military. The increasing threat from the popular-leftist forces softened resistance within the military to reform, giving credibility to the argument that such changes were necessary to preempt the program of the left and to give the government some measure of legitimacy. North American officials undoubtedly accompanied such arguments with considerable pressure, making it clear that reform was the price for continued U.S. support. Finally, the military was given a central role in the implementation of the reform, which meant that the program could be used as an instrument of repression to combat the growing leftist insurgency.

Repression

Because reform was largely forced on the Salvadoran government from the outside, the domestic distribution of power was insufficient to insure faithful implementation of a reformist program. In this situation, it was probably inevitable that the reform process would be used by those with power to pursue other objectives, such as counterinsurgency and intimidation. The promulgation of the reform was followed by the announcement of a state of siege. The large estates marked for expropriation were occupied by the military. It was in these areas that the flow of refugees and the numbers of peasants killed by security forces in 1980 were the highest (LeoGrande 1981). Over the next few years the peasant death toll mounted rapidly. As one authoritative account noted in 1982, "*Campesinos* suffer unspeakable brutality at the hands of the military and paramilitary forces" (AWC and American Civil Liberties Union [ACLU] 1982:51). Tens of thousands of peasants were to die, either as the direct objects of attack or as a consequence of military counterinsurgency tactics. While there was a sharp controversy in the early 1980s among observers over the extent to which the reform and the repression were analytically distinct,[13] clearly they often were inseparable in practice.

Various sources have documented that the most frequent rural victims of the Salvadoran violence have been identified with three groups: agrarian reform workers, peasant leaders, and members of peasant communities suspected of being sympathetic to the guerrillas (Central American Information Office [CAMINO] 1982:71). By September 1981, forty employees of the agrarian reform agency (ISTA) had been murdered (AWC and ACLU 1982:63). Indeed, the agency's director himself was assassinated in January while dining at the San Salvador Sheraton Hotel. Gunned down with José Rodolfo Viera were two AIFLD advisors to the reform, Michael Hammer and Mark Pearlman.

Peasant leaders who emerged during the reform process were murdered in large numbers. Some estimate that in the first year of the agrarian reform, more than five hundred peasant leaders were killed by security forces or allied right-wing paramilitary groups (CAMINO 1982:73). There were various reports of security forces occupying newly expropriated estates asking peasants to elect leaders, whom they executed in subsequent days. Many of the victims were members of UCS, which gave strong support to the reform. In fact, Viera was the head of UCS when he was selected to run ISTA. According to a UCS report, ninety-two of its members were killed in the two years ending December 10, 1981; only nine of these deaths could not be attributed to the security forces or death squads (United States, House 1982:337).

Finally, there were the thousands of victims of the rural pacification prong of the war against the guerrillas. According to a 1981 report of the legal aid office of the archbishop of El Salvador,

> the assassinations, the massacres, the robberies and burning of ranches are frequent, especially in the northern and eastern zones. The testimonies heard and read, most coming from persons not affiliated to organizations, have shown that to be a victim of the repression it is enough to be a relative of a militant or to be suspected of having collaborated with the insurgents. The concept of collective responsibility is being progressively extended to the individual family, town and even the Province. (quoted in CAMINO 1982:74)

Although efforts were made in later years to clean up military practices, the increasing reliance on air power to pursue the counterinsurgency campaign introduced a new source of noncombatant casualties and loss of homes.[14]

The Reform Program

The initial agrarian reform package of March 6, 1980 was largely taken from the unsuccessful proposal of the previous fall. Of its two parts, only the first was implemented. Its Phase One expropriated the 472 properties that were in excess of 1235 acres and converted them into 317 cooperatives with over thirty-one thousand members (about 8 percent of all peasant families). Covering more than 548,800 acres, the reform affected about 15 percent of the country's farmland, much of which had been devoted to the cultivation of export crops (United States, House 1984:271).[15] Phase Two, which applied to farms of between 605 and 1235 acres, has never been implemented.

A third phase of the program was initiated on April 28, 1980. Often referred to as "land to the tiller" (or "tenant"), Phase Three allowed those farming all rented or sharecropped land under 17.3 acres to claim title to it. At the time of its legal expiration (June 1984), about 63,660 of the estimated hundred fifty thousand eligible peasants had registered for title to some 240,000 acres—about 6.6 percent of the country's farmland. Another ten thousand peasants who had not completed the cumbersome filing procedures were told that they would be allowed to finish the process. The U.S. State

Department has estimated that altogether the reform benefited more than one-quarter of El Salvador's rural poor (about 12 percent of the total population) and affected around 22 percent of the agricultural land (United States, Department of State 1985).

There is some evidence that the United States was less than happy with the cooperative nature of Phase One (Buckley 1984: 116); however, this form of organization is central to the Christian Democratic ideology of leaders such as Duarte, who were brought into the government at that time.[16] This situation was more than reversed with "land to the tiller"; the evidence is clear that it was forced on reluctant and dubious Salvadoran officials. Journalist Tom Buckley (1984:118), for example, reported that Duarte informed him that he had accepted the program under heavy pressure and after having been promised substantial financial assistance to pay for the requisite compensation. The architect of the program was Roy Prosterman, who was brought to El Salvador by AIFLD, the "foreign office" of the AFL–CIO.[17] A primary formulator of a similar land reform program in South Vietnam, Prosterman had long been an enthusiastic supporter of programs that turned tenants into small farmers. In addition to their merits as social and economic reforms, such programs are seen as invaluable in the "fight against communism" because they rob radicals of their major appeal to the peasantry. Given the concerns of the Carter administration in El Salvador at the time, "land to the tiller" was a most attractive concept. It was even more appealing to the Reagan administration, which was less ambivalent about its preference for individualist as opposed to collective reforms.

Although Phase Three eventually benefited tens of thousands of peasant families, it was nonetheless hastily devised by U.S. advisors who did not consult with relevant Salvadoran officials (Chapin 1980:20).[18] The major criticism brought against the program is that it was based on a model that only partially fit Salvadoran reality. The transformation of smallholder tenants into property owners would work most smoothly if their land belonged to absentee owners with large holdings and if the state security forces enforced the reform faithfully. To the contrary, in El Salvador many of the affected plots were owned by local residents with only minor holdings, many of whom were very bitter over the possible expropriation of their property. As detailed below, many owners resisted implementation of this reform, often evicting their tenants. They were assisted in many cases by local security forces and paramilitary groups. Obstruction was also facilitated by the amazingly cumbersome implementation process established for the program (see Diskin 1982:33; Strasma et al. 1983:145–153).

Implementation of the Reform

Implementation of the various phases of the reform was complicated by shifting political fortunes in both Washington and San Salvador. Phase Two was postponed virtually as soon as it was announced. The Carter administration was divided about its merits, and the Reagan administration was solidly opposed to it (Bonner 1984:197, 239). This phase would have affected lands of 605 to 1235 acres, which belonged to about 10.5 percent of rural families and represented 18.5 percent of the farmland, including much of the country's crucial coffee crop.[19] A right-of-center coalition dominating the Salvadoran Constituent Assembly elected in March 1982 annulled Phase Two in its first legislative session. Not only did the owners of the targeted land possess considerable political power, but in addition, officials in both Washington and San Salvador have been receptive to their argument that redistribution of these lands would seriously reduce the country's foreign exchange earnings. It was also argued that the first phase alone had overtaxed the capabilities of the Salvadoran government; therefore, it lacked the financial, administrative, and technical capacity to undertake further expropriations. The issue was settled, at least for the present, by a provision in the 1983 constitution establishing a ceiling of 605 acres on the amount of land that an individual can own. Owners were given up to three years to sell property in excess of this limit (with sale to close relatives prohibited), after which time the excess would be subject to expropriation. The end result, then, has been to eliminate large estates from El Salvador, but with no benefit to the very sizable landless population.

The history of Phase Three has been more complicated, given the support it has received from the United States on the one hand and the struggle over its implementation in El Salvador on the other. The conflict within the country has involved a multiplicity of actors, with many landowners, local security-force officers, and rightist politicians seeking to frustrate its implementation pitted against peasants, rural organizations, agrarian reform workers, and centrist politicians attempting to maximize the reform potential of the program.

"Land to the tiller" was intended to be virtually self-executing. All tenanted and sharecropped land under the ceiling of 17.3 acres was expropriated and transferred to the families working it. They had until April 1981 to register their claims but, because of their insufficient initiative and the government's inadequate response, the program was extended three times until it finally expired at the end of June 1984. Although Prosterman (Prosterman, Riedinger, and Temple 1981) talked of a hundred fifty thousand families as immediate beneficiaries, AID data indicated that by June 1981 only 14,735 peasants had registered with the government and only 1,440 provisional titles had been granted, representing 54,961 acres. By March 1983 the number of applicants had reached 49,517, with 194,895 acres affected (United States, Department of State 1983). As previously mentioned, the final total was 63,660 beneficiaries, with another ten thousand in the process of completing their applications.

Considering that the program was begun in the middle of a civil war marked by a tremendous level of rural repression in a country with a long history of repression of peasants by both the state and landowners, it it not at all surprising that individual peasants were hesitant to undertake what was in effect their own expropriation process. A December 1981 UCS report to President Duarte, for example, claimed that the entire reform effort was near collapse because of repression backed by the military, illegal evictions, and a "frequently hostile" bureaucracy (DeYoung 1982:A1). The problem of evictions of beneficiaries of Phase Three land reform continued. In 1983 UCS charged that about ten thousand of the beneficiaries had been turned out since the beginning of the program.[20] Even more to the point, an internal AID audit of the program in January 1984 found that as many as one-third of its "beneficiaries" were not farming the land they had filed for "because they had been threatened, evicted or had disappeared" (AP 1984:A3). The State Department concurred in its 1984 certification report to Congress, noting that "Landowners affected by Phase III have resisted strongly, often with violence and forced eviction of campesinos" (United States, House 1984:284).

Attempts to frustrate Phase Three occurred not only on the individual level but also through the political system. The rightist-controlled Constituent Assembly elected in March 1982 quickly moved to undermine the program; one of its first acts was to suspend the law for one crop year. This setback occurred just before the July 1982 date when the Reagan administration needed to certify to Congress that the Salvadoran government was "making continued progress in implementing essential economic and political reforms, including the land reform program," as legislation passed the previous year required.[21] When President Alvaro Magaña voided the assembly's action and reaffirmed the program by decree, it was assumed that he was acting at least partly in response to pressure from the Reagan administration, which regarded the continuation of Phase Three as crucial to its strategy for El Salvador. Not only was the reform important to its "centrist" solution for that country, but it was also perceived as vital to avoiding further constraints mandated by legislators wary of the administration's Salvadoran policy. Such pressures probably also explain the reinstallment by the Salvadoran military of several thousand families who had been evicted and an effort by mobile teams in fall 1982 to inform potential beneficiaries of their rights and to encourage their participation. Also crucial was the fact that

160

LAND, POWER, AND POVERTY

responsibility for Phase Three had been placed not in ISTA but in a separate agency, FINATA. Since mid-1982 FINATA had been headed by Colonel Torres, an active-duty military officer who was able to resist ideological direction from the conservative administration and who has been praised by observers for his intelligence and energy (United States, House 1984: 162).

A countervailing presence was maintained by the Salvadoran right, however, through control of the ministry of agriculture and its agencies responsible for the land reform programs.[22] The right lost these positions to Christian Democrats following Duarte's presidential victory in May 1984, but the next month it was able to end further land distribution through Phase Three when the legislature refused to extend the program's life once again. Although North American pressure had been crucial to the three prior extensions, it was reported that this time U.S. officials were willing to accept termination (LeMoyne 1984:A1+).

Implementation of the Salvadoran agrarian reform has been greatly assisted by financial support from the United States. Total assistance (mostly in loans) through fiscal 1985 was estimated at $120.8 million (USAID 1985:76). Most of this amount was for agricultural credit, though support was also provided for technical assistance and for the implementing institutions. Funds were not provided to help the government of El Salvador with the burden of compensation, however, because of legislative restrictions promoted by Senator Jesse Helms in both 1980 and 1981. As one observer noted,

> This put the United States in the somewhat anomalous position of requiring that the Salvadoran government continue to implement the agrarian reform program, while refusing to permit U.S. assistance to be used to provide compensation to former owners affected by the reform. (Storrs 1981:131)

Compensation has been difficult for the Salvadoran government to raise. It had paid as of November 1982 for 29 percent of expropriated Phase One land, and agreement had been reached for another 24 percent of the land, but the government lacked the necessary cash resources to pay it (Browning 1983:414; also see Strasma et al. 1983:80–86). In early 1985 AID reported that compensation had been paid for 54 percent of the properties— almost all of it in bonds (United States, House 1985b:282). Even more financially strapped are the cooperatives; the Phase One beneficiaries are required to repay to the government over a twenty- to thirty-year period the total cost of the expropriation (land, improvements, livestock, machinery, and so on) and of any government-funded improvements (Browning 1983:417–418; Diskin 1984a:107; Strasma et al. 1983:86). A consultant's report to AID pointed out that as of November 1984, 95 percent of the cooperatives lacked the financial resources to pay their debt (then totaling around $800 million); in fact, three-quarters of them lacked the resources just to keep up with the service payments (United States, House 1985b:284).

CONCLUSION

The Salvadoran tragedy has many causes, but among the most important are those pertaining to rural society. The agrarian transformations of the colonial period and the nineteenth century created a highly unequal system that could only be maintained through repression—either directly, as occurred in 1932, or through the threats woven into the fabric of day-to-day life. In the 1970s the dislocations of the contemporary agrarian transformation, along with other factors such as rapid population growth and the organizational efforts of outside agents, caused peasants to begin challenging the ground rules of the traditional agrarian structure. In response, repression from the right increased; by 1980, however, the right could no longer veto agrarian policy. When the regime change of 1979–80 led to a substantial agrarian reform, the right reacted with ferocious brutality. Much of the reform has now been implemented, but the price paid by the peasantry has been very high.

Indicative of the complex currents of contemporary El Salvador are the fates of the three peasant organizations discussed in this chapter. The dissolution of the rightist paramilitary group ORDEN was a primary demand of the civilians brought in to the October 1979 government and one of that regime's few accomplishments. But much of ORDEN's repressive apparatus continued on under different guises, such as the Democratic National Front (FDN) organized soon thereafter by General Medrano. Presumably, there was substantial continuity between ORDEN and the paramilitary squads responsible for much of the rural repression of the early 1980s (Dunkerley 1982:143, 164; McClintock 1985a:253–254, 317–320).[23] This violence was directed especially against autonomous progressive organizations such as FECCAS, which was destroyed along with the larger popular organizations in the early 1980s. Many of the survivors joined the revolutionary forces, and those groups grew significantly in strength and in support in 1980 and 1981.

The fate of the UCS has been more complicated. AIFLD returned to El Salvador in 1978 and began to reestablish its ties with the peasant organization. Within two years it was paying almost all of UCS's nearly $2 million budget. After the promulgation of the agrarian reform (substantially formulated under AIFLD auspices), the U.S. labor organization hired about four hundred UCS members at $160 a month to promote the reform in the countryside. Although there is obvious merit to Bonner's (1984) description of UCS as "little more than an alter ego for AIFLD and the U.S. policy" (p. 193), it is also true that the peasant organization had ample reasons for supporting the reform. And its members paid dearly for their participation in the process, as described earlier. The Christian Democratic party was also part of this relationship. UCS was the largest group in the Popular Democratic Unity (UPD), a labor coalition that was "the backbone of PDC electoral support" in the first half of the 1980s (Norton 1985:28). Following Duarte's 1984 presidential victory, UCS leaders received top agrarian policy-making positions in the government, but disenchantment soon set in because of the lack of progress in settling the war and extending the reforms. Serious tensions also developed with AIFLD (Norton 1985:30–36).

The United States has been the sponsor in El Salvador of a reform benefiting about a quarter of the rural poor. This undertaking, unique for the United States, was primarily the result of security concerns. In early 1980, a revolutionary situation was rapidly developing in El Salvador. To officials in the Carter administration, it appeared that the only hope for preventing the left from coming to power was to preempt its issues while giving firm support to a government of "the center." Whether the Reagan administration would have reacted to the situation in the same way is interesting to contemplate; what is clear is that upon coming into office, it continued support for the reform for the same reasons. Phase One of the Salvadoran reform was a major redistributive act; it expropriated the largest estates, which included about 15 percent of the country's farmland. Phase Three, which has benefited over twice as many peasants, has been far less redistributive in nature, not only because it has affected about half as much land but especially because it was not based on the amount of property a landholder owned. Consequently, it applied to relatively small and medium-sized landowners as well as to those with large holdings.

It is important not to slight the accomplishments of the Salvadoran reform, which occurred in the most difficult of circumstances. Still, it remains true that it did not reach most of the rural poor, while the real benefits for many who were reached by both Phase One and Phase Three are questionable. The accomplishments of the reform are inadequate when measured against the need, yet those accomplishments were gained only at a tremendous price. Had the United States not intervened to preempt the popular forces as it did in 1980, a result more favorable to the Salvadoran peasantry might have been obtained at a lower price.

NOTES

1. Huizer's (1972) formulation of this concept, which he applies generally to peasant societies, was undoubtedly influenced by his field experience in El Salvador.

2. This paragraph and the next two are based on Anderson's (1971) thorough account. Also see Dunkerley (1982:19–31), North (1985:29–41), and White (1973:93–101).

3. Anderson (1971) explains both the acceptance of this myth and the motivation behind the massacre in the following way:

> [The army and the bourgeoisie] had sensed for a long time dark rumblings among the masses of the people, as the plantation owners of the Old South must have sensed them. In the rebellion of January, 1932, their worst fears had been realized. Indian and peasant discontent had been linked to the dread spector of International Communism. It is hardly surprising that their actions against the now doubly "red" Indians were hysterical and violent. (p. 131)

4. This and the following three paragraphs are largely based on Webre (1979:122–160). Also see Dunkerley (1982:45–71).

5. Mooney (1984) explains the popular mobilization of the 1970s as a consequence of aspirations rising faster than the rate of change. Undoubtedly this explanation holds for many individuals, especially in urban areas.

6. These ties were ruptured for a time during the late 1970s but were healed in June 1979. During 1978 and 1979 peasants with a more leftist orientation became increasingly active in the UCS (Forché and Wheaton 1980:14–16).

7. For background on this area, see Montes (1980:47–58, 222–239).

8. Because these events are crucial to the unfolding of the civil war and because interpretations vary, the reader should consult several sources, such as Baloyra (1982:64–74, 86–104), Berryman (1984:140–146), Dunkerley (1982:132–152), LeoGrande and Robbins (1980), and Montgomery (1982:7–23, 159–165).

9. Most prominently, they included Alvarez, who became the secretary-general of the Democratic Revolutionary Front (FDR) upon its formation in April as an umbrella organization of leftist opponents of the government; Guillermo Ungo, who replaced Alvarez after he was assassinated in November 1980; and Rubén Zamora, who has also been a primary spokesperson for this opposition.

10. This rhetoric eventually was continued by the Reagan administration. For example, Secretary of State George Shultz wrote to Congress in 1984, "Promotion of land reform stands at the very heart of El Salvador's effort to encourage social equity, political stability and economic development. It has our strong support" (United States, House 1984:263).

11. The coffee export trade had been nationalized in the fall by the first junta; the March decree affected the other major export commodities. The October junta had also frozen all transactions involving landholdings over 100 hectares (about 247 acres) pending passage of an agrarian reform law.

12. Four years later the State Department noted, "Enactment of the land reform removed one of the key appeals used by the violent left to attract the rural poor. . . . There is general agreement that land reform was a critical factor undercutting the far left's potential political support" (United States, House 1984:269).

13. Compare the criticisms of Deere (1982), LeoGrande (1981), and Lehoucq and Sims (1982) to the positions of Gómez and Cameron (1981), Prosterman (1981), and Prosterman, Riedinger, and Temple (1981).

14. The intentions and consequences of the air war were the matter of some controversy;

contrast, for example, AWC (1984:291–342), Lawyers Commitee for International Human Rights (LCIHR) and AWC (1984), and Norton (1986) with Williams (1985). Duarte issued stricter regulations governing air force bombings in September 1984, in itself an indication of earlier civilian casualties (see Cody 1984).

15. Of the original properties, 194 were in excess of the limit; the rest were multiple holdings of the same owner that totaled over the limit. The properties expropriated in Phase One of the program comprised about 31 percent of the country's cotton land, 24 percent of its sugar land, and 14 percent of its coffee land (Simon and Stephens 1982:13). By 1982 twenty-eight of the cooperatives had been abandoned, with another twenty-one in danger of abandonment (Browning 1983:413). For discussions of Phase One in addition to those mentioned in note 13, see Browning (1983:413–418), Diskin (1984a:107, 111–115, 1984b:84–86), Simon and Stephens (1982:9–14), Strasma et al. (1983), Thiesenhusen (1981), and United States, Department of State (1984:280–283).

16. Cooperatives are not always as progressive as promised. Long and Winder (1981) note that in unequal societies, "in practice the beneficiaries are denied effective control over such organizations. In such situations the State will tend to take steps to prevent the emergence of independent organizations representing the interests of beneficiaries" (p. 86). Their analysis is a good counterpoint to Mason's (1986) abstract approach to the Salvadoran reform.

17. Prosterman denies that Phase Three was forced on El Salvador; see Prosterman, Riedinger, and Temple (1981).

18. For discussions of Phase Three, see Browning (1983:419–423), Diskin (1982:33–35; 1984a:115–122), Simon and Stephens (1982:17–22), Strasma et al. (1983:129–153), United States, Department of State (1984:283–285), and the articles by Prosterman and Prosterman, Riedinger, and Temple cited in note 13.

19. Although some early reports gave much higher figures, Prosterman (1983:597) provides evidence suggesting that Phase Two would have affected about 30.6 percent of the coffee land, 30 to 41 percent of the cotton land, and 21 percent of the sugar land.

20. Although it would be virtually impossible to substantiate the actual number of evictees, the magnitude of the problem has been great. A survey in June 1983 by an agency of the Salvadoran government, using a more restricted definition than had UCS, estimated 5634 evictees in the country (United States, House 1984:284). A report by an independent consultant to AIFLD in 1983 found that 284 peasants in a sample of 703 potential beneficiaries had been evicted (Chavez 1983:A1, A5).

21. The requirement that the administration certify progress by the Salvadoran government in six areas as a prerequisite for U.S. assistance was in effect for two years until it was killed at the end of 1983, when President Reagan vetoed its continuation. Certification of land reform progress, however, continued at least through fiscal 1984.

22. For a discussion of the consequences for the reform of this period of rightist control, see Diskin (1984a:104–122).

23. Some members of ORDEN suffered from reprisals in areas where they lost their dominance; see Dunkerley (1982:175) and Montgomery (1982:136).

CHAPTER 8

Nicaragua:
From Obstruction to Revolution

The elites of Nicaragua, along with those of El Salvador, were for many decades the most successful in the region at avoiding any reforms in land tenure arrangements—perhaps one reason why the reforms now underway in these two countries are the most significant implemented in Central America. The essential pattern in both countries had been minor colonization programs accompanied by the avoidance of serious discussion of the need for land redistribution and by escalating rural repression. This combination of unconcern for deteriorating rural conditions with increasing repression clearly was among the primary causes of the Nicaraguan revolution, as it was of the Salvadoran civil war.

But the similarities between the two countries' situations ended in July 1979 when the Nicaraguan civil war resulted in victory for the revolutionary forces and a sharp break with the patterns of the past. Agrarian reform was a central component of the revolutionary government's projects of national reconstruction and socialist transformation. As a result, the new regime brought substantial change to aspects of the agrarian system ranging from land distribution and tenancy arrangements to marketing structures and the provision of credit.

The fundamental lesson of the earlier chapters in this study was that prevailing agrarian structures in Central America have bound much of the rural population to lives of poverty and oppression and, consequently, have generated social tension and political conflict. The case of Nicaragua teaches that victory is possible over the beneficiaries of the old order, permitting substantial changes in socioeconomic structures so as to create a more humane society. This case also teaches, however, that intentions cannot be realized quickly nor easily. There are always constraints on policymaking, especially in poor, vulnerable Third World countries. In Nicaragua, economic and political constraints have operated at both the domestic and inter- national levels to limit and frustrate the regime's objectives. Although this chapter will give attention both to the prerevolutionary situation and to the major outlines of agrarian policy under the revolutionary government, its major objective will be to utilize the case of Nicaragua to analyze the factors that limit the possibilities for restructuring Central American agrarian systems.

THE RURAL
ROOTS OF REVOLUTION

The expansion of commercial and especially export agriculture greatly trans- formed rural life in Nicaragua, as documented in Part I. The boom in coffee of the late nineteenth and early twentieth centuries, and then those in cotton and cattle after World War II, strengthened and enriched a small elite and eroded the economic security of much of the rural population. By the late 1970s, the amount of land devoted to the leading export crops had increased 219 percent while that planted in the major food crops had grown by only 92 percent; accordingly, per capita production of the leading food crops declined by 13 percent across the same period (see Tables 3.1 and 4.3). This meant that the average daily caloric intake of half the population was only 79 percent of the amount recommended by the U.N. Food and Agriculture Organization for the average Nicaraguan.[1]

During the commercial boom, peasants lost land and the ability to compete in land markets; by 1975 the largest 1.8 percent of landowners held 46.8 percent of the land, while the largest 12.1 percent owned 74.9 percent (see Table 4.1). Consequently, many rural people migrated to urban areas, and both the rural and urban poor attempted to make ends meet by joining the seasonal work force on the large commercial farms. Only 12.7 percent of the economically active agricultural population had sufficient access to land by the late 1970s to meet subsistence requirements. Close to 40 percent of that population consisted of landless wage earners—most of whom could obtain only seasonal work (Deere and Marchetti 1981:42).

Foremost among the beneficiaries of the agro-export development model in Nicaragua was the reigning Somoza family. The dynasty began in the mid-1930s after the United States withdrew from the country, ending (for the time being) its decades of military intervention there. The legacy of the U.S.

was the National Guard, which it had trained for the purpose of maintaining order. This the guard did very effectively, providing the crucial force that enabled Anastasio Somoza García and then his two sons to dominate Nicaraguan society until the revolutionary victory in 1979 (Booth 1985; Millett 1977; T. W. Walker 1981). The vast economic empire that the Somozas built was the result not of honest work but of "unchallenged conflict of interests, theft, embezzlement, and graft" (Booth 1985:69) based on unlimited political power. For example, the elder Somoza used his political position to acquire a number of the German-owned coffee plantations during World War II; by 1944, he was Nicaragua's top coffee producer and landowner (Booth 1985:68).

What little attention was given to rural problems under the Somozas was largely symbolic. An Alliance for Progress–stimulated agrarian reform law, for example, was approved in 1963. Although it included ambiguous language about the social function of the land, its actual implementation was restricted to minor colonization and titling programs. Overall, 16,500 families received land titles, while sixty-three colonies were initiated with 2651 families on 70,000 acres (Núñez Solo 1981). The colonies did provide land to the landless, but they also worked to the advantage of the state in at least two ways. Beneficiaries of the resettlement programs had often been moved from areas of rural conflict, their departure diminishing the level of tension in those regions. Second, Núñez Solo (1981:80–81) claims that the resettled were in effect working for the state, to which they were indebted, from which they bought, and to which they sold—the same argument, it will be recalled, that has been advanced by Honduran scholars concerning resettlement colonies in their country (e.g., Posas 1979).[2]

The most important direct connection between the state and the peasantry during the last decade of Somoza rule, however, was the repression carried out by the National Guard. Starting in the 1960s the passive stance of the peasantry began to be transformed by two forces, both of them threats to the system of domination pervading rural society: progressive church workers and the Sandinista National Liberation Front (FSLN).

As they did throughout Central America, Catholic clergy in Nicaragua began to organize Christian Base Communities in rural areas in the late 1960s and early 1970s, with consequences that were political as well as religious. Especially important were the Jesuit-created Evangelistic Committee for Agrarian Promotion (CEPA), which trained peasant leaders both to organize self-help projects and to make demands on political institutions in their own behalf, and nine hundred Delegates of the Word trained by the Capuchins in the outlying department of Zelaya. With this encouragement on the one hand and the attack on their economic security on the other, peasants began to respond; for the decade up to 1973, official records list 240 "land invasions" in just two departments, the major cotton-growing region of Chinandega and León (Berryman 1984:51–89; Booth 1985:116–121, 134–137; Collins 1986:22–25).

The FSLN was formed in 1961 but remained a relatively inconsequential and unsuccessful force until a decade later, when, with more experience and better ties to the peasantry, it became a greater threat to the regime.[3] Accordingly, the National Guard initiated attacks on the peasantry as part of its counterinsurgency campaign. Repression was already widespread in rural areas before the declaration of martial law at the end of December 1974. Following a successful Sandinista hostage-taking operation at a Christmas party honoring the U.S. ambassador, it became even more vicious.

In the rural areas where the FSLN operated—the north central and northeastern regions—whole families and even whole villages were systematically eliminated. As Amnesty International (1977) pointed out, the Northeast came to be under "virtual military occupation . . . with frequent, apparently arbitrary, killings, torture, massive detentions and disappearances, as well as the confiscation of goods, occupation of property, and the burning of crops, homes and farm buildings" (p. 26). One National Guardsman later estimated that that organization executed at least three thousand peasants (quoted in Booth 1985:311, n. 30); this is the standard estimate for the number murdered during the thirty-three months of the state of siege (Black 1981:89). Many more peasants were detained and tortured (AI 1977; Cardenal 1976). The purpose of this state terrorism was, in the words of Amnesty International (1977) "to intimidate the *campesinos* who might, in the future, be impelled to collaborate with or conceal insurgents, to discover those *campesinos* who are already doing so and to locate the guerrillas" (p. 26).

This repression did constrain the development of rural organizations, but at a more fundamental level, its results were largely the opposite. It further eroded the legitimacy of the regime for both rural and urban groups. It also radicalized church workers and peasants, many of whom forged closer ties with the Sandinistas, if not out of ideological affinity, then out of self-defense and rage. For example, the Association of Rural Workers (ATC), which played an important role in the struggle against Somoza in the Pacific coastal area, received much organizational assistance from both CEPA and the FSLN. Formed in 1977, by the following year it was working closely with the FSLN to oppose the regime because of the repression it was experiencing.

Although the eventual overthrow of the Somoza dynasty was largely the result of its loss of support in all sectors of society and of a series of insurrections carried out by urban popular forces, rural society incubated the FSLN. The prolonged period of rural struggle served in the eyes of many Nicaraguans to legitimate the Sandinistas' claim to be the vanguard of the revolution. Moreover, the urban-rural distinction is misleading. Many of the urban participants in the struggle, or their families, were migrants recently driven to the cities by the commercialization of agriculture, and many still worked in the cotton fields during the harvest. "To a surprising extent," as Paige (1985:107) has pointed out, "Nicaragua's agricultural proletariat was urban."

REVOLUTIONARY AGRARIAN POLICY

Agrarian policy was necessarily one of the primary concerns of the new revolutionary government; it has also been one of the most difficult policy areas because of the numerous contradictory needs and conflicting interests involved.[4] About one-half of Nicaragua's people lived in the countryside in the late 1970s, and about the same proportion of the economically active population worked in agriculture. In the same period, agriculture accounted for about two-thirds of the country's foreign exchange earnings and one-quarter of its GNP (Deere, Marchetti, and Reinhardt 1985:104, n. 2). The government faced strong pressures from the peasantry for land redistribution, it also confronted production imperatives to meet urban consumption requirements and foreign exchange needs. The leadership's policy response emerged gradually and has been noted for its pragmatism and flexibility (Deere, Marchetti, and Reinhardt 1985:75; Thome and Kaimowitz 1985:209) and for its ability to encompass the lessons of other countries' experiences.[5] The evolution of this policy can be divided into three stages.

Stage One:
1979–1981

The most significant redistribution of wealth affected by the revolutionary government occurred almost automatically. Because the Somoza family had concentrated so much of the land (as well as comparable assets in urban areas) in its own hands, with the defeat of the tyrant and his departure from Nicaragua these possessions were easily confiscated. With the addition of the property of his supporters, who also fled the country, about 23 percent of the cultivable land (and 43 percent of the farms of over 850 acres) passed from the private to the public sector. The Somoza family's greed, then, allowed the new revolutionary government to undertake a major redistributive action without attacking the class of large landholders, many of whom opposed

Somoza at the end of his rule and whose cooperation was now necessary in order to sustain agricultural production.

Consisting of about fifteen hundred estates, the confiscated lands were primarily large commercial operations devoted to export production. They were reorganized into state farms which, along with other nationalized properties, were collectively known as the Area of People's Property (APP). By 1984 there were over a thousand state farms employing close to sixty-five thousand workers. The decision to maintain these farms as large, collectively worked units under state control was partially a result of the ideological commitments of the leadership, but it was also a response to economic and political constraints (to be discussed more fully below). The most important of these constraints were the needs to maintain export earnings and to limit peasants' demands for the redistribution of private holdings. The implementation of the nationalization policy was facilitated by the fact that many of the confiscations had been conducted by the workers themselves, often during the revolutionary struggle. As wage workers, they were more amenable to the decision for large state farms than land-hungry peasants would have been. Their acquiescence also demonstrated the legitimacy the Sandinistas had established with the large force of landless rural workers and their union, the ATC.

Despite the Sandinista commitment to socialist transformation, during this first period any further land redistribution was preempted by the need to reactivate production and by the state's limited capacity to administer any larger program. Both industrial and agricultural production had dropped sharply during the civil war; their restoration depended in large measure on the willingness of individual producers to reinvigorate their activities. Reassurances by the Sandinistas of their commitment to a mixed economy were seen as a necessary incentive to restore private production, but the consolidation of the state sector was of no benefit to much of the rural population, nor was it salient to the need to improve basic grain production. By early 1980 peasants' discontent, especially as focused through the ATC, encouraged new policy initiatives dealing with rental relationships and the provision of credit.

Government decrees that spring lowered land rents by 85 percent and made all lands rented within the last two years and all idle lands available to their tenants and to landless workers. The eviction of tenants was prohibited, as were certain tenancy relationships such as sharecropping. At the same time, the allocation of credit to renters and owners of small and medium-sized holdings expanded tremendously. Small producers received seven times more credit in 1980 than they had in 1978; altogether, about one-half of small farmers received credit from the government in 1980 (Collins 1986:52). The effect of these policies was to improve rural living standards and basic grain production. The amount of land covered by credit more than doubled between 1977 and 1980. Furthermore, 67 percent of such land in the earlier year was used for export production, but in 1980 almost 59 percent of it was used for domestic production (Austin, Fox, and Kruger 1985:21). And the state used the provision of credit to encourage the formation of cooperatives: subsidized rates were offered through both production and credit and service cooperatives.[6] The ATC was enlisted to organize the cooperatives, and the results were impressive. About 60 percent of peasant households belonged to cooperatives by June 1980, while membership in the ATC boomed to 120,000 members (Deere, Marchetti, and Reinhardt 1985:83).

Stage Two:
1981–1984

Although the accomplishments of the policy initiatives of the first stage were substantial, they were incomplete. Pressures from the peasantry continued to mount, as did conflicts between the government and the agrarian bourgeoisie. Many rural people had yet to benefit much from the revolution, while many larger landowners were leaving land idle or running their operations at minimal production levels for reasons ranging from oppositional strategies to insecurity. Insufficient food production also continued to be a problem. To settle these issues, an agrarian reform law was announced in July 1981.

The law attempted to reassure private owners through a guarantee of the right to private property and by not setting size limits on efficiently utilized landholdings. (In this respect, it was less radical than its Guatemalan and Salvadoran counterparts.) At the same time, it permitted the confiscation of abandoned land and legitimated the expropriation of all idle, underutilized, or rented land on holdings above certain ceilings, which varied by region (350 hectares in the Pacific area and 700 hectares in the rest of the country). Sharecropped land also was subjected to expropriation if it was on holdings over 35 hectares in the Pacific area and 70 hectares elsewhere. Compensation would be paid with agrarian reform bonds, with the property values to be established by the values declared for tax purposes over the preceding three years. To prevent the concentration or fragmentation of holdings, beneficiaries were enjoined from selling or subdividing the titles to their grants.

At the time of the law's announcement, officials estimated that as much as 30 percent of the country's agricultural land could be expropriated under its provisions (Collins 1986:89). The form of its redistribution, however, occasioned much controversy among government officials and between them and representatives of peasants and rural workers. As the discussion advanced, it was agreed not to expand the state farm sector but to utilize state resources to encourage the gradual socialization of rural production through cooperatives, and to allow recipients to decide the form of their grant. In practice, through October 1982 most of the land was awarded through production cooperatives (Deere, Marchetti, and Reinhardt 1985:92–97).

Redistribution of land under the law began rather slowly but escalated in 1983, largely in response to the increasing counterrevolutionary threat from the U.S.–supported Contra armies based in Honduras and Costa Rica. During 1983 two and a half times as much land was granted under the law as had been available during its first eighteen months (Deere, Marchetti, and Reinhardt 1985:94). In addition, thousands of peasants in the war zones received individual title to the land they occupied. About 32 percent of rural families benefited directly from land redistribution and titling through July 1984.

Stage Three:
1985 to the Present

Agrarian policy entered a new phase in 1985 in response to national defense needs and the difficulties of maintaining a multiclass coalition. With support from the Reagan administration, the Contra forces had grown in strength to approximately ten to fifteen thousand men. By the end of 1984, it was estimated that they had killed over twenty-eight hundred Nicaraguans and wounded more than two thousand others (Rohter 1985:A1). Hundreds of these casualties were civilian noncombatants; as one of the former Contra directors has testified, "It was premeditated policy to terrorize civilian noncombatants to prevent them from cooperating with the Government" (Chamorro 1986:A22; also see AWC 1985). The most potent of the Contra forces, the Nicaraguan Democratic Front (FDN), operated out of Honduras, where it could easily strike across the border into north-central Nicaragua, a remote, mountainous region whose deeply conservative people had been a stronghold of support for the Somozas and some of whom were now joining the Contras (Kinzer 1985a:A2).

Peasant support for the revolutionary regime was weakening in other regions as well.[7] Despite the escalation of land grants, thousands of landless and land-poor peasant families remained; their disenchantment had grown with the years of frustration in their desire for their own land. Many others were unhappy because their grants had been made as part of production cooperatives rather than as individual holdings. Dissatisfaction was especially acute in the Pacific region, where most of the land had remained in large export estates, either privately or state owned. Consequently in the department of Masaya, the country's most densely populated rural area, only 15 percent of the landless and land-poor families had received land. Their declining support for the Sandinistas was demonstrated in their low vote for the party's candidate (Daniel Ortega) in the 1984 presidential election, their avoidance of the draft, and their decreasing participation in political ceremonies.

In response to such factors, a number of changes were made in agrarian policy in 1985 and 1986. Peasant demands triumphed over party ideology as new land grants were as likely to be made in individual holdings as in production cooperatives. In addition, some state farms were privatized, especially in the war zones of the north. Individual grants increased almost tenfold in 1985 over the previous year; individual holdings as a percentage of land granted to production cooperatives rose from 6 to 79 percent (Reinhardt 1986:Table 5). To obtain more distributable land, especially in the Pacific region, the government began in 1985 to purchase property from large landowners or to trade other properties with them. In the following year, the agrarian reform law was modified to lower the ceiling on land that was free from expropriation from 850 down to 85 acres. The pace of land grants and titling accelerated; in 1985 23 percent more land was distributed than during the year before (Reinhardt 1986:Table 5). From mid-1985 to mid-1986, four times more individual land titles were given to peasants than during the previous four years combined (Wallace 1986). Peasants also benefited as price controls were lifted on corn and beans. But thousands of peasant families were relocated, regardless of their wishes, out of the north-central war zone. Begun in March 1985, this policy was intended both to remove peasants supportive of the Contras from the border areas and to create "free fire zones" where the army could operate freely against the rebels (*New York Times* [NYT] 1985).

Preliminary Results

The Sandinista commitment to mixed ownership in the agricultural sector is portrayed in Table 8.1. Close to two-fifths of the land had been confiscated or expropriated by 1986 and divided rather equally between state farms and cooperatives (which were in turn almost equally divided between the two types of cooperatives).[8] The amount of land held in the largest private estates (over 850 acres) was only about a third of what it had been under the old regime, while the amount in the smallest holdings also had been cut, in this case almost in half. The guarantee of private property rights continued, however; nearly two-thirds of the land was still in the unorganized privately owned sector. When the individual holdings organized into credit and service cooperatives are taken into account, 74 percent of the cultivable land remained in private hands after over five years of Sandinista leadership.

TABLE 8.1
Nicaragua: Changes in Land Ownership, 1978 to 1985[1]

Type and Size of Holding	1978	1980	1985
Private Property			
Unorganized			
Over 850 acres	36.2	21.5	11.9
86–850 acres	46.3	43.5	41.5
Under 86 acres	17.5	15.5	9.5
Subtotal	100.0	80.5	62.9
Credit and service cooperatives	—	0.4	11.2
Production Cooperatives	—	1.0	8.8
State Farms	—	18.0	17.0
Total	100.0	99.9	99.9

NOTE: 1. Percentage of cultivable land in each category.
SOURCE: Calculated from Collins 1986:271.

Furthermore, the amount of land in the middle size category remained relatively constant. Private property rights also were guaranteed through the granting of titles to farmers lacking this legal security; by the beginning of 1986, about 60 percent of the country's peasants had received titles to about one-third of the total farmland (Collins 1986:247).

The revolution has also had a significant impact on land usage, a result both of the destruction brought about by the civil war and of the new regime's policy. As Table 8.2 indicates, land harvested in almost every crop fell during the last year of the civil war. (The decline is registered in different calendar years because of seasonal differences in crop years.) All of them have recovered, with the very important exception of cotton. The most impressive improvement has been for rice, which has nearly doubled in area harvested. The recovery of corn was interrupted by a bad year of drought and floods in 1982. When the two categories of crops are compared, it is clear that the historic trend has been reversed: the amount of land in export crops as a percentage of basic food crops declined from 1976–78 to 1983 by 30 percent. (The classification of sorghum is ambiguous; when it is placed with the food crops, then the decline is 22 percent.) In addition to representing a shift in priorities, however, this reversal in land usage was also the consequence of the difficulties in restoring cotton production.

The reactivation of production of all agricultural crops was a primary concern of the new government when it assumed power. The country desperately needed the foreign exchange earned by export crops, but several revolutionary objectives were dependent on the achievement of food crop production increases. By encouraging peasants to expand food production and by increasing the prices of food crops, the government could raise rural

TABLE 8.2
Nicaragua: Area Devoted to Food and Export Crops, 1976–78 to 1983[1]

	1976–78	1979	1980	1981	1982	1983	Change (%)
Food Crops							
Beans	66	49	77	89	68	68	3
Corn	228	140	197	200	164	220	–4
Rice	25	19	42	42	45	47	88
Total	319	208	316	331	277	335	5
Export Crops[2]							
Coffee	88	85	94	88	90	91	3
Cotton	185	174	45	94	93	95	–49
Sorghum	50	55	60	56	39	39	–22
Sugar	43	42	32	39	44	44	2
Total	366	356	231	277	266	269	–27
Export as % of Food	115	171	73	84	96	80	–30

NOTES: 1. Area harvested in thousands of hectares; many figures are estimates by either country or UNFAO, especially for 1981–83.
2. Data not available for bananas.
SOURCE: Calculated from UNFAO, various years.

incomes. Increased production would also provide more adequate diets for urban consumers while reducing dependence on food imports, thereby freeing scarce foreign exchange earnings for other purposes.

The degree of success these productions goals have met is indicated in Table 8.3, which standardizes the data on each crop as percentages of production in the base year of 1977–78. As can be seen, the restoration of export production has been problematic for all crops, but especially for the most crucial one, cotton, which in the mid-1980s was still at only one-half of the pre–revolutionary production level. The decline in coffee production occurred later and is primarily the result of attacks by Contra forces. Much of the coffee-producing area lies within or close to the war zones, and the rebels have selected coffee production as a particular target of their campaign of economic sabotage. Beef production also fell after the revolution as consumption and decapitalization reduced cattle herds by 25 to 35 percent. In 1983 beef production was still at only 81 percent of 1977 levels (Austin, Fox, and Kruger 1985:24). Bean and corn production fell as a consequence of the revolutionary struggle, and through the early 1980s corn production still was viewed as unsatisfactory. In contrast, rice and sorghum production have been great successes. The production of the three basic food crops taken together has expanded more rapidly than the population; per capita production of the three crops increased 13 percent from 1976–78 to 1984.

TABLE 8.3
Nicaragua: Indices of Agricultural Production, 1977–78 to 1984–85[1] (1977–78 = 100)

	1977–78	1979–80	1981–82	1983–84	1984–85
Export Crops					
Bananas	100	95	104	113	99
Coffee	100	98	110	85	89
Cotton	100	15	45	62	50
Sugar	100	87	119	115	95
Sorghum	100	148	225	239	265
Food Crops					
Beans	100	71	101	137	144
Corn	100	80	107	121	119
Rice	100	132	193	213	185
Food Production					
per capita[2]	261	—	285.1	301.3	294.9

NOTES: 1. Dates are for crop years.
2. Pounds per capita of beans, corn, and rice; actual dates are 1976–78, 1980–82, 1983, and 1984.
SOURCE: Collins (1986:274–276).

The goals of nutritional adequacy and agricultural self-sufficiency were embodied in the National Nutritional Plan (PAN), adopted in 1981, and in the development of the state's role in the marketing of staples. Through its agency ENABAS (Nicaraguan Agency for Basic Foods), the government controls the import of foodstuffs and establishes consumer and producer staple prices. Given the country's financial straits, the subsidy for urban consumers has been considerable—almost 6 percent of the national budget in 1982 (Austin, Fox, and Kruger 1985:27). The adequacy of the state policy toward producers is a matter of some disagreement, however. Many analysts claim that in its first years the government was sensitive to the need for adequate price incentives for producers of basic foods (mainly small and medium-sized producers), and some claim that producer prices kept up with inflation (e.g., Austin, Fox, and Kruger 1985:27; and Spalding 1985:210–214). But Colburn (1986:95–100) reaches a different conclusion. When measured against the prices peasants pay for basic consumer goods, their terms of trade have deteriorated, in many cases substantially. This conclusion is based on his interviews with peasants, especially corn producers, who claimed that their real incomes had declined. Consequently, Colburn blames inadequate price incentives as a major cause of a poor production performance in the food sector, especially for corn (also see Collins 1986:199–201). The government responded more fully to this problem in 1984 through major policy changes discussed in the following section.

CONSTRAINTS ON
REVOLUTIONARY POLICY MAKING

On the one hand, the accomplishments of Sandinista agrarian policy have been considerable; on the other, they fall far short of the need. This shortcoming can be blamed in part on disagreements within the leadership, policy errors, and mismanagement.[9] More important, though, are the numerous constraints facing any Third World government.[10] Furthermore, the Nicaraguan regime has confronted additional difficulties that are specific to small countries transgressing the boundaries of permissible policy established by a hegemonic power. The context of Sandinista agrarian policy, then, has been political and economic constraints operating both domestically and internationally. The economic factors can most fruitfully be discussed together; separate discussions of the domestic and the international political constraints will then follow.

Economic Constraints

A poor country to begin with, Nicaragua was devastated by the war against Somoza. Up to fifty thousand people were killed in the last five years of the struggle, and another hundred thousand were wounded—this out of a total population of only 2.5 million. Many of the deaths occurred not in combat but when Somoza unleashed his armed forces in indiscriminate urban attacks, including bombings by the air force. Accordingly, material damages were great to residential, commercial, and industrial areas. When the cost of this destruction is combined with both the substantial capital flight that occurred during the war and the debt inherited from the dictator, the total comes to $4.1 billion, according to a U.N. study (Collins 1986:10; T. W. Walker 1981:41–42).

Nicaragua would need under any circumstances to maintain export earnings in order to cover the cost of its considerable imports. The huge expense of reconstruction, however, created an additional imperative for the recovery of those earnings from the serious declines they registered during the last months of the civil war. The diversification of exports was a long-term policy goal, but these pressing short-term considerations meant that emphasis had to be placed on the traditional export commodities. Ironically, it was the development of these exports, especially coffee, cotton, and beef, that revolutionary leaders blamed for the devastating disruption suffered by rural society (see Núñez Solo 1981 and Wheelock Román 1980)—an argument substantiated in Part I of this study. Now in power, the revolutionaries were committed to widespread reform that would give rural people access to land

and employment sufficient to support them adequately. They also intended to reduce the country's dependence on imported food while insuring that all Nicaraguans, urban and rural, obtained nutritionally adequate diets. Theoretically, there is perhaps no essential conflict between these goals and the need to maintain agricultural export earnings (Collins 1986:111). In practice, though, serious tension developed between economic constraints on the one hand and egalitarian objectives and the desire to diversify exports on the other.

Aggravating this tension was the international economic context. All of the Central American economies slumped in the years after the Nicaraguan revolution; in 1979–83, real GDP for the region declined by 5.7 percent, while the per capita decline was 14.7 percent (Conroy 1985:224).[11] A major cause of this slump was a deterioration in agricultural prices through the late 1970s and early 1980s. Consequently, restoring export production to the pre-1979 level would not be sufficient; previous levels would have to be surpassed just to achieve the same earnings. Using 1970 as the base year (100), Nicaragua's terms of trade of goods index stood at 112.3 in 1977 and then declined to 91.9 in 1979 and to 72.9 in 1982 (Maxfield and Stahler-Sholk 1985:252); it then dropped another 17 percent by 1985 (Collins 1986:279).

The results of the declines in export production and in the terms of trade were starkly manifested in the balance of payments. For 1980 through 1983 the trade deficit averaged $322 million a year, which was about 73 percent of export earnings. As a result of these trends, the external public debt as a percentage of export earnings grew catastrophically: it increased by 161 percent from 1978 to 1980 and then almost doubled again during the next two years. By 1984, it had increased over tenfold from 1978 (see Table 3.8). Consequently, the program of egalitarian rural reform was constrained by the imperative to restore export earnings, as can be seen most clearly in the reorganization of confiscated properties, the treatment of private cotton and coffee growers, and rural labor shortages.

Because the properties they confiscated after taking power were almost all large, highly mechanized commercial farms, Sandinista officials believed that dividing them would have been economically irrational; instead, the properties were further concentrated into about eight hundred State Production Units. These farms were among the most important of the agricultural export producers, and consequently it was believed that there was no alternative but to continue using them for export production. They were organized as state farms rather than cooperatives for various reasons, but especially because officials realized that if peasants were given direct control, they would probably switch production from export to food crops (Collins 1986:60–62; Deere, Marchetti, and Reinhardt 1985:79–80).

Most of export crop production, however, remained in the private sector, especially with medium-sized and large producers. The first data available to the revolutionary government estimated that these private growers' share of production was 72 percent for cotton and a little above 50 percent for cattle, coffee, and sugar (Collins 1986:39). The tension between socialist ideology and the need for export earnings, with its attendant dependence on the agrarian bourgeoisie, was especially great in the case of cotton, the country's most important earner of foreign exchange, the export crop suffering the greatest decline in production during and after the civil war, and (unlike coffee) a crop for which production decisions can be made on an annual basis. Hypothetically, this sector could have been nationalized and reorganized as part of the state farm system, but practically, such a move was impossible because the government was overburdened with organizing and administering the initial State Production Units and because of its desire to maintain national unity in face of the threat from the United States. One purpose of the 1981 agrarian reform law was to reassure capitalist farmers; as long as they worked their land efficiently, they were freed from the threat of expropriation. Furthermore, the revolutionary government attempted to provide capitalist producers with sufficient incentives through the provision of credit and the establishment of purchase prices more generous than those offered to producers of other crops (as well as through the threat of expropriation for failure to produce).

If this dependence on the agrarian bourgeoisie was difficult for the Sandinistas, it was equally unpleasant for the planters. Colburn (1986) expresses it nicely: "Cotton producers are torn between the realization that 'there is money to be made in every tragedy' and Lenin's sobering adage that 'capitalists will make the very rope they will be hung by'" (p. 59). While many people continued with their plantings in order to protect their investments, many others left the country. Cotton production partially recovered from the eightfold drop of 1979–80, but as Table 8.3 indicates, it has essentially remained at a rough plateau since the following year, at an average of about 56 percent of 1977–78 production (Colburn 1986:45–62; Colburn and De Franco 1985; Collins 1986:39–50; Gilbert 1985; Sholk 1984).

Through its control of foreign trade and domestic prices, the revolutionary government is able to determine growers' profit level. If cotton growers believe that their profits are squeezed in order to maximize foreign exchange earnings going to the public treasury, it is not surprising that the Sandinistas are unsympathetic to their position. The situation of coffee growers is more complicated, however. Although larger farmers dominate coffee production, most producers have small holdings. As smallholders they are part of the poor majority that is the intended beneficiary of the revolution, but as coffee growers they experience the same profit squeeze as the larger producers. They could be assisted most directly by policies that would encourage and aid them in investing in improved cultivation practices that would increase their yields and incomes. Through the early 1980s, though, they experienced the same disincentives as large growers because of their insufficient profit levels (Colburn 1986:62–84; see also Kaimowitz 1980). As the counterrevolutionary war accelerated, the government was forced to face this problem, which it did in 1985, as discussed below.

At the same time, export production and earnings were harmed by policies that did help the rural poor. In prerèvolutionary Nicaragua, coffee and especially cotton growers depended on temporary workers to provide much of their labor during the harvest period. With the high rates of un- and underemployment, securing this seasonal labor was not difficult. But after the revolution, this cheap labor pool shrank. Many of the landless and land-poor received acreage. Poor farmers, who in the past had needed to supplement their incomes through seasonal labor, found their positions improved in 1980 by the extraordinary increase in available credit and by the higher prices paid for their crops. In addition, in 1980–81 the new government applied the minimum wage laws long on the books to rural employment, but it established a wage too low to attract sufficient labor. Neither did the wage keep pace with inflation in future years. Finally, as the counterrevolutionary attacks escalated, a larger percentage of potential labor was absorbed by national defense requirements (Collins 1986:69–78, 175–182; Enriquez 1985:270–275).

Even when labor was available to export growers, it was not as "dependable" and "disciplined" as in the past. In place of the repressive presence of the National Guard, workers now expected the state to be at their side in their attempts to organize, win a fair wage, create decent working conditions, and free themselves from demeaning subservience to the *patrón*. This rapid revolutionary transformation of the rural workforce was a major factor in many large landowners' decisions to decapitalize their holdings and leave the country with as much wealth as they could take (Collins 1986:42–48). Meanwhile, the production imperative soon constrained the regime's revolutionary commitment. Work stoppages, strikes, and seizures of centers of production were prohibited in July 1981 in order to "combat labor indiscipline" (Colburn 1986:103–120). Because of the difficulties in reactivating production, rural laborers have suffered "from an enforced policy of austerity and efficiency" (Colburn 1986:127).

Policymakers' attempts to determine the best balance between these competing goals did not occur within a political vacuum. Decisions about how to restore export earnings while pursuing redistributional goals were influenced not only by ideology and economic constraints but also by considerable political pressures.

Domestic Political Constraints

Peasant organization received substantial support from the Sandinistas during the struggle against Somoza and in the months after the revolutionary victory. Before 1979 was over, the membership of the ATC had reached fifty-nine thousand; by June 1980, it was about 120,000. Peasant mobilization was fully congruent with revolutionary aspirations, but it could also threaten regime objectives. Through the revolutionary struggle the landless and land-poor were empowered to act, taking land either spontaneously or in actions organized by the ATC. These land takeovers jeopardized the government's program to reactivate export production, however, both by switching production to food crops and by diminishing the labor supply. Consequently, in the months after taking power, the government attempted to discourage land takeovers, with some success. But as the months passed peasants grew restive, and takeovers increased in frequency. During 1980 the government tried to respond to the twin demands for adequate land and sufficient income by lowering land rental rates by 85 percent and by providing the huge increase in credit to smallholders.[12]

The government came close to promulgating an agrarian reform in 1980, but in the end it did not do so because of pressures from two very different quarters. Relations between the Sandinistas and the bourgeoisie, always tense, came close to the breaking point that spring as the bourgeois representatives in the governing junta resigned amid growing concern within that sector over the course of the revolution. The strained alliance held for the time being, in part because of Sandinista reassurances concerning respect for property rights. It was certainly not the right time to announce a new agrarian reform program (Gilbert 1985:169–170).

From the other side, the ATC was dissatisfied because of its insufficient involvement in the formulation of the proposed program. The union had included virtually all of the organized rural popular forces, making it very heterogeneous. In 1981 it was split and the National Union of Farmers and Cattle Ranchers (UNAG) was formed to represent small and medium-sized producers, leaving rural wage earners as the base for the ATC. For the government, the motive was largely tactical. The smaller producers were beginning to join the agricultural producers' union controlled by the larger commercial farmers (UPANIC), perceiving a greater commonality with other producers than with the rural laborers in the ATC. Obviously, this alliance with the agrarian bourgeoisie rather than with the rural proletariat ran counter to the regime's ideology and strategy, and so the new organization was formed.[13]

Within the year, about 60 percent of the small and medium-sized producers had joined the UNAG, giving it a membership of about seventy-five thousand (Austin, Fox, and Kruger 1985:23). The group forcefully pressed the demand for more land. Land seizures continued, and reports from the field described a peasantry that could not be appeased much longer. Furthermore, basic food production still had not recovered fully from the civil war, a problem aggravated when the new Reagan administration eliminated credits for U.S. wheat purchases. In response to these various pressures, deliberations concerning the agrarian reform law were renewed in the spring of 1981, this time with the substantial involvement of the ATC and the UNAG.

Implementation of the reform was slow, though, for a variety of administrative and political reasons. Officials in the agricultural ministry (MIDINRA) generally preferred an orderly, socialist transformation of agriculture; they focused on the needs of the state farms and were committed to producer cooperatives as the best form for the reorganization of redistributed land to take. By contrast, peasants who wanted land generally desired it as soon as possible, and they wanted freedon to determine how to organize it—usually as individual holdings. The peasants' position was promoted by the rural organizations, which had increasing success as the counter-revolutionary war sponsored by the United States escalated. In 1983 the amount of land transferred to the peasantry was more than twice as great as that distributed during the previous eighteen months. Although the government remained committed to the objective of socialist transformation, peasants were given more latitude in determining the form of agrarian reorganization. In addition, an ambitious program of titling was initiated in late 1982; most of the recipients were settlers with individual holdings in frontier regions, often in the war zones. As the fighting expanded, so did the program: in the first half of 1985, the average number of titles awarded monthly was 42 percent higher than it had been the year before, and the rate of awards increased again the next year (Collins 1986:247).

These pressures continued to escalate through the mid-1980s. The Contra forces grew in size and expanded their operations, reinforcing the government's need to secure the border region and to solidify its popular support. At the same time, disenchantment on the part of many peasants increased because the revolution had not brought them the hoped-for benefits, especially land and improved incomes, and because of a military draft instituted in 1985. As discussed earlier, the pace and form of land redistribution changed in 1985 in response to these pressures. Changes were also enacted to provide more attractive incentives to workers and producers (Collins 1986:253–255; Wallace 1986). Wage increases and other material incentives instituted in 1985–86 closed the gap between industrial and agricultural incomes for coffee workers and promoted increased productivity for all of the major export crops. State-set grain prices were increased dramatically in 1985 to keep up with rapidly rising inflation (250 percent); more significantly, price controls were then lifted on beans and corn, much to the satisfaction of peasant producers, who were expected to respond to this financial incentive with higher production.[14]

International Political Constraints[15]

Once the 1979 transition of power was completed in Nicaragua, the Carter administration reconciled itself to working with the revolutionary government. Emergency aid was delivered, and large appropriations for Nicaragua were requested from Congress. The continuation of U.S. influence and the desire to moderate the course of the revolution were paramount concerns, but the administration also argued explicitly for the need to work with and for social change. This approach altered substantially under the Reagan administration, first in rhetoric and then in substance.[16] Implementation of the new policy has been incremental, however, because of a wary public, a skeptical Congress, and divisions within the administration's own ranks.

The first substantive steps were taken in early 1981, when the United States suspended Nicaraguan credit for wheat purchases and discontinued further financial aid. The more critical step occurred that November: the National Security Council approved a plan to build a counterrevolutionary force. Small groups of anti-Sandinistas were already forming in the region; U.S. financial and organizational support were critical to their viability. The initial appropriation was $19 million for a five-hundred-man force. By 1983, the United States was known to have spent over $100 million in building a Contra force of ten to fifteen thousand. Further expansion was limited by growing congressional concern and vigilance; appropriations for fiscal years 1984 and 1986 were limited to $24 and $27 million respectively (the second sum only for "humanitarian" purposes); no aid was approved for fiscal 1985. Congressional apprehension over Sandinista intentions also increased, however. Caught between contradictory concerns, in 1986 Congress approved $100 million in new aid.

The United States also utilized its considerable leverage to limit international financial assistance to Nicaragua. According to one report, the Reagan administration instructed U.S. representatives to international lending institutions "to prepare technical excuses to veto any loans proposed for Nicaragua" (Maxfield and Stahler-Sholk 1985:258). This policy was fully implemented; consistent U.S. opposition restricted World Bank loans after 1981 and greatly limited Inter-American Development Bank credit. Other economic sanctions included the virtual elimination in 1983 of Nicaragua's sugar quota in the United States and the imposition in 1985 of a complete trade embargo (honored by no other country).

The consequences of these U.S. actions for Nicaragua have been severe. Clearly, the counterrevolutionary war would never have assumed the dimensions that it has without U.S. backing. By late 1986 close to eleven thousand Nicaraguans had died in the war (Booth 1986:408). Many of them were the victims of the Contras' deliberate policy of terrorism directed against the civilian population. In addition, tens of thousands more Nicaraguans were displaced from their homes by fighting, many forced to take refuge in squatter settlements or government relocation camps. As the conflict dragged on, political polarization heightened and civic morale deteriorated. The combined effects of these actions have aggravated the various economic and political constraints discussed earlier.

A key strategy of the Contras has been economic sabotage. Particular targets have been the vulnerable coffee crop (especially on agricultural cooperatives), agricultural technicians, and storage facilities for basic grains. The strategy has been one not just of sabotage but also of terror; production has been attacked both by direct destruction and by eliminating or terrorizing those who have provided the labor. In the 1984–85 season, more than two hundred coffee pickers were murdered and fifty-nine farms burned. By the mid-1980s over a thousand civilians in the north-central coffee region of Matagalpa-Jinotega had been assassinated by the Contras. Consequently, in 1984–85 more than 20,000 acres of coffee were not harvested because of danger to the pickers (Collins 1986:143–149, 252–253). Terrorism and infrastructure sabotage also damaged grain production and distribution, harming food supply and peasants' incomes (Collins 1986:218–221). It is estimated that the combined economic cost of the Contra operations through 1984 amounted to $380 million ($97 million in damage to the infrastructure and $283 million in damage to production) (Collins 1986:282). When other costs (such as deferred investment and extra defense spending) are included, the total damages for 1982 through 1986 are estimated at $1 billion to $1.5 billion (Booth 1986:408)—35 to 53 percent of 1984 GDP.

The opposition of the Reagan administration also reinforced the pressures from the bourgeoisie and the peasantry. Given the clash between the interests of the bourgeoisie and the ideological commitments of the Sandinistas, tensions were unavoidable. In light of the region's historical political patterns, it is an open question whether, left to itself, either group would have been willing to continue to compromise with the other rather than seeking its elimination as a serious political contender. Whatever possibilities there were for domestic reconciliation were greatly reduced by the Reagan administration's hostile policy toward the Nicaraguan government. The point has been well made by Gilbert (1986):

So long as the internal opposition had the hope that Washington would remove the FSLN, they had little incentive to seek any sort of accommodation with the regime. And so long as the FSLN saw the internal opposition as the disloyal ally of the contras and the Yankees, it had little incentive to offer any concessions toward accommodation. (p. 115)

The effect of U.S. policy and the counterrevolutionary war on government-peasantry relations was contradictory, causing strain on the one hand and leading to beneficial policy changes on the other. Limited by the U.S. Congress and public in its ability to pursue its objectives more forcefully, the administration undertook what in essence was a war of attrition, one that "bleeds Nicaragua's economy and threatens to do the same to the spirit of the people" (Collins 1986:238). Reinforcing the impact of economic hardship on popular support for the government was a military draft instituted in October 1983 in the face of the Contra build-up (Lantigua 1985) and justified in terms of national defense. It was un-popular with many youths and their families. Fifteen months later, it was estimated that around fifty thousand young men had fled the country and thousands of others were in hiding (Kinzer 1985b). The draft also affected economic performance; whether in compliance, in flight, or in hiding, workers were in acutely short supply in the harvest of all principal crops, the result being decline in production (Rohter 1985).

There was a conflict between the socialist vision of the Sandinistas and the desires not only of the bourgeoisie but also of much of the peasantry. Whether under different circumstances the original Sandinista project of a gradual socialist transformation of the agrarian sector, the support of the peasantry for this project won through improved benefits and education, would have been successful will remain unknown. Actual improvements in material conditions have been much smaller than expected for many peasants because of the combined effects of several variables: the initial impoverished and devastated condition of the economy; the deteriorating international economic situation; policy mistakes and administrative mismanagement; the counterrevolutionary war; and the financial and trade restrictions pursued by the United States. The relative importance given to these factors would vary with the observer.

Frustrated in their desire for land and facing continuing economic hardship, many peasants expressed their dissatisfaction through both the assertion of their viewpoint and the withdrawal of their support. The regime responded in a manner unparalleled in Central America. The pace of land redistributions was accelerated, their form increasingly altered from coop-eratives to individual grants; tens of thousands of private holdings were legitimated through the awarding of titles; and price restrictions on key crops were lifted. In the following years, the fundamental question has been whether the regime's responsiveness and a strong nationalist tradition will continue to triumph over the toll extracted by the relentless war of attrition pursued by the Reagan administration.

CONCLUSION

The processes that have created the agrarian systems of Central America and many of the region's most serious problems have also limited the ability of policymakers to alter those systems. The agrarian transformations, fueled by agro-export expansion and the spread of commercial agriculture, marginalized much of the peasantry, depriving many of their land and their self-sufficiency while making the region's economies vulnerable to international forces. Regimes that would seek to address these problems seriously are constrained in their ability to do so. The agrarian transformations created and strengthened elites with vested interests in maintaining the resulting structures and with substantial power to protect them.

Sandinista agrarian policy has consequently been confronted with the necessity of dealing with an agrarian bourgeoisie that has considerable incentives and resources to resist and frustrate the government. Reinforcing that group's position was the fact that, at least in the short run, the economy would be dependent on agricultural exports and therefore on the cooperation of numerous medium-sized and large producers of coffee, cotton, and sugar, especially as world prices for those commodities deteriorated. But these economic imperatives needed to be balanced with the demands and needs of the rural majority. The consequences of the past agrarian transformations guaranteed that the revolutionary government would face insistent demands for land, not only from land-poor peasants but also from many of the landless rural laborers who dreamed of regaining their landed status, even if only in the form of a small plot.

Under the best of circumstances, balancing the pressures from the bourgeoisie on the one hand and the peasantry and landless workers on the other, meanwhile attempting to transform society along socialist lines, would have been difficult. However, these problems were seriously compounded by the hostility of the United States and the counterrevolutionary army it organized and financed. International economic and political constraints, then, had conspired to frustrate a promising attempt at a new type of agrarian transformation in Central America. While the Sandinista government continues to show a unique responsiveness to peasant needs and demands in the mid-1980s, its capability to do so has been greatly limited.

NOTES

1. In 1970 the average daily caloric intake of the poorest 50 percent of the population was estimated to be 1767 (Collins 1986:157); the FAO recommendation for Nicaragua is 2244. Reports on Nicaraguan food consumption often mistakenly use as their standard the U.N. suggestion for the average person, which is 2600 calories.

2. The colonies were supported by substantial international assistance, including some from the United States. U.S. rural development assistance to Nicaragua became controversial during the late 1970s: questions arose as to whether it was actually beneficial to the poor; and whether it should be used as leverage to influence Somoza's human rights performance (Goshke and DeYoung 1977; Mudge 1979; Sigmund and Speck 1978; and United States, Senate 1978).

3. For background on the FSLN, including its evolution, ideological and organizational disputes, and role in the overthrow of Somoza, see Black (1981), Booth (1985), Nolan (1984), and T. W. Walker (1981).

4. Perhaps the best North American accounts of contemporary Nicaraguan agrarian policy are Collins (1986) and Deere, Marchetti, and Reinhardt (1985). Useful discussions also can be found in Austin, Fox, and Kruger (1985), Barraclough (1983), Colburn (1986), Deere and Marchetti (1981), Fitzgerald (1985), Kaimowitz and Stanfield (1985), Peek (1983), Sims (1982), Spalding (1985), and Thome and Kaimowitz (1985).

5. The Sandinistas solicited the advice and assistance of many international experts on agrarian reform. A number of the authors cited above provided help, including Collins, Fitzgerald, Kaimowitz, and Marchetti. See, for example, Collins (1986:ix, x, 1, 5).

6. In the credit and service cooperatives, farmers own the land individually but purchase inputs collectively and receive assistance from the cooperative in obtaining credit and technical assistance. In the production cooperatives, land and other resources are held collectively. The government has favored the latter arrangement, peasants the former. For further discussion, see Collins (1986:97–106).

7. This paragraph and the next are based on Collins (1986:241–250); also see Wallace (1986).

8. Total beneficiaries as of December 1985 were as follows: individual holdings, 7,213 families (341,000 acres); production cooperatives, 39,364 families (1,409,000 acres); titles for existing holdings, 33,397 families (2,488,000 acres); titles for indigenous community land, 3,348 families (177,000 acres); for a total of 83,322 families (4,416,000 acres), according to official data compiled by Reinhardt (1986:Table 5).

9. These factors are amply discussed in the sources cited in note 4 and will not be examined here.

10. This argument is most fully developed by Colburn (1986), who argues that

> the uniformities of contemporary post-revolutionary regimes in small developing countries [such as Nicaragua] suggest that the parameters of choice are limited. Predictable decisions are thrust on revolutionary elites by circumstances beyond their control. Thus, the effect of leadership on events seems to be of degree (and perhaps sequence) and not of kind. (p. 23)

11. In each of the four last years of the period 1979 to 1983, the performance of the Nicaraguan economy exceeded the regional average. However, the 1979 decline was so severe (25.9 percent) that the 22.5 percent growth in real GDP for this period was insufficient to bring the economy back to the level of 1978, which in turn was 7.2 percent below that of 1977 (Conroy 1985:224).

12. This section draws heavily on Collins (1986:48–50, 79–85) and Deere, Marchetti, and

Reinhardt (1985:81–101). Also see Colburn (1986:85–102), Deere and Marchetti (1981), Thome and Kaimowitz (1985:303–308). For discussions of the mixed results of the massive flow of credits, see Collins (1986:51–58) and Colburn (1986:89–91).

13. The extent to which these organizations truly represent their constituencies is a matter of some controversy. Contrast the views, for example, of Deere, Marchetti, and Reinhardt (1985) and Colburn (1986:97–109).

14. According to one economist, there "has emerged a quite remarkable consensus of the left, center, and right that governmental intervention in agricultural commodity markets has had undesirable results in almost every instance, in every country" (Bruce Gardner, quoted in Johnson and Schuh 1983:219).

15. Helpful in preparing this section have been Central American Historical Institute (CAHI) (1983), Gilbert (1986), LeoGrande (1979, 1982, 1985), Muravchik (1986–87) and Schoultz (1984).

16. Establishing the true intentions of the Reagan administration always has been difficult, both because of divisions within it (which Reagan typically would not settle) and because domestic and international laws would discourage admission of the intention to overthrow the government of another country. Nonetheless, Reagan came close to confessing such a goal during the first press conference of his second administration when he stated, according to one report, "that his objective is to 'remove' the 'present structure' of the Government in Nicaragua" (Smith 1985:A1). In order to secure congressional support for aid to the Contras, he stated the opposite later in the year: "We do not seek the military overthrow of the Sandinista government or to put in its place a government based on supporters of the old Somoza regime" (Cannon and Shapiro 1985:A1).

CHAPTER 9

Conclusion:
Land, Power, and Poverty

This study has argued that to understand the rural dimensions of the crisis of contemporary Central America properly, one must view political dynamics in their socioeconomic context and from a historical perspective. Accordingly, the scope of this investigation has been broad, ranging from export development in colonial days to labor systems in the nineteenth century to religiously inspired development work in the 1970s to revolutionary and counterrevolutionary armies in the eighties. The purpose of this final chapter is to summarize the earlier arguments and findings and to extend their conclusions. The following areas will be examined: the impact of the major agrarian transformations, the sources of peasant mobilization, the responses by the region's governments, and the role of the United States.

AGRARIAN TRANSFORMATIONS

The fundamental constraint that has continually plagued development-oriented Central American elites has been the inadequate size of domestic markets; there has been too little domestic demand to stimulate production and therefore economic growth. Accordingly, a primary orientation of such groups has been to discover and develop exports for foreign markets. What elites have conveniently and consistently downplayed is the relationship between internal demand and social stratification. Colonial society was structured by a relatively few Spaniards dominating a much larger Indian population for the purpose of extracting surplus for their own enrichment. The Indians, as conquered people, were the source of tribute and forced labor; they certainly were not copartners in the creation of a new society.

As decades and then centuries passed, new social groups were created, but society remained highly stratified. Consequently, elites continued to face the same dilemma: the creation of healthy domestic markets would necessitate a change in the distribution and utilization of resources. Peasants would have to be allowed access to sufficient land and other resources to meet their needs and to produce surplus for their own disposal. Peasant labor could no longer be so exploited through coercion, be it legal or extralegal. In short, the system of domination implanted at the time of the Conquest and reinforced across the succeeding centuries would have to be dismantled in order for healthy domestic markets to evolve.[1]

Production for export has offered elites a way around their dilemma. The solution foreign markets provide to the demand problem does not require social upheaval or the diminution of elite privilege. Furthermore, it is a solution that can be justified as not just in the elite's interest but as in the best interest of society. The profits made from selling indigo, coffee, bananas, cotton, sugar, or beef overseas can be plowed back into the economy, promoting economic development from which all groups can benefit. Self-interest, then, is reinforced by capitalist ideology and the doctrine of comparative advantage. The agro-export development model has consequently had a powerful appeal to Central American elites across the centuries, and also to many reformist groups. Although such groups may have the desire to create viable programs of widespread social reform, they have lacked the necessary political leverage. When in power, they have therefore faced many of the same economic constraints as elites.

The implementation of the agro-export development model has been successful in furthering the interests of elites; they have been enriched, often substantially so. When the standard of evaluation is economic development, the results have been more mixed. On the one hand, exports and economies have expanded and diversified. Incomes have grown, not only for elites but also within the middle sectors and for part of the peasantry. On the other hand, the region's dependence on its exports (as a percentage of GNP) has increased, and so too has its vulnerability to the international system. At the same time, foreign debt burdens have climbed, creating a new imperative for export expansion. But it has been difficult for the Central American economies to keep up; as a percentage of export earnings, both total debt and debt service have increased dramatically in all of the countries since 1970.

When the agro-export development model is evaluated in terms of its impact on the lives of rural people, the results in Central America are clear. The material and psychological interests of rural people throughout the region have been harmed—often devastated—by the periodic export-fueled agrarian transformations, including that of the postwar period. Through physical force and market forces, elite interests have expropriated land and labor in order to further their objectives. The quantitative data provided in this study uphold the numerous descriptive reports from and about the region. The share of land devoted to export crops in recent decades has increased relative to that used for food crops. Consequently, per capita domestic production of basic foods has declined, aggravating already serious malnutrition problems. As population has increased and land pressures intensified, peasants have been forced off of their land. Because sufficient new employment opportunities have not been generated, both landlessness and unemployment have risen in rural areas, as have near-landlessness and under-employment. As a result of the postwar agrarian transformation, then, a growing percentage of Central America's people are of marginal utility to the region's stratified systems.

The findings of this study do not contest the necessity for leaders of countries with small economies to discover and expand new exports nor the viability of the agro-export development model itself. The focus here has been narrower: the impact of this model on countries with highly stratified agrarian systems. Because Central American agrarian elites have relied con-sistently across the centuries on coercion to obtain the land and labor necessary to pursue their objectives, the approach under consideration in this study is most properly termed "the repressive agro-export development model." Although important political changes had occurred in each of the countries, elites retained as late as the 1970s the prerogative and the power to prevent innovations that would restructure their systems of domination. There were, of course, important variations among countries in these systems, depending on such factors as the nature of the indigenous civili-zations at the time of the Conquest, topography, climate, location, and the availability of land, labor, and capital. As a result, the most exploitive and repressive systems were created in Guatemala and El Salvador, followed by Nicaragua and then Honduras, with Costa Rica the least exploitive.[2]

PEASANT MOBILIZATION

The first notable expression of peasant discontent in the postwar period occurred in Guatemala as the system of domination loosened under the progressive governments of 1944–54. Next, a substantial percentage of the peasantry was organized in Honduras by the late 1960s; these peasants continued to play a major role through the middle of the next decade. Indeed, the 1970s witnessed the awakening of the peasantry as a political force throughout the region. Rejecting submissiveness, increasing numbers of rural people asserted their interests through cooperatives, unions, and other peasant organizations; political parties; and finally, revolutionary armies.

The attempt to explain the sources of peasant mobilization has generated a fruitful dialogue among scholars. Emphases differ among authors, but more recent works generally acknowledge the important roles played by three types of factors. First, the commercialization of agriculture erodes economic security, upsets traditional social relations, and weakens traditional value systems (see, for example, Paige 1975, Scott 1976, and Wolf 1969). Second, political organizers from outside of peasant communities provide needed sources of economic assistance, protection, organizational expertise, and new value systems (for example, see Migdal 1974, Singelmann 1981, and White 1977). Third, the response of the state, especially the mix it chooses between reform and repression, has important effects on the scope and intensity of mobilization (see, for example, McClintock 1984, Skocpol 1982, and Tilly 1978).

Each of these factors has been important in contemporary Central America. The earlier agrarian transformations in the region were resisted by peasants, especially Indians, but in the end, with little success. Then as in the present period, the immediate cause of their resistance was the attack on their economic security. This "subsistence crisis"—a factor most closely associated with Scott's (1976) account of peasant resistance in Southeast Asia—is not sufficient to account for the widespread mobilization of the peasantry in recent decades in Central America, however. What is distinctive about the present period is the critical role played by political factors, especially the activities of outside organizers and government policies.

The most important of the new political forces in rural Central America has been church people. With easier access and greater legitimacy than other actors because of shared religious beliefs (and, in the case of priests, status), church workers in each country have played a central role in peasant mobilization. Especially notable have been the influence of Catholic Action and foreign missionaries in Guatemala, the Church radio school program in Honduras, base communities in El Salvador, and Jesuit and Capuchin activities in Nicaragua. Throughout the region, these workers' efforts eroded the values and power relationships that perpetuated peasants' passivity. Whether those efforts were directly religious, developmental, or political, they often served to foster the transformation of attitudes from fatalistic to activistic and to create new organizations that nurtured this transformation and facilitated its expression. Eventually, peasants in each country changed, and supported by this process, they took the lead in asserting their rights to a better life, participating in demonstrations, marches, and land invasions.

The efforts of church people were reinforced by those of secular actors. In Guatemala during the reform period, substantial peasant organization was encouraged by the efforts of radical organizers and political party activists. Similar actors in the 1970s were joined by development workers from other countries, often the United States. Urban leftists were also active during the 1970s in the countryside of the other four nations. Especially prominent were the roles played in El Salvador by organizers from the popular organizations and in Nicaragua by the Sandinistas. Like the church workers, the secular activists brought a message and support that served to undermine traditional authority relations and to facilitate popular organization. When these efforts were combined with the subsistence crisis facing many rural people, the result was substantial mobilization by peasants in an effort to defend and improve their position. The actual results, however, were heavily dependent on the nature of each government's response to the popular threat to the status quo.

THE GOVERNMENT RESPONSE

The government response to peasant mobilization and organization in postwar Central America ranges across the full spectrum of possibilities. These responses can be broadly classified as positive, neutral, or negative, but further distinctions within the first and especially the final category are possible and useful. On the basis of the evidence described in Part II, the following classifications would seem to be the relevant ones: actively supportive, permissive, facilitative, neutral, preventative, repressive, and systematically repressive. Of these, probably the most characteristic stance has been the preventative.

In the traditional agrarian structure, the passivity of the peasantry was maintained through patron-client relationships and fatalistic value systems. Power was concentrated, and peasants had few alternatives, if any. Behind this stratified network stood the state. Should its coercive capability be required, it was ready to harass and intimidate potential rural leaders. Until recent decades, however, such preventative action was required only infrequently. In the postwar period, this stance has been most characteristic of the Honduran state, where it was interrupted only in the late 1960s and early 1970s under López Arellano. For most of the sixties, peasant mobilization was discouraged through harassment and jailings. Since the midseventies, Honduran administrations have had to accept the existence of a well-organized peasantry, but its activities have been constrained by government restriction such as the repeated jailings of peasant leaders in the 1980s. But to this point Honduran officials have not fallen to the level of relying on the

194   LAND, POWER, AND POVERTY

consistent use of torture and murder to enforce their will. Unfortunately, that
has not been true of other regimes.

Government officials and private groups have been willing to move
beyond preventative intimidation to more widespread violence (i.e., repression) in El Salvador, Guatemala, and Nicaragua in order to pursue their
objectives and protect their interests. The results, however, were not always
as intended. Rather than beating the population back into submissiveness,
repression in each country during the 1970s provoked further popular
resistance. The reliance on unjustified violence stiffened the resolve of many
people who were already in opposition to the regime and delegitimized it for
numerous others, many of whom were politicized and radicalized as a result.
When the villages and families of peasants were the victims of repression,
many of the survivors moved into opposition out of rage and in self-defense.

As terrible as it was, at this stage the repression was not sufficient to
protect the regimes of these three countries. Consequently, the violence was
escalated, becoming more indiscriminate and systematic. The application of
widespread repression from 1980 to 1983 in El Salvador and to 1984 in
Guatemala accomplished, for a time, its purpose. Although revolutionary
forces continued their struggles in both countries, the tens of thousands of
murders in each were sufficient to destroy popular organizations and restore
fear and passivity to the countryside. In Nicaragua, by contrast, Somoza's
willingness even to destroy the nation's cities with his air force was not
sufficient to save his regime. Although his forces killed on levels approaching
those of the other two countries, his personalistic dictatorship had alienated
all sectors of society and did not have the institutional capacity to implement
state terrorism on the same systematic level.

At other times governments in Central America have promoted peasant
mobilization and organization. The foremost examples are the active support
given the peasants by the Arbenz regime in Guatemala and the Sandinista
government in Nicaragua. With this support, rural people felt free to organize
and to assert their interests. Peasant organizations proliferated, and their
memberships skyrocketed. Other governments have been more permissive in
their orientation, especially in Costa Rica; there, peasant mobilization is
viewed favorably, but little active government support is offered. Some
administrations there and elsewhere have been closer to neutral, however. A
final possibility is the facilitative. Here the government is neutral in its
position on peasant mobilization, but the impact of its policies is nonetheless
to encourage it. The best example is Honduras in the late 1960s. It was not the
regime's intention to encourage peasant mobilization, but its adjudication of
land disputes in favor of peasants ignited a burst of organizing.

Which stance toward peasant mobilization a government will assume is a
function of a variety of factors, some specific to a particular time and place,

others general to postwar Central America. The most important have been the level of popular mobilization, the degree of repression inherent in the agrarian system, and constraints on resources. The first factor requires no explanation. For reasons discussed throughout this study (such as the availability of exportable crops, land, labor, and capital), the cumulative impact of the earlier agrarian transformations resulted in more repressive systems in Guatemala, El Salvador, and to a lesser extent Nicaragua. Consequently, these systems already had built into them a reliance on coercion and a disposition toward settling conflict through repression. Any level of peasant mobilization would accordingly be a greater threat to such a system than would a comparable level in Costa Rica or Honduras.

Finally, governments have varied in their access to resources with which to meet peasants' demands, especially the primary demand for land. Land distribution was facilitated in Guatemala in the 1950s and in Honduras and Costa Rica up to the mid-1970s by the availability of public lands. Similarly, the early stages of the Sandinista reform were made easier by the fact that the flight of Somoza and his supporters created a vast public sector that could be used for revolutionary objectives at relatively low cost. Large tracts of unused or underused private lands have also made it easier to meet the demands, especially if the acreage was owned by multinational corporations. Such foreign-owned lands were most plentiful, again, in Guatemala during the Arbenz reform and in Honduras and Costa Rica; underutilized domestically owned lands were important for the reforms in Guatemala and Nicaragua.

Putting these factors together, generally Costa Rica and Honduras had less repressive structures to begin with as well as less constraints on the ability of committed governments to meet peasants' demands for land. Although serious agrarian problems remain in both countries, their regimes have been sufficiently responsive to hold rural discontent below the level that would represent a serious threat to the maintenance of the system. In Guatemala in the 1950s, the underutilized lands of the United Fruit Company and of domestic *latifundistas*, together with the national farms, were sufficient to permit a major redistribution without an attack on large-scale commercial agriculture. But by the 1970s, the further expansion of commercial agriculture and population growth in Guatemala and El Salvador had created land pressures that intensified elite opposition to any serious consideration of agrarian reform or other needs of the peasantry. Given that both countries' systems were based on highly exploitive labor arrangements, intensifying land pressures heightened the probability that peasant mobilization would be experienced as an intolerable threat to the status quo.

In Nicaragua, by contrast, land pressures were not as acute, nor was the labor system relatively as coercive. Furthermore, the Somoza dynasty had preempted the landowning class from exercising state power. These are some of the reasons why the agrarian bourgeoisie in Nicaragua did not at first experience the country's popular mobilization as the kind of threat it represented to their counterparts in Guatemala and El Salvador.

These variations in constraints are important to keep in mind when comparing the agrarian reforms of the five countries. As Table 9.1 indicates, clearly the most far-reaching of the Central American reforms has been the Nicaraguan. When workers on state farms are included among its beneficiaries, as they are in this table, then the percentage of the rural population reached by the reform has been much the greatest in Nicaragua, followed by Guatemala under Arbenz and then by El Salvador, Honduras, and Costa Rica. Because beneficiaries invariably have families, the reform sector is substantially larger than this percentage indicates; a multiplication factor of five or six people is commonly used. For the percentage of farmland distributed, the rankings are the same except for a reversal between Costa Rica and Honduras at the low end of the scale. Although Nicaragua again leads its neighbors, the gap is much less than that for beneficiaries.[3] Note, however, that the time period covered in the table ends with 1984, but land distribution accelerated in Nicaragua in 1985. Accordingly, the actual disparity between it and the other two countries is greater than that indicated by the table.

There are important differences in the politics of the three major agrarian reforms in Central America. The Arbenz reform in Guatemala was facilitated

TABLE 9.1
Central America: A Comparison of Agrarian Reform Programs

Country	Years Covered	Cropped Land[1] per Rural Person	Beneficiaries[2] as % of Rural Population	Land Distributed[3] Total Area	as % of Farmland
Costa Rica	1962–84	.37	1.1	637	13
El Salvador	1980–84	.34	3.3	789	24
Guatemala	1952–54	.44	4.6	1800	27
Honduras	1962–84	.94	2.2	725	6
Nicaragua	1979–84	1.15	7.9	3854	32

NOTES: 1. Cropped Land: Arable land plus land under permanent crops for 1978 in hectares per person in rural areas. Calculated from International Agricultural Development Service 1978:17.

2. Beneficiaries: Total number of recipients of distributed land in years covered; includes national lands as well as expropriated lands. Nicaragua includes workers on state farms (about two-thirds of total).

3. Land Distributed: Total area is in thousands of acres. Farmland combines 1980 estimates of arable land, land permanently under cultivation, and permanent pasture land from CEPAL 1983:601.

SOURCES: Costa Rica: *La Nación* 1984a:16a; Seligson 1984:34; El Salvador and Nicaragua: Reinhardt 1986:Table 3; Guatemala: Aybar de Soto 1978:181, 210; Honduras: Morris 1984:101; Ruhl 1985:70.

by the availability of extensive unused lands on private and foreign-owned estates as well as by the government-operated national farms. As a result, it could be implemented without attacking productive commercial farms. But although domestic politics made the expropriation of foreign-owned lands relatively easier, United Fruit's ability to propagandize in the United States was a critical factor, leading to the overthrow of the Arbenz government and the undoing of the reform.

Only in El Salvador and Nicaragua, then, have large, productive commercial farms represented a substantial proportion of the lands redistributed—and in each case, under unique circumstances. Nicaragua is unique not only because of its revolutionary process but also because the prerevolutionary concentration of land in the hands of the Somoza family and a small number of its supporters allowed a revolutionary regime to redistribute land in its first years without attacking the agrarian bourgeoisie or having to face the problematic issue of compensation. In El Salvador, by contrast, meaningful reform was not possible without confronting the bourgeoisie. What is often overlooked in the justifiable criticisms of the Salvadoran reform is that it is the only case in Central America of the expropriation of a substantial number of productively used large commercial farms.

The number of landless and land-poor peasants in the region increases constantly, as do the ranks of the rural unemployed and underemployed. Unfortunately, as the need for land redistribution has grown, so too has its difficulty. The "easiest" lands to expropriate and/or distribute, accessible public property and unused lands on large estates, dwindle all the time. The conditions that gave rise to the peasant demands and movements discussed in this study, then, will continue into the future; so too, undoubtedly, will rural tensions and conflicts. As in the past, critical to the outcome of these conflicts will be the actions of the United States.

THE UNITED STATES AND AGRARIAN REFORM

The case material presented in Part II indicates that U.S. policy toward agrarian reform in Central America in the postwar period has been the result of policymakers' perceptions of three factors, listed in order of increasing importance: the nature of the reform itself, the effect of the reform on the economic interests of U.S. corporations, and the relationship of the reform to U.S. security concerns.

The reforms described in this study range from minor distributive programs with limited scope and few beneficiaries, such as colonization projects, to major land redistributions adversely affecting major economic actors and benefiting large numbers of impoverished peasants. The distributive programs have been unproblematic for the United States, which has been a primary financial benefactor of many of them. They threaten neither vested economic interests nor the principle of private property, but some of the needy are benefited and also, sponsors hope, immunized against the inducements of radical movements. The limitation of the distributive programs is that, for the same reasons they are unproblematic, they are incapable of responding effectively to the growing issues of landlessness and near-landlessness, as the cases of Costa Rica and Honduras so clearly demonstrate.

The redistributive programs have been a greater challenge to U.S. policymakers. Governments implementing two of the three most thorough reforms have incurred the enmity of the United States government and become the target of North American counterrevolutionary efforts. Arbenz was overthrown in Guatemala, and the Sandinistas are fighting for the life of their revolution in Nicaragua. Neither this opposition nor U.S. support for the reform in El Salvador can be explained without reference to the other two factors, economic interests and security concerns.

For the most part, Central American agrarian reforms have not substantially affected U.S. economic interests. Neither in Nicaragua nor in El Salvador did lands falling within the scope of the reforms include any notable holdings of North American companies, and the Costa Rican reform has not seriously affected the sizable holdings of United Fruit/United Brands in that country. However, the threat to the fruit company's holdings in both Guatemala and Honduras was central to the demise of reform efforts in each country. Although it is questionable whether domestic forces would have allowed serious implementation of the 1962 Honduran reform, any such effort was precluded by successful United Fruit opposition. The company was also triumphant in its battle against the Guatemalan government in the early 1950s, though, as argued earlier, United States intervention in Guatemala is explicable in anticommunist, not direct economic, terms. Nevertheless, it remains true that no agrarian reform has been successful in Central America that threatened serious harm to major U.S. economic interests.

This does not mean that lands owned by U.S. interests cannot be expropriated. In Honduras in 1975, United Brands lost 57,000 acres and Standard Fruit 84,000 acres to a government expropriation order. This action came at the peak of several years of increasing peasant mobilization, including growing numbers of land invasions and occupations. Significantly, the action was taken by a conservative military commander who had recently replaced a populist military leader. The expropriations were not presented as an attack on the fruit companies but rather as part of a package of moves intended to defuse an explosive situation. Furthermore, the fruit companies were at a point of extreme vulnerability; only months before, it had been disclosed that

United Brands had bribed the previous government into reducing the banana export tax. A year later, when the director of the Agrarian Reform Institute attempted further fruit company expropriations, his actions were overturned and he was forced out of office.

In the cases of the three redistributive land reforms, U.S. policy has been a function of a more fundamental concern, the security of the United States as perceived by policymakers. The Arbenz government was attacked not because it was conducting an agrarian reform but because the nature of that reform reinforced the perception of top U.S. officials that Guatemala was falling to the Communists. To the Reagan administration, the situation in Nicaragua has been similarly clear from the beginning: the Sandinistas are Communists and thus inherently a threat to the United States and the rest of Central America. Questions concerning the necessity or justice of the Nicaraguan reform are secondary, perhaps even irrelevant.

In El Salvador, in contrast, the United States has been the sponsor of a reform benefiting about a quarter of the rural poor. This undertaking, unique for the United States in Central America, was also the result of security concerns. Both the Carter and Reagan administrations have believed that the only hope of preventing the left from coming to power lies in preempting its issue of agrarian reform while giving firm support to a government of "the center."

That the basic commitment has been to U.S. security interests rather than to agrarian reform becomes clear when the Reagan policy toward El Salvador is contrasted with that toward Honduras. Although the need for land redistribution in Honduras is also pressing, it has not been part of the administration's approach to that country. Instead, the philosophy guiding both the United States and Honduras in the 1980s was, as AID (1982) noted, "an agrarian reform based on the principles of private property" (p. 6). The major manifestation of this strategy was the titling program discussed in chapter 6. That program provided needed security to tens of thousands of rural families, but such an approach does nothing for the plight of the growing number of landless and near-landless families. Land titling would, however, create support for the regime in a country whose stability was central to the Central American policy of the Reagan administration.

An analysis of the Central American cases in light of the security interests of the United States leads, then, to the following set of conclusions. The fundamental determinant of policy toward agrarian reform in Central America is U.S. security interests as they are perceived by policymakers. Major redistributive agrarian reforms will be supported only when they are viewed as furthering the security interests of the United States; but this is an uncommon occurrence. If no major security interests are seen as relevant, then policy will be determined by the nature of the reform and by economic considerations.

More generally, the result of this study correspond to those of other analyses of United States policy toward Latin America. They are particularly congruent with Blasier's (1976) account of the U.S. response to revolutionary change, which explains U.S. reconciliation to two revolutions (those in Mexico and Bolivia) and opposition to two others (those in Guatemala and Cuba). In the first two cases, revolutionary leaders were willing to compromise with the United States; in the second pair, they were not. Washington in turn found that it could best advance its security interests (excluding from the hemisphere a Great Power rival) by accommodating itself to revolutionary change in Mexico and Bolivia. In this context, the most interesting comparison is that of Bolivia with El Salvador.

In 1953 the Eisenhower administration reconciled itself to a progressive regime in Bolivia that had nationalized the tin mines and was conducting an extensive land reform. One of the crucial actors was the president's brother, Milton Eisenhower, who explained that "rapid peaceful social change is the only way to avert violent revolution in Bolivia; physical strife would be surest way of giving the Communists control" (quoted in Blasier 1976:133). The Bolivian government made major efforts to facilitate the perception that it was not only uninfluenced by communism but even a bulwark against such a threat. As a result of this accommodation, U.S. influence in Bolivia increased substantially, and the course of the revolution was moderated (Blasier 1976:133–145). Between 1952 and 1964, United States economic assistance to Bolivia averaged more per capita than that to any other country (Blasier 1976:144). However, from 1955 to 1983 Bolivia's position as the second-lowest-ranking country in the Western Hemisphere in per capita gross national product (after Haiti) remained unchanged. Although it would be a mistake to overstate the comparison, U.S. motivations and policy approaches were similar in both cases. U.S. interests (as perceived by policymakers) were protected more successfully than the quality of life was improved for impoverished Bolivians and Salvadorans.

The dilemma for advocates of major land redistribution in Central America is clear, then. Substantial redistributive programs attack the fundamental interests of powerful groups, which will use their power to oppose major reforms. The result will be considerable political conflict. Because compensation in cash is not feasible for widespread expropriations, such reforms can be portrayed as attacks on the principle of private property. Consequently, their opponents can find receptive audiences in the United States for claims that they are socialist in nature and harmful to economic development. The credibility of the opponents' case is enhanced when they can point to self-identified Marxists in positions of power in Central America. Scholars have argued for years that a Marxist or Marxist-influenced government in Central America would not necessarily become an agent of the

Soviet Union (and/or of Cuba),[4] but this distinction has seldom been perceived by U.S. policymakers.

The possibilities for major land redistribution in Central America continue to be constrained by the preeminent influence of anticommunism on U.S. policy toward the region. This is a tragedy for Central America. The present study has documented the injustices perpetrated through the creation of the structures of domination in rural Central America and through their perpetuation. Until agrarian society is transformed along more equitable lines, the number of people whose land, employment, and income are insufficient will continue to grow. Until such a transformation occurs, the contradictions of rural society will generate political conflicts that threaten the stability of societies and at times even that of the whole region. And until the United States accepts significant structural change, its policymakers will continue to confront challenges in Central America to their perception of their nation's security interests.

NOTES

1. Similarly, Paige (1975) points out that the "continued existence of the landed upper class in the agricultural export economy depends . . . on political restrictions on the workings of the markets in land, labor and capital. . . . The economic weakness of the landed upper class forces it to rely on political means to attain economic objectives" (p. 17).

2. For more extended discussions of the importance of such factors for intercountry variations, see, among others, Chinchilla (1983) and Stone (1983).

3. These results are for 1980 data on area for Guatemala. If 1950 data are used, however, the Arbenz reform shows the largest percentage of farmland distributed. Guatemala's farmland comprised 2,704,000 hectares in 1980, but in 1950 it comprised 1,998,000 hectares (FAO 1953:4), 36 percent of which was distributed.

4. One of the best and most recent discussions of these issues is Blachman, LeoGrande, and Sharpe (1986).

CHAPTER 10

Epilogue

Central America entered the 1990s with substantial structural constraints still retarding the sustained equitable development of the region. Throughout Latin America the 1980s were economically the "lost decade" as the promising growth rates of earlier years ended and living standards declined across classes and countries. In Central America the 1980s were a lost opportunity politically as well.

Popular forces in Nicaragua and El Salvador began the decade with a zestful optimism unleashed by the overthrow of hated dictators in the previous half year. They arrived at the 1990s with devastated economies, huge civilian death tolls, and polarized societies. Civilians occupied the seats of government in both Guatemala and Honduras, but the real power continued to be the military. Although the scale was vastly different, political killings increased through 1989 in both countries, provoking fears in Guatemala of another descent into barbaric military terrorism. Costa Rica managed to maintain its identity as a peaceful and free society, but fears for its future in a context of regional militarization, violence, and stagnation were widespread.

There were, of course, countervailing trends. Regular presidential elections with close international scrutiny were at least partially institutionalized in each country. Substantial progress was made toward ending the U.S./Contra war against Nicaragua. Insurgents and governments were intermittently talking to each other in El Salvador. Enough political space had been created in El Salvador, Guatemala, and Nicaragua that exiles returned to participate through regular nonviolent political channels.

204

LAND, POWER, AND POVERTY

Nonetheless, what was most striking at the end of the decade was how little of the decade's initial promise had been realized. The 1980s in Central America retaught a series of tragic lessons. First, socioeconomic structures are hard to change. Second, they are especially hard to change in small countries when the beneficiaries of those structures enjoy the support (for whatever the reasons) of a hegemonic great power. Third, the consequences of socio-political conflict are not an abstraction but are measured by the blood, tears, death and anguish of real individuals ... by the hundreds of thousands.

THE 1980s ECONOMICALLY: THE LOST DECADE

Earlier chapters of this book documented that the benefits of the economic growth of the 1960s and 1970s were unequally shared.[1] Indeed, the commercialization and internationalization of Central American agriculture, although promoting growth, often lead to a deterioration in the economic security of many rural people. During much of the 1980s the story was simpler: there was no growth.

Table 10.1 provides the stark data. Alongside the healthy growth rates of gross domestic product per (GDP) capita of the 1961–80 period is the negative mirror of the first half of the 1980s—a decline in per capita growth for each country. Costa Rica pulled out of this tailspin in 1986, Honduras and Guatemala the following year, but through 1988 economic decline had not ended in either El Salvador or (especially) Nicaragua. The result is portrayed in the last column of the table: in each country, 1988 per capita

TABLE 10.1
Growth Rate of Gross Domestic Product Per Capita

Country	Average[1] 1961–80	1981–85	1986	Annual 1987	1988[2]	1988 as % of 1980[3]
Costa Rica	2.6	−2.6	2.7	2.6	1.1	94
El Salvador	1.5	−2.9	−1.0	.9	−1.5	85
Guatemala	2.7	−3.9	−2.7	.2	.6	80
Honduras	2.2	−2.5	−0.3	.9	.6	89
Nicaragua	.4	−2.7	−4.3	−4.0	−11.1	71

NOTES: 1. Cumulate growth.
2. Preliminary estimate.
3. GDP per capita in 1988 as percentage of 1980.
SOURCE: IDB 1989: Tables 11-3 and B-1.

income was less than it had been in 1980. In fact, 1987 Costa Rican per capita GDP had regressed back to the level of 1974; for Honduras, it had regressed back to 1973; for Guatemala, back to 1971; for El Salvador, 1964; and for Nicaragua, all the way back to the level of 1960, according to the Inter–American Development Bank (*Times of the Americas*, Sept. 20, 1989:16).

The causes of this miserable performance were both external and internal. With their economies based on the export of a small number of commodities, the Central American countries continue to be vulnerable to variations in the international system—a system on which these weak economies have virtually no impact. A major cause of the economic stagnation of the region during the first half of the decade was a worldwide recession. In addition, the recession-induced reduction of demand for Central American products was paralleled by deteriorating terms of trade, as the relative costs of imports outpaced the value of regional exports. The terms of trade dropped for each country through the decade to 1985 and then recovered by 1988 for Costa Rica, Honduras, and Nicaragua, as indicated by the first column of Table 10.2, part B, but still had not for El Salvador or Guatemala.[2] For these reasons, as well as some production declines, the total value of exports in actual dollars declined during the 1980s by substantial percentages in three of the countries (El Salvador, Guatemala, and Nicaragua).

Central America ended the 1980s, then, still locked into its centuries-old dilemma: its economies are structured for export production yet world demand for its exports continues to be insufficient to stimulate sustained development. The Caribbean Basin Initiative (CBI) is a notable example of the difficulties. Started earlier in the decade by the Reagan administration with the intention of improving the U.S. market for the region's exports, the CBI has been judged as providing relatively inconsequential benefits for the region.[3]

The economic situation is actually even worse. Now much of the region's export earnings do not go into the promotion of economic development or into social programs but rather are required to service an ever-larger international debt. And even worse still, the debt grew faster than export earnings during the 1980s for each of the Central American countries, (see Table 10.2). As a result, the size of the debt relative to export earnings was much larger in 1988 than at the start of the decade, as the top half of the table shows. The harmful change in this ratio was astronomical in Nicaragua, where it grew from a debt 474 percent larger than export earnings in 1980 to 3395 percent in 1988, for an increase in the ratio itself of 616 percent. This change across the decade was also pronounced in El Salvador and Guatemala, as their debt-to-export earning ratios more than

TABLE 10.2
Performance of the External Sector in the 1980s

A. External Public Debt Outstanding as Percentage of Export Earnings,
   1970–1988

Country	1970	1980	1982	1984	1986	1988[1]
Costa Rica	98	253	412	399	417	425[2]
El Salvador	55	87	213	239	226	282
Guatemala	61	69	140	208	263	258
Honduras	80	203	328	312	334	373
Nicaragua	124	474	826	1327	2510	3395

B. Percentage Changes in External Performance, 1980 to 1988[1]

Country	Terms of Trade	Exports Value	External Debt	Debt Exports
Costa Rica	0	23	72	68[2]
El Salvador	−31	−41	96	224
Guatemala	−8	−29	137	274
Honduras	0	5	126	84
Nicaragua	12	−53	232	616

NOTES: 1. Preliminary estimates for 1988.
2. Data are for 1987.
SOURCES: Calculated from IDB 1986: Table 43 and IDB 1989: Tables
11-2, D3, and E1.

doubled. In Costa Rica and Honduras the ratio grew at a slower pace. However, it should not be overlooked that the actual size of the ratio of debt to export earnings was worse in these two in 1987–88 than in El Salvador and Guatemala. In summary, the essential point is this: the international debt that the Central American countries must service with their export earnings is growing faster than the earnings themselves, leaving less for productive use at home.

The causes of economic decline were internal as well, especially the continuing political violence. Economic performance was the worst in the three countries with the most conflict. When world economic conditions improved in the second half of the decade, domestic performance did not follow in either El Salvador or Nicaragua. The problem was not just the diversion of resources away from productive use and into military expenses but also the economic warfare waged by the opposition in both countries. A major tactic of the FMLN in El Salvador was economic sabotage, with damages estimated at $1.2 billion (U.S. State, 1988:4). Even more important was the economic warfare directed against Nicaragua by the Contras and the United States. The Contras attacked not only economic targets but also civilians involved in productive activities, such as the murders of 147 agricultural experts and 130 teachers by the Contras through 1988. Total economic damages (both direct and indirect) as a result of the war were estimated at $12.2 billion through 1988 by the Nicaraguan government. This included an estimated $315.5 million in losses resulting from the U.S. trade embargo and another $422.9 million in losses in international funding due to United States pressures (*Envio*, February 1989:16).

The elimination of destructive conflict is necessary for sustained development because a healthy intraregional trade is an economic necessity for each to prosper. Nor is the return of peace a sufficient condition. Future development is still constrained by grossly unequal agrarian structures that deny to substantial numbers of the rural population the opportunity to earn a sufficient income to support themselves adequately. Consequently, domestic demand is limited because too many people have too little income for consumption. Finally, inherent in these systems are the grievances that will fuel new rounds of popular mobilization in the future and, most likely, further destructive political conflict.

The situation was desperate for much of the rural population in 1979. A decade later it was even worse for many. One measure of this deteriorating quality of life is presented in Table 10.3, which gives the changes across the decade in the real minimum wage. With the exception of Costa Rica, the results have been catastrophic, especially in El Salvador and even more so in Nicaragua. Although these data stop with 1985 for these two countries, other evidence (such as Table 10.1) indicates a continuation of these tragic trends through the second half of the decade.

TABLE 10.3
Changes in Real Minimum Wage (1980 = 100)

Country	1980	1982	1984	1985	1986[1]
Costa Rica	100.0	85.8	103.8	111.7	118.6
El Salvador	100.0	83.0	73.7	63.6	—
Guatemala	100.0	120.8	111.6	93.9	68.7
Honduras	100.0	105.0	91.9	90.3	86.1
Nicaragua	100.0	78.0	66.8	44.1	—

NOTES: 1. Provisional data.
SOURCES: 2. IDB 1989: Table II-6.

208 LAND, POWER, AND POVERTY

THE 1980s POLITICALLY: FURTHER POLARIZATION

As the Central American countries entered the 1990s, the capabilities of their governments to respond adequately to these serious problems were limited. The various external and internal economic constraints reduced available resources. In addition, the configuration of political forces for each country restricted possibilities for effective government action. The countries fall into three groupings. Nicaragua is unique, not only because of the ideological orientation of its leadership, but also because of the terrible consequences of the enmity of the U.S. government. Costa Rica also continued to stand apart in the region because of its distinct political and social systems and also because of its superior economic performance in the late 1980s. Since the recent trends in Costa Rica are not much different from those analyzed in previous chapters, it will not be discussed further here.

The differences among the remaining three countries are substantial, yet they also shared important common characteristics. Each made progress in institutionalizing the electoral process but as the 1990s began, the military was at least as powerful as ever. Popular forces, therefore, confronted an ambiguous situation. They did benefit from more political space for overt political activities. However, the repressive apparatus persisted as a menacing deterrent force. Indeed, death squad/military killings increased through 1989 in each of the three countries.

Nicaragua

Nicaragua celebrated the tenth anniversary of its revolution on July 19, 1989, a milestone marked "by a cloud of uncertainty, political discontent, and economic hardship" (*Christian Science Monitor*, July 17, 1989:1). The revolutionary regime's redistributive policies had achieved major successes in meeting basic needs through the literacy campaign, agrarian reform, and health care policies. Popular forces had been empowered through the creation of a variety of participatory channels. But, popular support for Sandinista leadership eroded with the continuation of the war, the draft, political restrictions, and economic decline. Even if the Sandinistas were to win the February 1990 elections, the prospects for their continuing political hegemony were not propitious and those for their original project of socialist transformation were even less.

The disastrous decline in economic performance showed a drop in per capita gross domestic product for 1988 to only 71 percent of the level of 1980 (Table 10.1). Corresponding with this decline was the acceleration of inflation, from 747 percent in 1986 to 1,800 percent in 1987 and up to as much as 23,000 percent in 1988 (Moreno 1989:3; *Christian Science Monitor*, January 23, 1989:2)[4]. For Nicaraguans, the economic crisis meant falling living standards; rising unemployment; shortages of all supplies including even beans, rice, and sugar; and long waits in line for those goods in supply. Emigration increased, including by long-time supporters of the revolution. Up to one-third of the country's college-educated professionals were said to have left by the end of 1988, over a quarter of them just in the last year (*Christian Science Monitor*, January 23, 1989:2).

To combat the hyperinflation the Nicaraguan government instituted two packages of austerity measures in 1988 and another in January 1989. The harsh measures, which included a 20 percent cut in the budget, layoffs of close to 10,000 state workers, wage cuts, and credit and money supply restrictions, were described as "far more severe" than many of those mandated by the International Monetary Fund, but without its financial help (*Envio*, June 1989:11–12). Inflation did drop but fears of recession later resulted in an easing up—and less success (*Envio*, August 1989:10–11). This was the economic context, then, for the 1990 elections.

Supporters of the government of President Daniel Ortega blamed the problems largely on the war, and therefore the United States. Moderate critics cited the government's "great political and economic mistakes."[5] Meanwhile, hostile opponents spoke of "a decade of Marxist dictatorship, militancy, and mismanagement" (*Christian Science Monitor*, November 9, 1989:19).[6] This latter group certainly included the U.S. government, which pointed to the Nicaraguan government's "decision to pursue a costly military buildup, questionable state planning programs, and the elimination of most free-market incentives" (U.S. State 1988:6).

The combination of the economic crisis and the war had a number of consequences for agrarian policy, which largely meant a continuation of the latest trends discussed in chapter 9. Peasant demands for land continued and were frequently met, usually not through expropriations but rather through parceling.[7] While there were 460 expropriations in 1986, there were only seven in 1988 and just three in 1989 to August (*Envio*, August 1989:18). Parceling occurred both within Sandinista Production Cooperatives (CAS) and with idle and underutilized state lands. Unfortunately, the best source of this land was in the remote interior, while the greatest pressures were in the Pacific region of León and Chinandega. For example, in 1989 an estimated 2,000 landless peasants in the area were joined by 5,000 agricultural workers put out of work by the economic crisis. As a result, some twenty peasant-organized land takeovers occurred in the region in the year up to August 1989 (*Envio*, August 1989:17).

Undoubtedly the most significant set of events in Central America at the

end of the decade was the efforts of the countries' presidents themselves to
end the war against Nicaragua, demonstrating a surprising degree of
independence from Washington and the latter's efforts to disrail the peace
process. The war had been very costly for Nicaragua. In addition to the
economic devastation already discussed, total casualties were around
60,000 by 1989, including an estimated 29,000 killed by the Contras. The
Contra victims included close to 4,000 civilians killed and another 4,000
children disabled (*Envio*, February 1989:16; June 1989:24). The war was
also a destabilizing threat to the rest of the region, especially for contiguous
Costa Rica and Honduras. As it became clear that the Contras would not
win, Honduras in particular needed a resolution that would remove the
Contras from its territory (*Christian Science Monitor*, September 19, 1989).

The most important steps in the peace process occurred in August 1987,
March 1988, and January, February, and August 1989.[8] After years of
failed diplomatic initiatives by other countries, the Central American
presidents themselves met and signed an accord at Esquipulas, Guatemala in
August 1987 that established a foundation for the settlement of the region's
conflicts. The goals of the agreement were national reconciliation, peace,
and democratization in each country.[9] For Nicaragua, the plan called for an
end to external assistance to the Contras in return for a Sandinista pledge to
restore political freedoms. Although the government's performance was
spotty, it made major efforts toward compliance. The Reagan administration, however, sought to undermine the accord through pressures on its
regional allies and by attempting to keep the Contras together as a fighting
force by continuing the flow of "humanitarian" assistance.

Nonetheless, the Contras were finished as a real fighting force. Defeated
militarily and unable to command sufficient support in the U.S. Congress, in
March 1988 they agreed at Sapoá to a ceasefire with the Sandinista
government. Although small-scale attacks continued, the military battle had
been won by the government. Through 1988 the Reagan administration
attempted to provoke the Sandinistas into overly repressive acts that would
alienate supporters and embolden opponents.[10] But time ran out on the
Reagan administration in January 1989. The Sandinistas had outlasted their
fierce opponent. Although the administration of George Bush was no kinder
toward the Ortega government, it was clear to observers that the new U.S.
administration wanted a settlement of the conflict so that attention could be
shifted to other policy concerns and to avoid continual costly battles with
Congress.

Within this new political context, the Central American presidents were
able to formulate a more precise peace plan, which they signed on February
14, 1989, at a meeting in El Salvador. Referred to as Esquipulas IV, this
accord exchanged a Nicaraguan commitment to presidential elections by

February 25, 1990, and specific electoral reforms for promises by the other presidents of a plan for the demobilization and relocation of the Contras and of verification mechanisms. The Bush administration hoped that it would be able to delay the disbanding of the Contras until at least after the elections. The Central American presidents, meeting at Tela, Honduras, however, renewed their commitment to the peace process on August 7, 1989, with an agreement described as "a sharp rebuff to the United States" (*Washington Post*, August 8, 1989:1). The Tela agreement called for the relocation of the Contras by December 8 with the implementation supervised by an international commission drawn from the Organization of American States and the United Nations.

Consequently, the struggle between Nicaraguans shifted to the electoral arena. The Bush administration even cut off funds to the Miami headquarters of its allies, encouraging them to return home to campaign. Agreement on a common candidate to challenge President Ortega, though, was difficult. By 1989 the Sandinistas were opposed by twenty different political parties, including three to their left. Fourteen of these parties united in the National Opposition (UNO), with Violeta Barrios de Chamorro eventually selected as their presidential candidate. Although she was an attractive choice for international purposes—the widow of the martyred publisher of *La Prensa* slain in 1978 and a short-term member of the first revolutionary junta—her political abilities were questionable.[11]

Regardless of who would win in 1990, the future of Nicaragua was dismal. Either candidate would face a devastated economy and a bankrupt treasury, as well as a polarized nation. A reelected Ortega would confront a much more thoroughly organized internal opposition and vigilant regional and international forces wanting to strengthen political pluralism in the country. Their leverage would be the external economic assistance absolutely required by Nicaragua. A victorious Chamorro would probably be pulled apart by the fragmentation and conflicts within her own coalition and by the contradictions between the interests of the conservative forces within her coalition and the policy measures that would need to be adopted to gain and sustain support among popular forces. The response of the Sandinistas would also, of course, be a major factor with which to contend.

Ronald Reagan left office having failed to obtain the major objective of his Nicaraguan policy: the overthrow of the Sandinista government. He did succeed, though, in a second goal, which was to destroy the Nicaraguan revolution as an example to be emulated by other countries. In doing so, he set Nicaragua back by decades and perhaps generations in its ability to provide for the basic needs of its population.

El Salvador

After ten years of intense conflict, El Salvador ended the 1980s no closer to a resolution of the conflict that had left some 70,000 dead. Furthermore, developments in 1989 demonstrated that the attempt by the United States to create and perpetuate a moderate solution in the country was a failure. Early in the year the party of the right, ARENA, won control of the political system through the electoral process. The year ended as the FMLN mounted its most successful attack of the war, even taking control of portions of the capital. Meanwhile, the slow death of Napoleón Duarte by cancer symbolized the evisceration of the political center.[12]

The democratic forces of El Salvador received little international support (or attention) in the 1970s as their victories in 1972 and 1977 were stolen by the military. In the 1980s, however, the institutionalization of the electoral process was at the heart of U.S. objectives in Central America. Consequently, the forces of the oligarchy and other rightists in El Salvador organized their own party, ARENA, to compete in the electoral arena. At the middle of this effort was Roberto D'Aubuisson, a charismatic figure from a military background repeatedly tied to death squad killings, including the assassination of Archbishop Oscar Romero. In the presidential election of 1984 and the legislative elections of 1985 D'Aubuisson and ARENA lost to Duarte and the Christian Democrats. The next round of elections, however, belonged to the right. In 1988 ARENA won control of the national legislature and most of the mayoralities. And in March 1989 it won the presidency. It also controlled the Supreme Court and the rest of the judiciary.

Throughout the 1980s ARENA changed; how much, though, was a matter of controversy. D'Aubuisson was a poor presidential candidate because of his infamy. Clearly if he were to hold that office, the U.S. Congress would cut off the funds vital to the operation of the Salvadoran government. Pressure from the Reagan administration in 1982 prevented the selection of D'Aubuisson as provisional president. When he ran for that office in 1984, substantial U.S. financial support went to the victorious campaign of Duarte. Finally recognizing this political reality, in the following years the party's elite attempted to moderate the image of ARENA and to broaden its base of support. Crucial to its efforts was the selection in 1986 of Alfredo Cristiani as the party's president. In addition to being the president of the country, Cristiani is a wealthy businessman and coffee cultivator, graduate of Georgetown University in Washington D.C., and has no known connection to the death squads. Prior to his election, though, D'Aubuisson remained the major power in the party. Whether this relationship would alter, after his victory increased Cristiani's stature and resources, remained to be seen.

The victories of ARENA in 1988 and 1989, however, were due to much more than a changing image. At least as important was the collapse of support for Duarte and the Christian Democrats. They had been elected on the twin promises of peace and reform. They failed miserably on both counts. In addition, the party was widely charged with rampant corruption (correctly) and then split in two when rival factions could not compromise on the 1989 presidential nominee. The nomination went to the leader favored by the United States. The loser bolted, forming a new party and taking many of the party's legislators with him.

Duarte and the United States made the fateful decision in 1980 to align the Christian Democrats with the military and other forces to their right rather than with the popular organizations to their left. The hope was to simultaneously defeat the FMLN and tame the military. It is hard to say which has been the greater failure. Popular support for the Duarte government could only be maintained by a reform program that would improve the material conditions of the desperately poor majority. This he could not do because of the policy restrictions placed on him by his coalition partners, the Salvadoran military and the Reagan administration.[13] Combined with the economic sabotage of the FMLN, capital flight, the devastating earthquake of 1986, the drought in 1987, a decline in world coffee prices, and the corruption and infighting of his party, Duarte was unable to deliver on his promises and his support fell. So too did support for the "centrist" strategy of the United States. It was reported in 1988 that "nearly everybody here, from conservative Army colonels to leftist political leaders, openly criticizes the U.S. 'project,' questioning whether it can produce genuine change or end the war" (*Christian Science Monitor*, October 19, 1988:14).

As the leading opposition party, ARENA was the major beneficiary of popular disenchantment with the Christian Democrats. How ARENA could perform any more successfully as the governing party, however, was not clear. Economically, the right talked of turning El Salvador into another Taiwan through free market forces and aggressive export promotion. But, as argued in chapter 4, Central America is not East Asia. The "growth with equity" experienced in the latter region came after major structural reforms, including the agrarian system. ARENA, in contrast, has attempted to reverse what was an already inadequate reform. Parcelization of cooperatives in Nicaragua was welcomed by peasants, but in El Salvador they had reason to be afraid that financial pressures and coercion would leave them vulnerable to attempts by former owners to regain control of the land (Boyd 1989). Indeed, following ARENA's 1988 national and local victories, reports increased of the harassment and eviction of land reform beneficiaries (Blachman and Sharpe 1988–89:124). Even if ARENA's economic strategy could promote growth, it seemed to promise a decline in the economic security of much of the rural population.

Certainly the hard right within the party believed that they had the solution to the war: "unleash" the military against the FMLN and its supporters and increase repression against the "unreliable" throughout society. Even if this were a viable strategy domestically (a controversial assumption), it is unlikely that the U.S. Congress would continue to provide the funds necessary to finance the effort, especially if the killing of civilians returned to high levels. Nonetheless, rightists were willing to take this chance. Death squad killings "intensified dramatically" during 1988 (Americas Watch 1988b:1).[14] After ARENA's 1989 victory, arrests, torture, and killings increased even further, culminating in the slaying of the six Jesuit priests in November of the same year.

Violence against civilians also became a more frequent abuse by the FMLN in the late 1980s, although it is important to emphasize that civilian casualties attributed to the insurgents remained far below those blamed on the security forces/death squads. Americas Watch (1988b:5) calculated that civilian executions by the guerrillas increased by 74 percent during the first half of 1988 compared to the previous year. One of their most controversial tactics was the assassination of mayors, whom the rebels portray as key units of the government's counterinsurgency strategy. An aggressive campaign of attacks against urban targets also led to a number of unintended civilian casualties, as did the use of land mines. In another controversial tactic, homes and family members of military personnel were attacked and some killed.

Each of these tactics generated debate within the FMLN, with its supporters on the democratic left, and each cost it support among the civilian population. The vast majority of Salvadorans are war-weary and partisans of neither side. Although there were examples during the FMLN's November 1989 urban offensive of spontaneous popular logistic support for the rebels, it is telling that the offensive did not ignite popular insurrectionary activities along the lines of the Nicaraguan revolution. Instead, Salvadorans retreated behind their doors to wait out the danger.

El Salvador ended the 1980s, then, with levels of violence and fear unparalleled since the early years of the decade. Unlike earlier, though, there was now no foundation upon which to fantasize the possibility of constructing a centrist solution. El Salvador's remaining hope was that the forces of the far right and of the far left, now both stronger than ever, would realize that neither could destroy the other without destroying the country in the process.

Guatemala

The Guatemala of 1986–89 bore a chilling resemblance to the earlier period of 1976–79. Just as during the earlier period, an opening of political space in the last half of the 1980s facilitated the rapid formation of a number of popular organizations. The activities and demands of these popular groups then led to a counterresponse from the right. While the tactics of the popular forces were assemblies, demonstrations, and strikes, elements on the right relied on terror. As the 1980s ended in Guatemala, political violence from the right was escalating once again.

The major difference between the two periods was that Guatemala had a civilian for president in the latter rather than an "elected" general. Christian Democrat Vinício Cerezo's election in 1985 was an encouraging development, although many observers were dubious that he would have the power to accomplish much. Indeed, by the end of the decade some thought that if he were able to last through the election of his successor in March 1990 and to the end of his term, that a completed term would be his only major accomplishment.

As indicated in chapter 5, Cerezo began his presidency with his power significantly circumscribed by the military. His position was limited even further in May 1988. An attempted coup by junior officers was put down by the army high command but only with Cerezo's acquiescence to almost all of the demands of the military plotters. The concessions included restrictions on the political opening that had facilitated mass politics, the cancellation of a mild agrarian reform program, an increase in the military budget, freedom for the military from civilian interference in security policy, and cancellation of the government's dialogue with the revolutionary armies[15] (Americas Watch 1988a:1–5; *New York Times*, November 19, 1988:1).

Within the half year kidnappings, torture, and murder were reported to have "sharply increased," both in urban and especially rural areas, with 75 people assassinated in just September (*New York Times*, November 19, 1988). The August and September of the following year were similarly bloody, following another unsuccessful May coup attempt. A leading Christian Democrat, a prominent banker, a university professor, and four students were killed in Guatemala City, while in the rural province of San Marcos alone at least twenty-seven people were killed or disappeared (*Times of the Americas*, October 4, 1989:1 ff. and October 18:8). Observers blamed the escalating violence on rightist efforts to destabilize the government and to discredit the center as a governing force.

A major concern of the right was the resurgence of mass mobilization. Popular groups bravely took advantage of the democratic opening to organize and to assert their demands. In the first three years of civilian government, it was reported that there were more strikes and protests than in the previous thirty years (*Christian Science Monitor*, March 14, 1989:2). What was perhaps most notable, given the tragic history of the past decade, was the development of rural organizations, including the reappearance of the Committee for Peasant Unity (CUC).[16] The greatest attention, though, was given to the activities of Father Andres Giron. His National Peasant Union, which claimed a membership of 115,000 by the end of 1988, organized marches, protests, and hunger strikes in behalf of the continuing desperate plight of the country's peasantry (*New York Times*, December 27, 1988:3). The efforts for agrarian reform received additional support in March 1988 when the Catholic bishops issued a pastoral letter calling for land reform.

This was the sociopolitical context of the rightist coup attempt of May and of the subsequent political pressures and violence from the right. And these rightist activities are the larger context facing advocates of democratic reform in Guatemala. The electoral path can bring political office, but has not yet brought sufficient power to undertake significant reforms. The guerrilla path has yet to succeed either, bringing instead the horrific counterinsurgency detailed in chapter 5. Meanwhile, Gen. Efraín Ríos Montt reemerged in late 1989 as a leading candidate for the presidency, telling readers of a Guatemalan magazine, "A government for the people, by the people is no more than a French idiocy that's never happened" (*New York Times*, September 3, 1989:8).

Honduras

Honduran politics have been far less violent in recent decades than those of its neighbors, as explained throughout the preceding chapters of this book. Within its own traditions, though, the 1980s was a violent decade, with two serious rounds of rightist political killings. The first round was halted by popular revulsion and domestic political constraints. The second round, though, was still continuing at the decade's end, leaving serious concern for the country's near future.

It is now well established that some 123 people disappeared in Honduras during 1981–84, as reported by the United Nations Human Rights Commission (Americas Watch 1987:64).[17] Most of these deaths and disappearances were at the hands of a secret military unit organized in 1980 that functioned as an official death squad. A former member of the unit, now in exile, has testified that the special interrogation and kidnapping teams of "Batallion 316" detained, tortured, and killed over 100 suspected leftists in its network of secret jails between 1980 and 1984 (*New York Times*, May 2, 1987:1 ff.). There have been numerous reports that the C.I.A. knew of many of the kidnappings; the extent of its knowledge of the torture and killings has not been established (Americas Watch 1987:114–121).

This recourse to violence by the Honduran security forces corresponded to the initiation of its role as a staging base for the Contra war against Nicaragua and to the rise to power of General Gustavo Alvarez Martinez, who was the organizer of Batallion 316. When the Contra forces began coalescing in 1981 with U.S. money and Argentine trainers, Alvarez was the representative of the Honduran government to the joint staff organized to manage and coordinate the "secret war" (*Washington Post*, December 16, 1984:A27). He was even more helpful when he became the head of the armed forces in January 1982, working very closely with the hard-line U.S. ambassador, John D. Negroponte. Alvarez was forced out of his post in March 1984, for reasons unrelated to these abuses (*Washington Post*, April 2, 1984:A15). It is widely acknowledged that the human rights situation in Honduras improved substantially shortly after his departure; although torture of detainees continued, killings and disappearances virtually ceased through 1986 (Washington Office on Latin America 1987:69–70).

This widespread (for Honduras) violence of the early 1980s was said to have "shocked the nation" (Washington Office on Latin America 1987:69). When relatives of some of the victims filed suit against the government, the jurisdiction of the Inter-American Court of Human Rights was accepted by the civilian administration of José Azcona Hoyo. And, when the Court in 1988 found the Honduran government guilty in the 1981 disappearance of one of its citizens, the president's spokesman announced that the government "has no option but to respect the judgment fully (*New York Times*, July 30, 1988:1).

This encouraging record, though, was defiled by a resurgence of political violence at the end of the decade. Six political assassinations were reported in the first seven months of 1989, up from two the year before while 78 killings by the security forces and police were almost double the number of the prior year. Reports of torture and beatings were tripled over the previous year (*New York Times*, August 27, 1989). Government leaders deny any sanctioning of the violence but have acknowledged abusive behavior by soldiers and policemen at lower levels of their services. Officials claim that they are trying to prevent such abuses and to punish the guilty.

Honduran difficulties in strengthening the rule of law have been paralleled by shortcomings in the democratization of the country's political system. The president serving until 1986, Roberto Suazo Córdova, was generally perceived as "programmatically inept, venal, and corrupting"

(Rosenberg 1989:B321). His successor, José Azcona Hoyo, came to the end of his term perceived as a "caretaker," and as "little more than a firgurehead for the army" (*New York Times*, August 27, 1989). The political reality, realized by all, was that the military was the major power in the country, now more powerful than ever.

The impact of the United States has been contradictory on Honduran democratization. On the one hand, the United States played an important role in engineering the return to civilian government early in the decade and applied substantial pressure to ensure that Suazo Córdova would not succeed in his efforts to extend his tenure as president. In November 1989 Honduras had its third successive and successful presidential election.

On the other hand, the Honduran military received substantial financial assistance from the Reagan administration, in part to strengthen it against possible subversion, but also in part to reward the military for permitting its territory to be used by both the Contras and the U.S. military. As a result, the Honduran military's domination of the political system increased as a consequence of Reagan's Nicaraguan policy.[18] Honduras entered the 1990s, then, with a string of successful elections and a vibrant party system but with an enfeebled presidency shadowed by a domineering military.

CONCLUSION

This book has argued that substantial change in the agrarian systems of Central America is a precondition for justice and peace in the region. But history demonstrates that such changes infrequently occur. The record is also clear that there are limits to what an outside force can accomplish, even a hegemonic power as dominating as the United States is in Central America.

Occasionally, though, opportunities for change open due to shifts in the constellation of forces acting on a system. One of these rare opportunities occurred in Central America at the end of the 1970s. Dictators were deposed in Nicaragua and El Salvador at a time of high levels of popular mobilization, presenting a chance for significant and lasting structural change in both. Such successful reforms would have had an effect on Honduran politics and perhaps eventually on Guatemala.

A decade later, the outcome was otherwise. The Carter and Reagan administrations aligned the Salvadoran center with the military and eventually the right. This policy did not work, for which Salvadorans have paid a high price. In Nicaragua, the Reagan administration was unable to look past the rhetoric of the Sandinista leadership to the basic needs of Nicaraguan society. Resolving to crush the revolution, the Reagan policy crushed Nicaraguan society.

It is true that U.S. policy toward the region in the 1980s did emphasize democratization and important gains were registered in each country. However, a policy that emphasized the primacy of military solutions in El Salvador and Nicaragua also strengthened the position of the military in Honduras. Rather than being isolated in the region, then, the Guatemalan military and its dominating position were congruent with regional trends at the end of the decade.

The tragedy of U.S. policy toward the region, therefore, was more than the terrible record of deaths, devastation, and polarization. The tragedy was also the destruction of a historic opportunity. The claim here is not a naive one that if the opportunity had been seized, that change would have been easy and wholly beneficent. To the contrary, there would have been much conflict, tradeoffs, and individual suffering. A maximal outcome would have required sustained and intelligent international pressures to offset self-serving Leninism. There would have been a considerable cost for such change. The price paid by Central Americans because this opportunity was not seized, however, has been far greater.

The price could have been even more. Amid the analysis of systems and states, the efforts of individuals and their successes can be lost. How much greater the tragedy would have been without the courageous work of human rights monitors, school teachers, priests and other church workers, agricultural advisors, democratic politicians, health workers, labor and peasant organizers, of thousands of others working under dangerous conditions. And how much more excessive the Reagan policy would have been without the sustained commitment of U.S. citizen groups challenging his policy. And it will be the continuing efforts of such individuals that will help to create the next opportunity for change in Central America. Their sacrifices, including the lives of many, is one of the reasons why a better outcome is deserved.

NOTES

1. For a similar conclusion for agrarian reform since 1960, see Thiesenhusen (1989). Among the many case studies in this volume are several on Central American countries.

2. The decline in the terms of trade to 1985 for each country was as follows (in percentages): Costa Rica, 12; El Salvador, 31; Guatemala, 17; Honduras, 18; and Nicaragua, 2 (IDB 1989:Table II-2).

3. One of the most recent assessments finds the overall impact of the CBI to have been "modest" but when "measured against the expectations and standards set by the proponents of CBI in the Reagan administration, the initiative has clearly been a failure" (Paus 1988:208–209). In fact, just the cutting of the U.S. sugar quota (in response to domestic pressures) "possibly even outweighted" the gains for some of the region's countries. For supporting data, see Rosenberg (1989:B319).

4. For portrayals of the economic crisis and its human and political consequences see, in addition to these two sources, *New York Times* (December 20, 1987:20 and December 25, 1988:8).

5. The comment is by Francisco Mayorga, a former Sandinista economic advisor still living in Nicaragua. An example of the first position is the economist Father Xabier Gorostiaga, who estimates U.S. responsibility for the economic crisis at sixty percent, with the Sandinista policies perhaps ten percent responsible. For a report on a debate between the two, see *New York Times* (December 25, 1988:8).

6. The comment is from Joe Loconte, director of communications with the Council for Inter–American Security in Washington, D.C.

7. The sources for this paragraph are the May and August 1989 issues of *Envio*. Also see the informative interview in the June issue with Daniel Núñez, the president of the National Union of Farmers and Cattle Ranchers (UNAG). Núñez speaks, for example, of the importance to UNAG of maintaining a mixed economy and refers to a series of well-intended but inappropriate "top-down policies" (pp. 40–41).

8. This section is based on a number of press reports and two particularly clear and insightful analyses, *Envio* (March 1989:3–9) and Moreno (1989).

9. The accord is usually referred to as the Esquipulas Accord for the site of its signing or as the Arias Plan, in recognition of the leading role played by the president of Costa Rica, Oscar Arias, for which he was awarded the Nobel Peace Prize. The accord addressed the conflicts in each country but only the Nicaraguan dimension will be explored here. For a thorough evaluation of the varying degrees of compliance with the accord by the five countries, see Latin American Studies Association (1988).

10. This interpretation, often made by critics of the Reagan administration's purposes, was substantiated by House Speaker Jim Wright and subsequent press reports (*New York Times* September 21, 1988:6 and September 25:15).

11. The primary source for this section is an excellent survey of the "electoral map" by *Envio* (October 1989:3–17). She is described as follows: "With confusing speeches full of platitudes, incapable of debate, Violeta Chamorro could not make up for 60 years of political inexperience in just a few months" (p. 11).

12. Excellent and timely analyses of both ARENA and the FMLN are provided, respectively, by Miles and Ostertag (1989a) and (1989b). Also on newer thinking in the FMLN, see Karl (1989) and Villalobos (1989). For other useful and current analyses, see Blachman and Sharpe (1988–1989), *Envio* (May 1989), García (1989), and Smyth (1988–1989). Among the many press reports, insightful are *New York Times* (June 26, 1988:1+ and March 12, 1989:14) and a five-part series in the *Christian Science Monitor* beginning October 19, 1988.

13. As an example of the priorities of the Reagan administration, two-thirds of all of the funds that it gave to non-governmental organizations in El Salvador between 1985 and 1987 went to a right-wing think tank while only 9 percent went to groups involved in rural development (*Christian Science Monitor* August 28, 1989:1).

14. Americas Watch (1988b:7–8) blamed this increase in violence on rightist frustration with the political opening permitted by the Duarte administration and as a consequence of an amnesty approved in October 1987, which Americas Watch maintains

· has effectively given those who engage in political killings, especially the military and death squads allied with or tolerated by the military, the go-ahead for further killings by demonstrating that even the most heinous crimes can be forgiven by a sleight of hand.

It remains true that "no Salvadoran officer, nor any death squad member, has been prosecuted and criminally punished for a human rights violation" (p. 1).

15. The revolutionaries have formed an umbrella organization known as the National Revolutionary Guatemalan Union (URNG).

16. Among the more recent discussions of the rural reign of terror earlier in the decade, especially good are Carmack (1988) and Manz (1988).

17. For additional background also see, Americas Watch (1984), Committee for the Defense of Human Rights in Honduras (1985), and LeMoyne (1988).

18. When a new U.S. ambassador to Honduras, John Ferch, insisted on treating the civilian government as the highest authorities in the country, rather than the military high command, he was removed from his position in June 1986 after only ten months at his post (Americas Watch 1987:122). The overbearing presence of the United States in Honduras has had the unintended consequence of fueling anti-U.S. sentiment, intense expressions of which can be found across the political spectrum (*New York Times* April 9, 1988:6).

REFERENCES

AMERICAS WATCH (1984). *Honduras: On the Brink. A Report on Human Rights Based on a Mission of Inquiry.* New York: Americas Watch, Lawyers Committee for International Human Rights, and Washington Office on Latin America.

———(1987). *Human Rights in Honduras: Central America's "Sideshow".* New York: Americas Watch.

———(1988a). *Closing the Space: Human Rights in Guatemala, May 1987–October 1988.* New York: Americas Watch.

———(1988b). *Nightmare Revisited 1987–88.* New York: Americas Watch.

BLACHMAN, MORRIS J. and KENNETH E. SHARPE (1988–89). "Things Fall Apart in El Salvador." *World Policy Journal* 6, 1 (Winter):107–139.

BOYD, R. DEAN JR. (1989). "ARENA Policies Deepen Economic Crisis." *Times of the Americas* (September 20):12.

CARMACK, ROBERT M., ed. (1988). *Harvest of Violence: The Maya Indians and the Guatemalan Crisis.* Norman: University of Oklahoma Press.

COMMITTEE FOR THE DEFENSE OF HUMAN RIGHTS IN HONDURAS (1985). *Human Rights in Honduras 1984.* Translation of report by Committee for the Defense of Human Rights in Honduras. Washington, D.C.: Washington Office on Latin America and World Council of Churches.

GARCÍA, JOSE (1989). "El Salvador." In Abraham F. Lowenthal, ed., *Latin America and Caribbean Contemporary Record, 1986–1987, v. VI.* New York: Holmes & Meier.

KARL, TERRY (1989). "Negotiations or Total War: Salvador Samoyoa." *World Policy Journal* 6, 2 (Spring):321–355.

LATIN AMERICAN STUDIES ASSOCIATION COMMISSION on COMPLIANCE with the CENTRAL AMERICA PEACE ACCORD (1988). *Extraordinary Opportunities ... And New Risks.* Pittsburgh: Latin American Studies Association.

LEMOYNE, JAMES (1988). "Testify to Torture." *New York Times Magazine* (June 5):44–47.

MANZ, BEATRICE (1988). *Refugees of a Hidden War: The Aftermath of Counterinsurgency in Guatemala.* Albany: State University of New York Press.

MILES, SARA and BOB OSTERTAG (1989a). "D'Aubuisson's New ARENA." *NACLA Report on the Americas* XXIII, 2 (July).

———(1989b). "FMLN's New Thinking." *NACLA Report on the Americas* XXIII, 3 (September).

MORENO, DARIO (1989). "The Sandinistas and Their Opponents." Paper presented at annual meeting of the Southeastern Council on Latin American Studies, Myrtle Beach, S.C., April 13–15.

PAUS, EVA, ed. (1988). *Struggle Against Dependence: Nontraditional Export Growth in Central America and the Caribbean.* Boulder: Westview Press.

ROSENBERG, MARK B. (1989). "Honduras." In Abraham F. Lowenthal, ed., *Latin America and Caribbean Contemporary Record, 1986–1987, v. VI.* New York: Holmes & Meier.

SMYTH, FRANK (1988–89). "Consensus or Crisis? Without Duarte in El Salvador." *Journal of Interamerican Studies and World Affairs* 30, 4 (Winter):29–52.

THIESENHUSEN, WILLIAM C., ed. (1989). *Searching for Agrarian Reform in Latin America.* Boston: Unwin Hyman.

UNITED STATES, DEPARTMENT OF STATE (1988, November). "The Situation in Central America." Washington, D.C.: United States Department of State Bureau of Public Affairs.

VILLALOBOS, JOAQUÍN (1989). "A Democratic Revolution for El Salvador." *Foreign Policy* #74 (Spring):103–122.

WASHINGTON OFFICE on LATIN AMERICA (1987). *Police Aid and Political Will.* Washington, D.C.: Washington Office on Latin America.

References

ADAMS, DALE W., DOUGLAS H. GRAHAM, and J. D. VON PISCHKE (1984). *Undermining Rural Development with Cheap Credit*. Boulder, CO: Westview Press.

ADAMS, F. GERARD, and JERE R. BEHRMAN (1982). *Commodity Exports and Economic Development*. Lexington, MA: Lexington Books.

ADAMS, RICHARD N. (1968–69). "The Development of the Guatemalan Military." *Studies in Comparative International Development*, 10(5).

——— (1970). *Crucifixion by Power: Essays on Guatemalan National Social Structure, 1944–1966*. Austin: University of Texas Press.

ADAMS, RICHARD N., ed. (1957). *Political Changes in Guatemalan Indian Communities: A Symposium*. New Orleans: Middle American Research Institute.

ADELMAN, IRMA (1980). "Income Distribution, Economic Development and Land Reform." *American Behavioral Scientist*, 23(3), 437–456.

ADELMAN, IRMA, and SHERMAN ROBINSON (1978). *Income Distribution Policy in Developing Countries: A Case Study of Korea*. Stanford, CA: Stanford University Press.

ADLER, JOHN H., EUGENE R. SCHLESINGER, and ERNEST C. OLSON (1952). *Public Finance and Economic Development in Guatemala*. Stanford, CA: Stanford University Press.

AGUILERA PERALTA, GABRIEL (1979). "The Massacre at Panzós and Capitalist Development in Guatemala." *Monthly Review*, 31(7), 13–24.

ALAS, HIGINIO (1982). *El Salvador: ¿Por qué la Insurrección?*. San José: Permanent Secretariat of the Commission for the Defense of Human Rights in Central America.

ALEXANDER, ROBERT J. (1984). *Agrarian Reform in Latin America*. New York: Macmillan.

ALLEN, ROY, CLAUDIA DODGE, and ANDREW SCHMITZ (1983). "Voluntary Export Restraints as Protection Policy: The U.S. Beef Cases." *American Journal of Agricultural Economics*, 65(2), 291–296.

América Indígena (1974). 43(2).

AMERICAS WATCH COMMITTEE [AWC] (1982). *Human Rights in Guatemala: No Neutrals Allowed*. New York: Author.

——— (1983). *Creating a Desolation and Calling It Peace*. New York: Author.

——— (1984, January 26, February 6). *Protection of the Weak and Unarmed: The Dispute over Counting Human Rights Violations in El Salvador*. Reprinted in U.S., House, Committee on Foreign Affairs. *The Situation in El Salvador*. Hearings before subcommittees on Human Rights and International Organizations and on Western Hemisphere Affairs. 98th Congress, 2nd session, pp. 291–342.

——— (1985). *Violations of the Laws of War by Both Sides in Nicaragua 1981–1985*. New York: Author.

AMERICAS WATCH COMMITTEE and AMERICAN CIVIL LIBERTIES UNION (1982). *Report on Human Rights in El Salvador*. New York: Random House.

AMNESTY INTERNATIONAL [AI] (1977). *The Republic of Nicaragua*. London: Author.
——— (1981a). *"Disappearances": A Workbook*. New York: Author.
——— (1981b). *Guatemala: A Government Program of Political Murder*. New York: Author.
ANDERSON, CHARLES W. (1961). "Politics and Development Policy in Central America." *Midwest Journal of Political Science, 5*(4), 332–350.
ANDERSON, THOMAS P. (1971). *Matanza: El Salvador's Communist Revolt of 1932*. Lincoln: University of Nebraska Press.
——— (1981). *The War of the Dispossessed: Honduras and El Salvador, 1969*. Lincoln: University of Nebraska Press.
——— (1982). *Politics in Central America*. New York: Praeger.
ARROYO, GONZALO (1978). "Agriculture and Multinational Corporations in Latin America." In Vilo Harle, ed., *Political Economy of Food*. Farnborough, England: Saxon House, Teakfield.
ASHE, JEFFREY (1978). *Rural Development in Costa Rica*. New York: ACCION International.
ASSOCIATED PRESS [AP] (1981, May 5). "Military Aid to Guatemala Favored by State Department If It Is Sought." *Chattanooga (TN) Times*, p. A6.
——— (1984, February 15). "Salvadoran Land Program is Criticized." *New York Times*, p. A3.
ASTORGA LIRA, ENRIQUE (1975). *Evaluación de los Asentamientos y Cooperativas Campesinas en Honduras*. Tegucigalpa: National Agrarian Institute.
AUSTIN, JAMES, JONATHAN FOX, and WALTER KRUGER (1985). "The Role of the Revolutionary State in the Nicaraguan Food System." *World Development, 13*(1), 15–40.
AYBAR DE SOTO, JOSÉ M. (1978). *Dependency and Intervention: The Case of Guatemala in 1954*. Boulder, CO: Westview Press.
BAER, DONALD E. (1973). "Income and Export Taxation of Agriculture in Costa Rica and Honduras." *Journal of Developing Areas, 8*(1), 39–54.
BALOYRA, ENRIQUE (1982). *El Salvador in Transition*. Chapel Hill: University of North Carolina Press.
BARAHONA RIERA, FRANCISCO (1980). *Reforma Agraria y Poder Político*. San José: Editorial Universidad de Costa Rica.
BARKIN, DAVID (1982). "The Impact of Agribusiness on Rural Development." In Scott McNall, ed., *Current Perspectives in Social Theory: Vol. 1*. Greenwich, CT: JAI Press.
BARRACLOUGH, SOLON (1970). "Agricultural Policies and Strategies of Land Reform." In Irving L. Horowitz, ed., *Masses in Latin America*. New York: Oxford University Press.
——— (1973). *Agrarian Structure in Latin America*. Lexington, MA: Lexington Books.
——— (1983). *A Preliminary Analysis of the Nicaraguan Food System* (Report No. 83.1). Geneva: United Nations Research Institute for Social Development.
BARRY, TOM (1986). *Guatemala: The Politics of Counterinsurgency*. Albuquerque, NM: Inter-Hemispheric Education Resource Center.
BAUER PAÍZ, ALFONSO (1956). *Cómo Opera el Capital Yanqui en Centroamerica (El Caso de Guatemala)*. Mexico City: Editoria Ibero-Mexicana.
BELLI, PEDRO (1970). "Farmers' Response to Price in Underdeveloped Areas: The Nicaraguan Case." *American Economic Review, 60*(2), 385–392.
——— (1977). "Bitter Lemons: The Central American Experience in the Export of Fruits and Vegetables." *Baylor Business Studies, 8*, 23–33.
BERRY, R. ALBERT, and WILLIAM R. CLINE (1979). *Agrarian Structure and Productivity in Developing Countries*. Baltimore, MD: Johns Hopkins University Press.
BERRYMAN, PHILIP (1984). *The Religious Roots of Rebellion*. Maryknoll, NY: Orbis.
BLACHMAN, MORRIS J., WILLIAM M. LEOGRANDE, and KENNETH SHARPE, eds. (1986). *Confronting Revolution: Security through Diplomacy in Central America*. New York: Pantheon.
BLACK, GEORGE (1981). *Triumph of the People: The Sandinista Revolution in Nicaragua*. London: Zed Press.

———— (1983a). "Garrison Guatemala." *NACLA Report on the Americas*, 17(1).

———— (1983b). "Guatemala—The War Is Not Over." *NACLA Report on the Americas*, 17(2).

———— (1985). "Under the Gun." *NACLA Report on the Americas*, 19(6), 10–24.

BLASIER, COLE (1976). *The Hovering Giant: U.S. Responses to Revolutionary Change in Latin America*. Pittsburgh: University of Pittsburgh Press.

BLUTSTEIN, HOWARD I. [and others] (1971). *Area Handbook for Honduras*. Washington, DC: U.S. Government Printing Office.

BONNER, RAYMOND (1984). *Weakness and Deceit: U.S. Policy and El Salvador*. New York: Times Books.

BOOTH, JOHN A. (1980). "A Guatemalan Nightmare: Levels of Political Violence, 1966–1972." *Journal of Inter-American Studies and World Affairs*, 22, 195–220.

———— (1985). *The End and the Beginning: The Nicaraguan Revolution* (2nd ed.). Boulder, CO: Westview Press.

———— (1986, December). "War and the Nicaraguan Revolution." *Current History*, 88, 405–408+.

BOOTH, JOHN A., and MITCHELL SELIGSON (1979). "Peasants as Activists: A Reevaluation of Political Participation in the Countryside." *Comparative Political Studies*, 12(1), 29–59.

BOWEN, GORDEN (1983). "U.S. Foreign Policy Toward Radical Change: Covert Operations in Guatemala, 1950–1954." *Latin American Perspectives*, 10.

———— (1985). "The Political Economy of State Terrorism: Barrier to Human Rights in Guatemala." In George W. Shepherd, Jr., and Ved P. Nanda, eds., *Human Rights and Third World Development*. Westport, CT: Greenwood Press.

BOYER, JEFFERSON C. (1982). *Agrarian Capitalism and Peasant Praxis in Southern Honduras*. Unpublished doctoral dissertation, University of North Carolina, Chapel Hill.

BRINTNALL, DOUGLAS E. (1979). *Revolt Against the Dead: The Modernization of a Mayan Community In the Highlands of Guatemala*. New York: Gordon and Breach.

BROCKETT, CHARLES D. (1984a). "Malnutrition, Public Policy and Agrarian Change in Guatemala." *Journal of Inter-American Studies and World Affairs*, 26(4), 477–497.

———— (1984b). "The Right to Food and United States Policy in Guatemala." *Human Rights Quarterly*, 6(3), 366–380.

———— (1987a). "Public Policy, Peasants, and Rural Development in Honduras." *Journal of Latin American Studies*, 19(1), 69–86.

———— (1987b). "The Commercialization of Agriculture and Rural Economic Security: The Case of Honduras." *Studies in Comparative International Development*, 22(1), 82–102.

BROOKS, JOSEPH J. (1967). "The Impact of U.S. Cotton Policy on Economic Development: The Cases of El Salvador and Nicaragua." *Public & International Affairs*, 5, 191–214.

BROWN, ANTOINETTE B. (1983). "Communication." *Culture and Agriculture*, 21, 8+.

BROWN, MARION (1971). "Peasant Organization as Vehicle of Reform." In Peter Dorner, ed., *Land Reform in Latin America: Issues and Cases*. Madison: University of Wisconsin Land Tenure Center.

BROWNING, DAVID (1971). *El Salvador: Landscape and Society*. Oxford: Clarendon Press.

———— (1983). "Agrarian Reform in El Salvador." *Journal of Latin American Studies*, 15(2), 399–405.

BUCKLEY, TOM (1984). *Violent Neighbors: El Salvador, Central America and the United States*. New York: Times Books.

BURBACH, ROGER, and PATRICIA FLYNN (1980). *Agribusiness in the Americas*. New York: Monthly Review Press.

BURGOS-DEBRAY, ELIZABETH, ed. (1984). *I, Rigoberta Menchú: An Indian Woman in Guatemala*. London: Verso.

BURKE, MELVIN (1976). "El Sistema de Plantación y la Proletarización del Trabajo Agrícola en El Salvador." *Estudios Centroamericanos*, 31, 473–486.

Burrows, Charles R. (1962, November 18). Letter to Edward M. Rowell, Department of State. Dorchester, MA: John F. Kennedy Library. Presidential office files, countries, box 18.
——— (1969, September 4). Recorded interview by Dennis J. O'Brien. Dorchester, MA: John F. Kennedy Library. Oral History Program.

Caballero, José María (1984). "Agriculture and the Peasantry under Industrialization Pressures: Lessons from the Peruvian Experience." *Latin American Research Review*, 19(2), 3–42.

Cambranes, J. C. (1985). *Coffee and Peasants: The Origins of the Modern Plantation Economy in Guatemala, 1853–1897*. South Woodstock, VT: Plumsock Mesoamerican Studies.

Cannon, Lou (1982, December 6). "Latin Trip an Eye-Opener for Reagan." *Washington Post*, p. A17.

Cannon, Lou, and Margaret Shapiro (1985, June 12). "Democrats Soothed on Nicaragua." *Washington Post*, p. A1.

Cardenal, Fernando (1976, June 8). "Prepared Statement." U.S., House, Committee on International Relations. *Human Rights in Nicaragua, Guatemala, and El Salvador: Implications for U.S. Policy*. Hearings before Subcommittee on International Organizations. 94th Congress, 2nd session, pp. 17–29.

Cardona, Rokael (1978). "Descripción de la Estructura y Económica del Agro Guatemalteco 1954–1975." *Política y Sociedad*, 6, 5–43.

Cardoso, Ciro F. S. (1977). "The Formation of the Coffee Estate in Nineteenth-Century Costa Rica." In Kenneth Duncan and Ian Rutledge, eds., *Land and Labour in Latin America*. London: Cambridge University Press.

Carias, Marco, and Daniel Slutzky (1971). *La Guerra Inutil, Análisis Socio-económico del Conflicto entre Honduras y El Salvador*. San José: Editorial Universitaria Centroamericana.

Carmack, Robert M. (1983). "Spanish-Indian Relations in Highland Guatemala, 1800–1944." In Murdo MacLeod and Robert Wasserstrom, eds., *Spaniards and Indians in Southeastern Mesoamerica*. Lincoln: University of Nebraska Press.

Carter, W. E. (1969). *New Lands and Old Traditions: Kekchi Cultivators in the Guatemalan Lowlands*. Gainesville: University of Florida Press.

Carvajal, Manuel J. (1979a). *Bibliography of Poverty and Related Topics in Costa Rica*. Unpublished paper, U.S. Agency for International Development, Washington, DC.
——— (1979b). *Report on Income Distribution and Poverty in Costa Rica* (General Working Document No. 2). Washington, DC: U.S. Agency for International Development.

Central America Report [CAR] (1986, April 25). "UPEB No Match for Banana Companies." *Central America Report*, pp. 114–115.

Central American Historical Institute [CAHI] (1983). *A Chronology of U.S.–Nicaraguan Relations: Policy and Impact*. Washington, DC: Central American Historical Institute.

Central American Information Office [CAMINO] (1982). *El Salvador: Background to the Crisis*. Boston: Author.

Chamorro, Edgar (1986, January 9). "Terror Is the Most Effective Weapon of Nicaragua's 'Contras'" (Letter to the editor). *New York Times*, p. A22.

Chapin, Norman (1980). "A Few Comments on Land Tenure and the Course of Agrarian Reform in El Salvador." In *El Salvador: Agrarian Reform Organization Project Paper*, Annex IIA, *A Social Analysis*. Washington, DC: U.S. Agency for International Development.

Chavez, Lydia (1983, June 5). "Salvadoran Plan for Land Changes Suffers Setbacks." *New York Times*, pp. A1, A5.

Checchi, Vincent (1959). *Honduras: A Problem in Economic Development*. New York: Twentieth Century Fund.

CHENERY, HOLLIS (1979). *Structural Change and Development Policy.* Washington, DC: World Bank.

CHERNOW, RON (1979, May). "The Strange Death of Bill Woods." *Mother Jones,* pp. 32–41.

CHINCHILLA, NORMA STOLTZ (1983). "Interpreting Social Change in Guatemala: Modernization, Dependency, and Articulation of Modes of Production." In Ronald H. Chilcote and Dale L. Johnson, eds., *Theories of Development: Mode of Production or Dependency?* Beverly Hills, CA: Sage.

CLAIRMONTE, FREDERICK F. (1975). "Bananas." In Cheryl Payer, ed., *Commodity Trade of the Third World.* New York: Wiley.

CLARK, CAL (1985, August). "The Taiwan Exception: Regime Change as a Prerequisite for Economic Development." Paper presented at the annual meeting of the American Political Science Association, New Orleans.

CODY, EDWARD (1984, September 13). "El Salvador Tightens Rules For Bombing." *Washington Post,* p. 1+.

COLBURN, FORREST D. (1982). "Current Studies of Peasants and Rural Development: Application of the Political Economy Approach." *World Politics,* 34(3), 437–449.

——— (1986). *Post-Revolutionary Nicaragua: State, Class, and the Dilemmas of Agrarian Policy.* Berkeley: University of California Press.

COLBURN, FORREST D., and SILVIO DE FRANCO (1985). "Privilege, Production and Revolution: The Case of Nicaragua." *Comparative Politics,* 17(3), 277–290.

COLBY, BENJAMIN N., and PIERRE L. VANDEN BERGHE (1969). *Ixil Country.* Berkeley CA: University of California Press.

COLLINS, JOSEPH (1986). *Nicaragua: What Difference Could a Revolution Make?* (3rd ed.). New York: Grove Press.

CONROY, MICHAEL E. (1985). "Economic Legacies and Policies: Performances and Critique." In Thomas W. Walker, ed., *Nicaragua: The First Five Years.* Boulder, CO: Westview Press.

CONWAY, H. MCKINLEY, Jr. (1963). *El Salvador: A "Bright Spot" in Central America.* Atlanta: Conway Publications.

CORBO, VITTORIO, ANN O. KRUEGER, and FERNANDO OSSA, eds. (1986). *Export-Oriented Development Strategies: The Success of Five Newly Industrializing Countries.* Boulder, CO: Westview Press.

DAINES, SAMUEL R. (1977). *Analysis of Small Farms and Rural Poverty in El Salvador.* Unpublished report prepared for the U.S. Agency for International Development/El Salvador, San Salvador.

DAVIDSON, JOHN R. (1976a). *The Basic Village Education Project in Guatemala.* Washington, DC: U.S. Agency for International Development, Manpower Development Division.

——— (1976b). *The Rural Credit and Cooperative Development Project in Guatemala* (Case Studies in Development Assistance, No. 1). Washington, DC: U.S. Agency for International Development.

DAVIS, L. HARLAN (1973). "Foreign Aid to the Small Farmer: The El Salvador Experience." *Inter-American Economic Affairs,* 29(1), 81–91.

DAVIS, L. HARLAN, and DAVID E. WEISENBORN (1981). "Small Farmer Market Development: The El Salvador Experience." *Journal of Developing Areas,* 15(3), 404–415.

DAVIS, SHELTON H. (1983a). Introduction to *Voices of the Survivors: The Massacre at Finca San Francisco, Guatemala,* ed. by Julie Hodson. Cambridge, MA: Cultural Survival, Inc., and Anthropology Resource Center.

——— (1983b). "The Social Roots of Political Violence in Guatemala." *Cultural Survival Quarterly,* 7(1), 4–11.

——— (1983c). "State Violence and Agrarian Crisis in Guatemala." In Martin Diskin, ed., *Trouble in Our Backyard: Central America and the United States in the Eighties.* New York: Pantheon.

DAVIS, SHELTON H., and JULIE HODSON (1982). *Witnesses to Political Violence in Guatemala: The Suppression of a Rural Development Movement* (Impact Audit 2). Boston MA: Oxfam America.

DEERE, CARMEN (1982). "A Comparative Analysis of Agrarian Reform in El Salvador and Nicaragua." *Development and Change, 13*, 1–41.

DEERE, CARMEN, and PETER MARCHETTI, S. J. (1981). "The Worker-Peasant Alliance in the First Year of the Nicaraguan Agrarian Reform." *Latin American Perspectives, 8*(2), 40–73.

DEERE, CARMEN, PETER MARCHETTI, S. J., and NOLA REINHARDT (1985). "The Peasantry and the Development of Sandinista Agrarian Policy, 1979–1984." *Latin American Research Review, 20*(3), 75–109.

DESSAINT, ALAIN Y. (1962). "Effects of the Hacienda and Plantation System on Guatemala's Indians." *América Indígena, 22*(4), 323–354.

DEWITT, R. PETER (1977). *The Inter-American Development Bank and Political Influence.* New York: Praeger.

DEYOUNG, KAREN (1982, January 25). "Salvadoran Land Reform Imperiled, Report Says." *Washington Post,* pp. A1+.

DISKIN, MARTIN (1982). "1982 Supplement" to *El Salvador Land Reform 1980–1981: Impact Audit,* by Laurence R. Simon and James C. Stephens, Jr. Boston, MA: Oxfam America.

—— (1984a, January 26, February 6). "The Direction of Agrarian Reform in El Salvador." Reprinted in U.S., House, Committee on Foreign Affairs. *The Situation in El Salvador.* Hearings before subcommittees on Human Rights and International Organizations and on Western Hemisphere Affairs. 98th Congress, 2nd session, pp. 87–128.

—— (1984b, January 26, February 6). "Prepared Statement." U.S., House, Committee on Foreign Affairs. *The Situation in El Salvador.* Hearings before subcommittees on Human Rights and International Organizations and on Western Hemisphere Affairs. 98th Congress, 2nd session, pp. 84–86.

DORNER, PETER, ed. (1971). *Land Reform in Latin America: Issues and Cases.* Madison: University of Wisconsin Land Tenure Center.

—— (1972). *Land Reform and Economic Development.* Baltimore, MD: Penguin.

DOSAL, PAUL J. (1985). "Accelerating Dependent Development and Revolution: Nicaragua and the Alliance for Progress." *Inter-American Economic Affairs, 38*(3), 75–96.

DOZIER, CRAIG L. (1958). *Indigenous Tropical Agriculture in Central America.* Washington, DC: National Academy of Sciences.

DUNCAN, KENNETH, and RUTLEDGE, IAN, eds. (1977). *Land and Labour in Latin America: Essays on the Development of Agrarian Capitalism in the Nineteenth and Twentieth Centuries.* London: Cambridge University Press.

DUNKERLEY, JAMES (1982). *The Long War: Dictatorship and Revolution in El Salvador.* London: Junction Books.

DURHAM, WILLIAM (1979). *Scarcity and Survival in Central America.* Stanford, CA: Stanford University Press.

EBEL, ROLAND H. (1964). "Political Change in Guatemala: Indian Communities." *Journal of Inter-American Studies, 6*(1), pp. 91–104.

EDELMAN, MARC (1985). "Back from the Brink." *NACLA Report on the Americas, 19*(6), pp. 37–46.

ELLIS, FRANK (1983). *Las Transnacionales del Banano en Centroamerica.* San José: Editorial Universitaria Centroamericana.

ENRIQUEZ, LAURA J. (1985). "The Dilemmas of Agro-export Planning." In Thomas W. Walker, ed., *Nicaragua: The First Five Years.* Boulder, CO: Westview Press.

EVANS, PETER (1985). "After Dependency: Recent Studies of Class, State, and Industrialization." *Latin American Research Review, 20*(2), 149–160.

FALLA, RICARDO (1978). *Quiché Rebelde*. Guatemala City: Editorial Universitaria de Guatemala.

FEDER, ERNEST (1977). *Strawberry Imperialism*. The Hague: Institute of Social Studies.

——— (1981). "The World Bank—FIRA Scheme in Action in Tempoal, Veracruz." In Rosemary E. Galli, ed., *The Political Economy of Rural Devlopment*. Albany: State University of New York Press.

FFRENCH-DAVIS, RICARDO, and ERNESTO TIRONI (1982). *Latin America and the New International Economic Order*. London: Macmillan.

FIELDS, GARY S. (1980). *Poverty, Inequality, and Development*. New York: Cambridge University Press.

FITZGERALD, E. V. K. (1985). "Agrarian Reform as a Model of Accumulation: The Case of Nicaragua Since 1979." *Journal of Development Studies*, 22(1), 208–225.

FLETCHER, LEHMAN B., ERIC GRABER, W. C. MERRILL, and E. THORBECKE (1970). *Guatemala's Economic Development: The Role of Agriculture*. Ames: Iowa State Press.

FONCK, CARLOS O. (1972). *Modernity and Public Policies in the Context of the Peasant Sector: Honduras as a Case Study*. Unpublished doctoral dissertation, Cornell University, Ithaca, NY.

FORCHÉ, CAROLYN, and PHILIP WHEATON (1980). *History and Motivations of U.S. Involvement in the Control of the Peasant Movement in El Salvador*. Washington, DC: Ecumenical Program for Interamerican Commitment in Action.

FORD, PETER (1986, June 23). "Guatemala inches forward." *Christian Science Monitor (Boston)*, p. 1+.

Foreign Agriculture (1960). "Costa Rica's Livestock Industry." 12, 15–16.

FOX, JOHN W. (1978). *Quiché Conquest: Centralism and Regionalism in Highland Guatemalan State Development*. Albuquerque: University of New Mexico Press.

GALLI, ROSEMARY E. (1981). "Colombia: Rural Development as Social and Economic Control." In Rosemary E. Galli, ed., *The Political Economy of Rural Development: Peasants, International Capital, and the State*. Albany: State University of New York Press.

GAYOSO, ANTONIO (1970). *Land Reform in Guatemala* (Spring Review Country Paper). Washington, DC: U.S. Agency for International Development.

GHOSE, AJIT KUMAR (1983). *Agrarian Reform in Contemporary Developing Countries*. Boston, MA: St. Martin's.

GILBERT, DENNIS (1985). "The Bourgeoisie." In Thomas W. Walker, ed., *Nicaragua: The First Five Years*. Boulder, CO: Westview Press.

——— (1986). "Nicaragua." In Morris J. Blachman, William M. LeoGrande, and Kenneth Sharpe, eds., *Confronting Revolution: Security Through Diplomacy in Central America*. New York: Pantheon.

GOLDBERG, RAY A. (1981). "The Role of the Multinational Corporation." *American Journal of Agricultural Economics*, 63(2), 367–374.

GOLDBERG, RAY A., and LEONARD M. WILSON (1974). *Agribusiness Management for Developing Countries—Latin America*. Cambridge, MA: Ballinger.

GÓMEZ, LEONEL, and BRUCE CAMERON (1981). "American Myths." *Foreign Policy*, 43, 71–78.

GONDOLF, ED. (1981) "Community Development Amidst Political Violence: Lessons from Guatemala." *Community Development Journal*, 16(3), 228–236.

GORDON-ASHWORTH, FIONA (1984). *International Commodity Control: A Contemporary History and Appraisal*. New York: St. Martin's.

GOSHKE, JOHN M., and KAREN DeYOUNG (1977, October 24). "U.S. Aid to Nicaragua—'Garbled' Rights Message." *Washington Post*.

GOTT, RICHARD (1971). *Guerrilla Movements in Latin America*. New York: Doubleday.

GRABER, ERIC S. (1980). *Income Distribution, Employment and Social Well-Being in*

Guatemala: A Survey. Unpublished paper, U.S. Agency for International Development, Washington, DC.

GRIFFIN, KEITH (1978). *International Inequality and National Poverty.* New York: Macmillan.

GRIFFITH, WILLIAM J. (1965). *Empires in the Wilderness: Foreign Colonization and Development in Guatemala, 1834–1844.* Chapel Hill: University of North Carolina Press.

GRINDLE, MERILEE S. (1986). *State and Countryside: Development Policy and Agrarian Politics in Latin America.* Baltimore, MD: Johns Hopkins University Press.

GUDMUNDSON, LOWELL (1983). "Costa Rica Before Coffee: Occupational Distribution, Wealth Inequality, and Elite Society in the Village Economy of the 1840s." *Journal of Latin American Studies, 15*(2), 427–452.

GUESS, GEORGE M. (1979). "Pasture Expansion, Forestry, and Development Contradictions. The Case of Costa Rica." *Studies in Comparative International Development, 14,* 42–55.

HALL, CAROLYN (1985). *Costa Rica: A Geographical Interpretation in Historical Perspective.* Boulder, CO: Westview Press.

HANDY, JIM (1984). *Gift of the Devil: A History of Guatemala.* Boston, MA: South End Press.

HARNESS, VERNON, L., and ROBERT D. PUGH (1970). *Cotton in Central America* (Foreign Agricultural Service Publication No. M–154). Washington, DC: Department of Agriculture.

HARRISON, PETER D., and B. L. TURNER (1978). *Pre-Hispanic Maya Agriculture.* Albuquerque: University of New Mexico Press.

HATCH, JOHN K., and AQUILES LANAO FLORES (1977, August 19). *An Evaluation of the AIFLD/HISTADAUT Project Proposal to Assist Peasant Federations.* Paper prepared for U.S. Agency for International Development, Washington, DC.

HATCH, L. UPTON, GLENN C. W. AMES, and L. HARLAN DAVIS (1977). *Small Agricultural Producers Credit Programs: El Salvador; A Case Study* (Case Studies in Development Assistance, No. 3). Washington, DC: U.S. Agency for International Development.

HEMPHILL, ALAN K. (1976). "Livestock Prospects Mixed in Central America—Mexico." *Foreign Agriculture, 14,* 29.

HERRING, HUBERT (1964). *A History of Latin America from the Beginning to the Present.* New York: Knopf.

HERRING, RONALD J. (1983). *Land to the Tiller: The Political Economy of Agrarian Reform in South Asia.* New Haven: Yale University Press.

HEWITT DE ALCANTARA, CYNTHIA (1973–74). "The Green Revolution as History: the Mexican Experience." *Development and Change, 5*(2), 25–44.

——— (1976). *Modernizing Mexican Agriculture: Socioeconomic Implications of Technological Change, 1940–1970.* Geneva: United Nations Research Institute for Social Development.

HILDEBRAND, JOHN R. (1969). *Economic Development: A Latin American Emphasis.* Austin, TX: Pemberton Press.

HILLMAN, JIMMYE S. (1981). "The Role of Export Cropping in Less Developed Countries." *American Journal of Agricultural Economics, 63*(2), 375–383.

HOLLAND, BARBARA J. (1973). *The Dynamics of Health: Nicaragua.* Washington, DC: U.S. Government Printing Office.

HOUGH, RICHARD, JOHN KELLEY, STEVE MILLER, RUSSELL DEROSSIER, FRED L. MANN, and MITCHELL A. SELIGSON (1983). *Land and Labor in Guatemala: An Assessment.* Washington, DC: U.S. Agency for International Development and Development Associates.

HOY, DON R. (1984). "Environmental Protection and Economic Development in Guatemala's Western Highlands." *Journal of Developing Areas, 18*(2), 161–176.

HUIZER, GERRIT (1972). *The Revolutionary Potential of Peasants in Latin America.* Lexington, MA: Lexington Books.

ICKIS, JOHN C. (1983). "Structural Responses to New Rural Development Strategies." In David C. Korten and Felipe B. Alfonso, eds., *Bureaucracy and the Poor*. West Hartford, CT: Kumarian Press.

IMMERMAN, RICHARD H. (1982). *The CIA in Guatemala: The Foreign Policy of Intervention.* Austin: University of Texas Press.

INTER-AMERICAN DEVELOPMENT BANK [IDB] (1976). *Informe General sobre el Desarrollo Agropecuario y Rural de El Salvador*. Washington, DC: Author.

——— (various years). *Economic and Social Progress in Latin America*. Washington, DC: Author.

INTERNATIONAL AGRICULTURAL DEVELOPMENT SERVICE [IADS] (1981). *Agricultural Development Indicators*. New York: Author.

INTERNATIONAL BANK FOR RECONSTRUCTION AND DEVELOPMENT [IBRD] (1953). *The Economic Development of Nicaragua*. Baltimore, MD: Johns Hopkins University Press.

INTERNATIONAL INSTITUTE OF AGRICULTURE (1947). *The World's Coffee*. Rome: U.N. Food and Agricultural Organization.

International Labour Review [ILR] (1963), "Agrarian Reform Law in Honduras." 87(6). 573–580.

INTERNATIONAL WORK GROUP FOR INDIGENOUS AFFAIRS [IWGIA] (1978). *Guatemala 1978: The Massacre at Panzós*. Copenhagen: Author.

JACOBY, ERICH H. (1971). *Man and Land: The Fundamental Issues in Development*. New York: Knopf.

DE JANVRY, ALAIN (1981). *The Agrarian Question and Reformism in Latin America*. Baltimore, MD: Johns Hopkins University Press.

JOHNSON, D. GALE, and G. EDWARD SCHUH (1983). *The Role of Markets in the World Food Economy*. Boulder, CO: Westview Press.

JOHNSON, KENNETH F. (1972). "Guatemala: From Terrorism to Terror." *Conflict Studies, 23*, 4–17.

——— (1973). "On the Guatemalan Political Violence." *Politics & Society, 4*(1), 55–83.

JOHNSTON, BRUCE F., and WILLIAM C. CLARK (1982). *Redesigning Rural Development: A Strategic Perspective*. Baltimore, MD: Johns Hopkins University Press.

JONES, CHESTER LLOYD (1966, originally published 1940). *Guatemala: Past and Present*. New York: Russell & Russell.

JONES, JEFFREY R. (1984). "The Central American Energy Problem: Anthropological Perspectives on Fuelwood Supply and Production." *Culture and Agriculture, 22*, 6–9.

KAIMOWITZ, DAVID (1980). "Nicaraguan Coffee Harvest 1979–80: Public Policy and the Private Sector." *Development and Change, 11*(4), 497–516.

KAIMOWITZ, DAVID, and DAVID STANFIELD (1985). "The Organization of Production Units in the Nicaraguan Agrarian Reform." *Inter-American Economic Affairs, 39*(1), 51–78.

KARNES, THOMAS L. (1978). *Tropical Enterprise: The Standard Fruit & Steamship Company in Latin America*. Baton Rouge: Louisiana State University Press.

KARUSH, G. E. (1978). "Plantations, Population, and Poverty: The Roots of the Demographic Crisis in El Salvador." *Studies in Comparative International Development, 8*(3), 59–75.

KEENE, BEVERLY (1980). "Export-Cropping in Central America" (Background Paper No. 43). Washington, DC: Bread for the World.

KENT, GEORGE (1984). *The Political Economy of Hunger*. New York: Praeger.

KEPNER, CHARLES DAVID, Jr., and JAY HENRY SOOTHILL (1967, originally published 1935). *The Banana Empire: A Case Study of Economic Imperialism*. New York: Russell & Russell.

KESSING, DONALD B. (1981). "Exports and Policy in Latin American Countries: Prospects for the World Economy and for Latin American Exports, 1980–90." In Warner Baer and Malcolm Gillis, eds., *Export Diversification and the New Protectionism*. Champaign: University of Illinois Press.

KINCAID, DOUGLAS (1985). "'We Are the Agrarian Reform': Rural Politics and Agrarian Reform." In Nancy Peckenham and Annie Street, eds., *Honduras: Portrait of a Captive Nation*. New York: Praeger, 135–147.

KING, RUSSELL (1977). *Land Reform: A World Survey*. Boulder, CO: Westview Press.

KINLEY, DAVID (1982, May). "A Case Study Questions the Value of Reagan's 'Caribbean Basin Initiative.'" pp. 17–19.

KINZER, STEPHEN (1985a, January 23). "In Remote Nicaraguan Zone, Rebels Strike Boldly." *New York Times*, p. A2.

——— (1985b, April 11). "Nicaragua Men Fleeing Draft Fill Honduran Refugee Camp." *New York Times*, p. A1.

KRASNER, STEPHEN D. (1978). *Defending the National Interest*. Princeton: Princeton University Press.

KRIESBERG, MARTIN, ERVIN BULLARD, and WENDELL BECRAFT (1970). *Costa Rican Agriculture: Crop Priorities and Country Policies*. Unpublished report, U.S. Department of Agriculture, Washington, DC.

KUSTERER, KENNETH C., MARIA REGINA ESTRADA DE BATRES, and JOSEFINA XUYÁ CUXIL (1981). *The Social Impact of Agribusiness: A Case Study of ALCOSA in Guatemala* (Evaluation Special Study No. 4). U.S. Agency for International Development, Washington, DC.

LABARGE, RICHARD A. (1968). "Impact of the United Fruit Company on the Economic Development of Guatemala, 1946–1954." In Richard H. LaBarge, Wayne M. Clegern, and Oriol Pi-Sunyer, *Studies in Middle American Economics* (Publication No. 29). New Orleans: Tulane University, Middle American Research Institute.

LAFEBER, WALTER (1984). *Inevitable Revolutions: The United States in Central America*. New York: Norton.

LAIRD, LARRY K. (1974). *Technology versus Tradition: The Modernization of Nicaraguan Agriculture, 1900–1940*. Unpublished doctoral dissertation, University of Kansas, Lawrence.

LANDSBERGER, HENRY A., and CYNTHIA N. HEWITT (1970). "Ten Sources of Weakness and Cleavage in Latin American Peasant Movements." In Rodolfo Stavenhagen, ed., *Agrarian Problems & Peasant Movements in Latin America*. New York: Doubleday Anchor.

LANTIGUA, JOHN (1985, May 9). "Managua Suspending Draft and Freezing Size of Armed Forces." *Washington Post*, p. A31.

LAPPÉ, FRANCES MOORE, and JOSEPH COLLINS (1978). *Food First: Beyond the Myth of Scarcity*. New York: Ballantine.

LARDIZÁBAL, FERNANDO (1986). "Myths and Realities: Agricultural Policy or Agrarian Reform?" In Mark B. Rosenberg and Philip L. Sheperd, eds., *Honduras Confronts its Future*. Boulder, CO: Lynne Reinner.

LASSEN, CHERYL A. (1980). *Landlessness and Rural Poverty in Latin America: Condition, Trends, and Policies Affecting Income and Employment*. Ithaca, NY: Cornell University Center for International Studies.

LASSEY, WILLIAM R., JAMES HUFFMAN, BERTHA CLOW, LAYTON THOMPSON, CLIVE HARSTON, and MARY MOBLEY (1969). *The Lake Izabal Area of Guatemala: Communication, Social Change and Agricultural Development*. Unpublished report, Montana State University Center for Planning and Development, Bozeman.

LAWYERS COMMITTEE FOR INTERNATIONAL HUMAN RIGHTS AND AMERICAS WATCH COMMITTEE [LCIHR–AWC] (1984). *El Salvador's Other Victims: The War on the Displaced*. New York: Authors.

LEHOUCQ, EDWARD, and HAROLD SIMS (1982). "Reform with Repression: The Land Reform in El Salvador." (Occasional Paper in Social Change No. 6). Philadelphia: Institute for the Study of Human Issues.

LeMoyne, James (1984, June 30). "Salvadoran Right Blocks Land Plan." *New York Times*, pp. A1+.

LeoGrande, William M. (1979). "The Revolution in Nicaragua: Another Cuba?" *Foreign Affairs, 58*(1), 28–50.

——— (1981). "Land Reform and the El Salvador Crisis." *International Security, 6*(1), 27–52.

——— (1982). "The United States and the Nicaraguan Revolution." In Thomas W. Walker, ed., *Nicaragua in Revolution*. New York: Praeger.

——— (1985). "The United States and Nicaragua." In Thomas W. Walker, ed., *Nicaragua: The First Five Years*. Boulder, CO: Westview Press.

LeoGrande, William M., and Carla Anne Robbins (1980). "Oligarchs and Officers: The Crisis in El Salvador." *Foreign Affairs, 58*, 1084–1103.

Lethander, Richard W. (1968). *The Economy of Nicaragua*. Unpublished doctoral dissertation, Duke University, Durham, NC.

Libertad (San José) (1985, July 19–25). "Landless Peasants Stage Protest in Front of INA." In U.S. Joint Publications Research Service, *JPRS Reports*, No. LAM–85–079–90.

Linares, Olga F. (1979). "What Is Lower Central American Archeology?" *Annual Review of Anthropology, 8*, 21–43.

Lofchie, Michael F., and Stephen K. Commins (1982). "Food Deficits and Agricultural Policies in Tropical Africa." *Journal of Modern African Studies, 20*, 1–25.

Long, Norman, and David Winder (1981). "The Limitations of 'Directive Change' for Rural Development in the Third World." *Community Devlopment Journal, 16*(2), 82–87.

Lowenthal, Abraham F. (1973). "United States Policy Toward Latin America: 'Liberal,' 'Radical,' and 'Bureaucratic' Perspectives." *Latin American Research Review, 8*(3), 3–26.

McCamant, John (1968). *Development Assistance in Central America*. New York: Praeger.

MacCameron, Robert L. (1983). *Bananas, Labor, and Politics in Honduras: 1954–1963*. Syracuse, NY: Maxwell School of Citizenship and Public Affairs Syracuse University.

McCann, Thomas (1976). *An American Company: The Tragedy of United Fruit*. New York: Crown.

McClintock, Cynthia (1984). "Why Peasants Rebel: The Case of Peru's Sendero Luminoso." *World Politics, 37*(1), 48–84.

McClintock, Michael (1985a). *The American Connection: Vol. 1: State Terror and Popular Resistance in El Salvador*. London: Zed Books.

——— (1985b). *The American Connection: Vol. 2: State Terror and Popular Resistance in Guatemala*. London: Zed Books.

McCreery, David J. (1976). "Coffee and Class: The Structure of Development in Liberal Guatemala." *Hispanic American Historical Review, 56*(3), 438–460.

——— (1983). *Development and the State in Reforma Guatemala, 1871–1885*. (Latin American Series, No. 10). Athens: Ohio University Press.

MacLeod, Murdo J. (1973). *Spanish Central America: A Socioeconomic History, 1520–1720*. Berkeley CA: University of California Press.

MacLeod, Murdo J, and Robert Wasserstrom, eds. (1983). *Spaniards and Indians in Southeastern Mesoamerica*. Lincoln: University of Nebraska Press.

Marshall, C. F. (1983). *The World Coffee Trade*. Cambridge, England: Woodhead-Faulkner.

Martz, John D. (1956). *Communist Infiltration in Guatemala*. New York: Vantage Press.

Mason, David T. (1986). "Land Reform and the Breakdown of Clientelist Politics in El Salvador." *Comparative Political Studies, 18*(4), 487–516.

Maxfield, Sylvia, and Richard Stahler-Sholk (1985). "External Constraints." In Thomas W. Walker, ed., *Nicaragua: The First Five Years*. Boulder, CO: Westview Press.

May, Stacy, and Galo Plaza (1958). *The United Fruit Company in Latin America*. New York: National Planning Association.

MEIER, GERALD M., ed. (1984). *Leading Issues in Economic Development* (4th ed.). New York: Oxford University Press.

MERRILL, WILLIAM C. (1974). *The Long-Run Prospects for Increasing Income Levels in Guatemala's Highlands*. Guatemala City: National Council for Economic Planning.

METRINKO, MONIKA (1978, October 16). "Exports Fuel Growth of Central America's Beef Production." *Foreign Agriculture, 16*, 2–3.

MIGDAL, JOEL S. (1974). *Peasants, Politics, and Revolution: Pressures toward Political and Social Change in the Third World*. Princeton: Princeton University Press.

MILLETT, RICHARD (1977). *Guardians of the Dynasty*. Maryknoll, NY: Orbis.

MINKEL, CLARENCE W. (1967). "Programs of Agricultural Colonization and Settlement in Central America." *Revista Geográfica, 66*, 19–53.

MOLINA CHOCANO, GUILLERMO, and RICARDO REINA (1983). *La Evolución de la Pobreza Rural en Honduras* (Publication No. PREALC/223). Santiago, Chile: International Labour Organization.

MONTEFORTE TOLEDO, MARIO (1972). *Centro América: Subdesarrollo y Dependencia: Vol. 1*. Mexico City: National Autonomous University of Mexico.

MONTES, SEGUNDO (1980). *El Agro Salvadoreño (1973–1980)*. San Salvador: University of Central America.

MONTGOMERY, JOHN D. (1984). "United States Advocacy of International Land Reform." In John D. Montgomery, ed., *International Dimensions of Land Reform*. Boulder, CO: Westview Press.

MONTGOMERY, TOMMIE SUE (1982). *Revolution in El Salvador*. Boulder, CO: Westview Press.

MOONEY, JOSEPH P. (1984). "Was It WORSENING of Economic and Social Conditions that Brought Violence and Civil War to El Salvador?" *Inter-American Economic Affairs, 38*(2), 61–69.

MORLEY, SYLVANUS G., and GEORGE W. BRAINERD (1983). *The Ancient Maya* (4th ed.) Revised by Robert J. Shaver. Stanford, CA: Stanford University Press.

MORRIS, JAMES A. (1984). *Honduras: Caudillo Politics and Military Rulers*. Boulder, CO: Westview Press.

MORSINK-VILLALOBOS, JENNIFER, and JAMES R. SIMPSON (1980). "Export Subsidies: The Case of Costa Rica's Banana Industry." *Inter-American Economic Affairs, 34*(3), 69–86.

MOSK, SANFORD A. (1955). "The Coffee Economy of Guatemala, 1850–1918: Development and Signs of Instability." *Inter-American Economic Affairs, 9*(3), 6–20.

MUDGE, ARTHUR W. (1979). "A Case Study in Human Rights and Development Assistance: Nicaragua." *Universal Human Rights, 1*(4), 93–102.

MUNRO, DANA G. (1918). *The Five Republics of Central America*. New York: Oxford University Press.

MURAVCHIK, JOSHUA (1986–87). "The Nicaraguan Debate." *Foreign Affairs, 65*(2), 366–382.

MURPHY, BRIAN (1970). "The Stunted Growth of Campesino Organizations." In Richard N. Adams, ed., *Crucifixion by Power*. Austin: University of Texas Press.

MYERS, NORMAN (1981). "The Hamburger Connection: How Central America's Forests Became North America's Hamburgers." *Ambio, 10*(1), 3–8.

La Nación, San José (1982, April 4). "Deforestation Reaches 60,000 Hectares a Year." In U.S. Joint Publication Research Service, *JPRS Reports*, No. 80907–16.

———— (1983, June 2). "Government to Distribute Land to 10,000 Families." In U.S. Joint Publications Research Service, *JPRS Reports*, No. 83830–61.

———— (1984a, April 5). "IDA Responds." In U.S. Joint Publications Research Service, *JPRS Reports*, No. LAM–84–067–41.

———— (1984b, May 14). "Peasant Occupation of Farm Land Continues in Southern Region." In U.S. Joint Publications Research Service, *JPRS Reports*, No. LAM–84–079–63.

NAIRN, ALLAN, and JEAN-MARIE SIMON (1986, June 30). "Bureaucracy of Death." *New Republic,* pp. 13–17.

NATHAN ASSOCIATES (1969). *Agricultural Sectoral Analysis for El Salvador: Summary.* Unpublished paper prepared for the government of El Salvador.

NAYLOR, ROBERT A. (1967). "Guatemala: Indian Attitudes Toward Land Tenure." *Journal of Inter-American Studies, 9,* 619–640.

NEWFARMER, RICHARD S. (1983). "The Private Sector and Development." In John P. Lewis and Valeriana Kallab, eds., *U.S. Foreign Policy and the Third World: Agenda 1983.* New York: Praeger.

NEWSON, LINDA (1982). "The Depopulation of Nicaragua in the Sixteenth Century." *Journal of Latin American Studies, 14*(2), 253–286.

———— (1985). "Indian Population Patterns in Colonial Spanish America." *Latin American Research Review, 20,* 41–74.

New York Times (1985, March 19). "Sandinistas Forcing Thousands Out of War Zone." *New York Times,* p. A11.

NOLAN, DAVID (1984). *The Ideology of the Sandinistas and the Nicaraguan Revolution.* Coral Gables, FL: University of Miami, Graduate School of International Studies.

NORTH, LIISA (1985). *Bitter Grounds: Roots of Revolt in El Salvador* (2nd ed.). Toronto: Between the Lines.

NORTH AMERICAN CONGRESS ON LATIN AMERICA [NACLA] (1974). "Guatemala: Breaking Free." *NACLA'S Latin America & Empire Report, 8.*

NORTON, CHRIS (1985, November-December). "Build and Destroy." *NACLA Report on the Americas,* pp. 26–36.

———— (1986, February 6). "Salvador's Army Moves Civilians in Effort to Oust Rebels." *Christian Science Monitor* (Boston), p. 1+.

NÚÑEZ SOLO, ORLANDO (1981). *El Somocismo y el Model Capitalista Agro-exportador.* Managua: National Autonomous University of Nicaragua.

OLSON, GARY L. (1974). *U.S. Foreign Policy and the Third World Peasant: Land Reform in Asia and Latin America.* New York: Praeger.

OMANG, JOANNE (1985, January 16). "Administration Worries as Banana Operation Closes in Costa Rica." *Washington Post,* p. A15.

ORELLANA, SANDRA L. (1984). *The Tzutjil Mayas: Continuity and Change, 1250–1630.* Norman: University of Oklahoma Press.

ORGANIZATION OF AMERICAN STATES [OAS] (1966). *Domestic Efforts and the Needs for External Financing for the Development of Nicaragua.* Washington, DC: Organization of American States, Inter-American Committee on the Alliance for Progress.

———— (1974). *Situation, Principal Problems and Prospects of the Economic Development of Guatemala.* Washington, DC: Organization of American States, Inter-American Economic and Social Council.

———— (1975). *Situation, Principal Problems and Prospects for the Integral Development of El Salvador.* Washington, DC: Organization of American States, Inter-American Economic and Social Council.

PAIGE, JEFFERY M. (1975). *Agrarian Revolution: Social Movements and Export Agriculture in the Underdeveloped World.* New York: Free Press.

———— (1983). "Social Theory and Peasant Revolution in Vietnam and Guatemala." *Theory and Society, 12*(6) 699–737.

———— (1985). "Cotton and Revolution in Nicaragua." In Peter Evans, Dietrich Rueschemeyer, and Theda Skocpol, eds., *State Versus Market in the World-System.* Sage Political Economy of the World System Annuals, Vol. 8. Beverly Hills, CA: Sage.

PARSONS, JAMES J. (1965). "Cotton and Cattle in the Pacific Lowlands of Central America."

Journal of Interamerican Studies, 7(2), 149–159.

PARSONS, KENNETH H. (1976). *Agrarian Reform in Southern Honduras* (Research Paper No. 67). Madison: University of Wisconsin Land Tenure Center.

PASTOR, ROBERT A. (1982, July 20 and 22). "Agricultural Development in the Caribbean Basin." Prepared statement in U.S., House, Committee on Foreign Affairs. *Agricultural Development in the Caribbean and Central America.* Hearings before Subcommittee on Inter-American Affairs. 97th Congress, 2nd session, pp. 75–106.

PAYER, CHERYL (1975). *Commodity Trade of the Third World.* New York: Wiley.

PAYERAS, MARIO (1983). *Days of the Jungle: The Testimony of a Guatemalan Guerrillero, 1972–1976.* New York: Monthly Review Press.

PEARSE, ANDREW (1980). *Seeds of Plenty, Seeds of Want: Social and Economic Implications of the Green Revolution.* Oxford: Clarendon Press.

PEARSON, NEALE J. (1969). "Guatemala: The Peasant Union Movement, 1944–1954." In Henry Landsberger, ed., *Latin American Peasant Movements.* Ithaca: Cornell University Press.

———— (1980). "Peasant Pressure Groups and Agrarian Reform in Honduras, 1962–1977." In William P. Avery, Richard E. Lonsdale, and Ivan Völgyes, eds., *Rural Change and Public Policy.* New York: Pergamon Press.

PEARSON, ROSS (1963a). "Land Reform, Guatemalan Style." *American Journal of Economics and Sociology,* 22, 225–234.

———— (1963b). "Zones of Agricultural Development in Guatemala." *Journal of Geography,* 62(1), 11–22.

PECKENHAM, NANCY, and ANNIE STREET, eds. (1985). *Honduras: Portrait of a Captive Nation.* New York: Praeger.

PEEK, PETER (1983). "Agrarian Reform and Rural Development in Nicaragua, 1979–1981." In Ajit K. Ghose, ed., *Agrarian Reform in Contemporary Developing Countries.* New York: St. Martin's Press.

PETRAS, JAMES F., and ROBERT LAPORTE, Jr. (1973). *Cultivating Revolution: The United States and Agrarian Reform in Latin America.* New York: Random House/Vintage.

PFEIL, ULRIKE (1977). *Peasant Mobilization and Land Reform: A Theoretical Model and a Case Study (Honduras).* Unpublished master's thesis, University of Florida, Gainesville.

PLACE, SUSAN E. (1981). *Ecological and Social Consequences of Export Beef Production in Guanacaste Province, Costa Rica.* Unpublished doctoral dissertation, University of California, Los Angeles.

PLANT, ROGER (1978). *Guatemala: Unnatural Disaster.* London: Latin American Bureau.

POSAS, MARIO (1979). "Política Estatal y Estructura Agraria en Honduras (1950–1978)." *Estudios Sociales Centroamericanos,* 8, 37–116.

———— (1981a). *Conflictos Agrarios y Organización Campesina.* Tegucigalpa: Editorial Universitaria.

———— (1981b). *El Movimiento Campesino Hondureño: Una Perspectiva General.* Tegucigalpa: Editorial Guaymuras.

POSAS, MARIO, and RAFAEL DEL CID (1981). *La Constucción del Sector Público y del Estado Nacional en Honduras, 1876–1979.* San José: Editorial Universitaria Centroamericana.

La Prensa (San Pedro Sula) (1982, September 28). "Agrarian Reform Discussed at Peasants Meeting." In U.S. Joint Publications Research Service, *JPRS Reports,* No. 82258–89.

———— (1983, January 18). "Land Occupation Denounced." In U.S. Joint Publications Research Service, *JPRS Reports,* No. 83020–88.

PROSTERMAN, ROY L. (1981). "El Salvador Debate: Real Facts and True Alternatives." *Food Monitor,* 24, 13–19.

———— (1982, August 9). "The Unmaking of a Land Reform." *New Republic,* pp. 21–25.

———— (1983). "The Demographics of Land Reform in El Salvador since 1980." James W. Wilkie and Stephen Haber, eds., *Statistical Abstract of Latin America: Vol. 22*. Los Angeles: University of California, Latin American Center.

PROSTERMAN, ROY L., JEFFREY M. RIEDINGER, and MARY N. TEMPLE (1981). "Land Reform and the El Salvador Crisis." *International Security*, 6(1), 53–74.

PUCHALA, DONALD J., and JANE STAVELY (1979). "The Political Economy of Taiwanese Agriculture." In Raymond F. Hopkins, Donald J. Puchala, and Ross B. Talbot, eds., *Food, Politics, and Agricultural Development*. Boulder, CO: Westview Press.

QUIROS GUARDIA, RODOLFO (1973). *Agricultural Development in Central America: Its Origin and Nature* (Research Paper No. 49). Madison: University of Wisconsin Land Tenure Center.

REINHARDT, NOLA (1986). "Agro-Exports and the Peasantry in the Agrarian Reforms of El Salvador and Nicaragua" (unpublished draft). To be published in William Thiesenhusen, ed., *Searching for Agrarian Reform in Latin America*. Boston, MA: Allen & Unwin.

La República (San José) (1983, July 24). "Land Ownership." In U.S. Joint Publications Research Service, *JPRS Reports*, No. 84297–13.

REUTLINGER, SHLOMO, and HAROLD ALDERMAN (1980). "The Prevalence of Calorie-Deficient Diets in Developing Countries." *World Development*, 8(5/6), 399–411.

RIDING, ALAN (1979, April 5). "Guatemala Opening New Lands But the Best Goes to Rich." *New York Times*, p. A2.

RIISMANDEL, JOHN N. (1972). *Costa Rica: Self-Image, Land Tenure, and Agrarian Reform, 1940–1965*. Unpublished doctoral dissertation, University of Maryland, College Park.

ROHTER, LARRY (1985, March 19). "Little in Nicaragua Escapes War's Onslaught." *New York Times*, p. A1.

ROSS, DELMER G. (1975). *Visionaries and Swindlers: The Development of the Railways of Honduras*. Mobile, AL: Institute for Research in Latin America.

ROUX, BERNARD (1978). "Expansión del Capitalismo y Desarrollo del Subdesarrollo: La Integración de América Central en el Mercado Mundial de la Carne de Vacuno." *Estudios Sociales Centroamericanos*, 1, 8–34.

ROWLES, JAMES P. (1985). *Law and Agrarian Reform in Costa Rica*. Boulder, CO: Westview Press.

RUHL, J. MARK (1984). "Agrarian Structure and Political Stability in Honduras." *Journal of Interamerican Studies and World Affairs*, 26(1), 33–68.

———— (1985). "The Honduran Agrarian Reform Under Suazo Córdova." *Inter-American Economic Affairs*, 39(2), 63–81.

SAENZ MAROTO, ALBERTO (1970). *Historia Agrícola de Costa Rica*. San José: University of Costa Rica.

SÁENZ P., CARLOS, and C. FOSTER KNIGHT (1971). *Tenure Security, Land Titling and Agricultural Development in Costa Rica*. San José: University of Costa Rica.

SALAZAR, JOSÉ M. (1962). *Tierras y Colonizacción en Costa Rica*. San José: Ciudad Universitaria.

———— (1979). "Política Agraria." In Chester Zelaya, ed., *Costa Rica Contemporánea, Vol. 1*. San José: Editorial de Costa Rica.

SANDERSON, STEVEN E. (1986). *The Transformation of Mexican Agriculture*. Princeton: Princeton University Press.

SATTERTHWAITE, RIDGWAY (1971). *Campesino Agriculture and Hacienda Modernization in Costal El Salvador: 1949 to 1969*. Unpublished doctoral dissertation, University of Wisconsin, Madison.

SCHLESINGER, STEPHEN, and STEPHEN KINZER (1983). *Bitter Fruit: The Untold Story of the American Coup in Guatemala*. New York: Doubleday.

SCHMID, LESTER (n.d.). "Some Effects of U.S. Foreign Policy Upon Farmers and Other Rural People of Guatemala." Unpublished paper, Land Tenure Center, University of Wisconsin, Madison.

SCHOULTZ, LARS (1983). "Guatemala: Social Change and Political Conflict." In Martin Diskin, ed., *Trouble in Our Backyard: Central America and the United States in the Eighties.* New York: Pantheon.

——— (1984). "Nicaragua: The United States Confronts a Revolution." In Richard Newfarmer, ed., *From Gunboats to Diplomacy: New U.S. Policies for Latin America.* Baltimore, MD: Johns Hopkins University Press.

SCHWARTZ, NORMAN B. (1978). "Community Development and Cultural Change in Latin America." *Annual Review of Anthropology, 7,* 235–261.

SCOTT, JAMES C. (1976). *The Moral Economy of the Peasant: Rebellion and Subsistence in Southeast Asia.* New Haven: Yale University Press.

——— (1985). *Weapons of the Weak: Everyday Forms of Peasant Resistance.* New Haven: Yale University Press.

SELIGSON, MITCHELL (1980a). *Peasants of Costa Rica and the Development of Agrarian Capitalism.* Madison: University of Wisconsin Press.

——— (1980b). "Trust, Efficacy and Modes of Political Participation: A Study of Costa Rican Peasants." *British Journal of Political Science, 10,* 75–98.

——— (1982). "Agrarian Reform in Costa Rica: The Impact of the Title Security Program." *Inter-American Economic Affairs, 35*(4), 31–56.

——— (1984). "Implementing Land Reform: The Case of Costa Rica." *Managing International Development, 1*(2), 29–46.

SELIGSON, MITCHELL, and EDWARD N. MULLER (1985, August). "Political Support under Crisis Conditions: Costa Rica, 1978–1983." Paper presented at the annual meeting of the American Political Science Association, New Orleans.

SEXTON, JAMES D., ed. (1985). *Campesino: The Diary of a Guatemalan Indian.* Tucson: University of Arizona Press.

SHANE, DOUGLAS (1980). *Hoofprints in the Forest.* Unpublished report, U.S. Department of State, Washington, DC.

SHAW, ROYCE Z. (1979). *Central America: Regional Integration and National Political Development.* Boulder, CO: Westview Press.

SHEPHERD, PHILIP (1985). "Wisconsin in Honduras: Agrarian Politics and U.S. Influence in the 1980s." In Nancy Peckenham and Annie Street, eds., *Honduras: Portrait of a Captive Nation.* New York: Praeger.

SHERMAN, WILLIAM L. (1979). *Forced Native Labor in Sixteenth Century Central America.* Lincoln: University of Nebraska Press.

SHOLK, RICHARD (1984). "The National Bourgeoisie in Post-Revolutionary Nicaragua." *Comparative Politics, 16*(3), 253–276.

SIGMUND, PAUL, and MARY SPECK (1978, October 4, 5, and 6). "Virtue's Reward: The United States and Somoza, 1933–1978." Prepared statement in U.S., Senate, Committee on Foreign Relations. *Latin America.* Hearings before Subcommittee on Western Hemisphere Affairs. 95th Congress, 2nd session.

SIMON, LAURENCE R., and JAMES C. STEPHENS, JR. (1982). *El Salvador Land Reform, 1980–1981: Impact Audit,* (2nd. ed.). Boston: Oxfam America.

SIMS, HAROLD (1982). "Sandinista Nicaragua: Pragmatism in a Political Economy in Formation" (Occasional Papers in Social Change, No. 5). Institute for the Study of Human Issues.

SINGELMANN, PETER (1981). *Structures of Domination and Peasant Movements in Latin America.* Columbia: University of Missouri Press.

SKOCPOL, THEDA (1982). "What Makes Peasants Revolutionary?" *Comparative Politics, 14*(3), 351–375.

SLUTZKY, DANIEL (1979). "Notes sobre Empresas Transnacionales, Agroindustriales y Reforma Agraria en Honduras." *Estudios Sociales Centroamericanos, 8,* 35–48.

SMITH, CAROL A. (1978). "Beyond Dependency Theory: National and Regional Patterns of Underdevelopment in Guatemala." *American Ethnologist, 5*, 574–617.

——— (1984a). "Does A Commodity Economy Enrich the Few while Ruining the Masses? Differentiation Among Petty Commodity Producers in Guatemala." *Journal of Peasant Studies, 11*(3), 60–95.

——— (1984b). "Local History to Global Context: Social and Economic Transitions in Western Guatemala." *Comparative Studies in Society and History, 26*(2), 193–228.

SMITH, HEDRICK (1985, February 22). "President Asserts Goal Is to Remove Sandinista Regime." *New York Times*, p. A1.

SMITH, ROBERT S. (1956). "Forced Labor in the Guatemalan Indigo Works." *Hispanic American Historical Review, 36*(2), 319–328.

SMITH, T. LYNN, ed. (1965). *Agrarian Reform in Latin America*. New York: Knopf.

SPALDING, ROSE J. (1985). "Food Politics and Agricultural Change in Revolutionary Nicaragua, 1979–82." In John C. Soper and Thomas C. Wright, eds., *Food, Politics, and Society in Latin America*. Lincoln: University of Nebraska Press.

SPIELMANN, HANS O. (1972). "La Expansión Ganadera en Costa Rica." *Revista Geográfica, 77*, 57–84.

STONE, SAMUEL (1983). "Production and Politics in Central America's Convulsions." *Journal of Latin American Studies, 15*(2), 453–469.

STORRS, K. LARRY (1981). "Congress and El Salvador." In Library of Congress, Congressional Research Service, *Congress and Foreign Relations: 1981*. Washington, DC: U.S. Government Printing Office.

STRASMA, JOHN, PETER GORE, JEFFREY NASH, and REFUGIO ROCHIN (1983). *Agrarian Reform in El Salvador*. Unpublished paper prepared by Checchi & Co. for U.S. Agency for International Development, Washington, DC.

STREETEN, PAUL (1974). "World Trade in Agricultural Commodities and the Terms of Trade with Industrial Goods." In Nurul Islam, ed., *Agricultural Policy in Developing Countries*. New York: Wiley.

STROUSE, PIERRE A. D. (1970). "Instability of Tropical Agriculture: The Atlantic Lowlands of Costa Rica." *Economic Geography, 46*, 78–97.

TAI, HUNG-CHAO (1974). *Land Reform and Politics: A Comparative Analysis*. Berkeley: University of California Press.

TAX, SOL (1963). *Penny Capitalism: A Guatemalan Indian Economy*. Chicago: University of Chicago Press.

TAYLOR, JAMES ROBERT, JR. (1969). *Agricultural Settlement and Development in Eastern Nicaragua* (Research Paper No. 33). Madison: University of Wisconsin Land Tenure Center.

TENDLER, JUDITH (1976). *Intercountry Evaluation of Small Farmer Organizations: Final Report [on] Ecuador and Honduras* (Program Evaluation Study). Washington, DC: U.S. Agency for International Development.

THIESENHUSEN, WILLIAM C. (1981). "El Salvador's Land Reform: Was It Programmed to Fail?" *Christianity and Crisis, 41*(8), 133–137.

THOME, JOSEPH, and DAVID KAIMOWITZ (1985). "Agrarian Reform." In Thomas W. Walker, ed. *Nicaragua: The First Five Years*. Boulder, CO: Westview Press.

TIEMPO (San Pedro Sula) (1982, May 5). "Peasants' Union Protests Arrests in Northwest." In U.S. Joint Publications Research Service, *JPRS Report*, No. 80872–122.

——— (1983, October 24). "Most Agrarian Reform Beneficiaries Fail to Receive Assistance." In U.S. Joint Publications Research Service, *JPRS Report*, No. 84872–122.

TILLY, CHARLES (1978). *From Mobilization to Revolution*. Reading, MA: Addison-Wesley.

TIME (1968, January 26). "Guatemala: Caught in the Crossfire." P. 23.

——— (1975, August 18). "Blood and Land." P. 36.

Timmer, C. Peter (1982). "Appropriate Technology, Food Production, and Rural Development: The Rural Sector from a Food Policy Perspective." In Ray A. Goldberg, ed., *Research in Domestic and International Agribusiness Management: Vol. 3*. Greenwich, CT: JAI Press.

Torres Rivas, Edelberto (1971). *Interpretación del Desarrollo Centroamericano*. San José: EDUCA.

Torres, James F. (1979). *Income Levels, Income Distribution, and Levels of Living in Rural Honduras: A Summary and Evaluation of Qualitative and Quantitative Data* (General Working Document). Washington, DC: U.S. Agency for International Development.

La Tribuna (Tegucigalpa) (1983, November 23). "Japanese Agricultural Development Aid." In U.S. Joint Publications Research Service, *JPRS Reports*, No. LAM–84–006:69.

Trudeau, Robert H. (1984). "Guatemala: The Long-Term Costs of Short-Term Stability." In Richard Newfarmer, ed., *From Gunboats to Diplomacy: New U.S. Policies for Latin America*. Baltimore: Johns Hopkins University Press.

Trudeau, Robert H., and Lars Schoultz (1986). "Guatemala." In Morris J. Blachman, William M. LeoGrande, and Kenneth Sharpe, eds., *Confronting Revolution: Security through Diplomacy in Central America*. New York: Pantheon.

Tuma, Elias (1965). *Twenty-Six Centuries of Agrarian Reform*. Berkeley: University of California Press.

United Nations (various years). *Statistical Abstract*. New York: Author.

United Nations, Economic Commission for Latin America [UNECLA] (1950). *The Economic Development of Latin America and Its Principal Problems*. Lake Success, NY: United Nations Department of Economic Affairs.

——— (1979). *Transnational Corporations in the Banana Industry of Central America*. (N.P.): Author.

——— (1983). *Statistical Yearbook for Latin America*. New York: Author.

United Nations, Food and Agriculture Organization [UNFAO] (various years). *Production Yearbook*. Rome: Author.

United States, Agency for International Development [USAID] (1970, March 27). "$3 Million Aid Loan to Help Small Farmers in Guatemala" (press release). Washington, DC: Author.

——— (1982). *Honduras, Project Paper: Small Farmer Titling*. Washington, DC: Author.

——— (1983). *Honduras, Project Paper: Small Farmer Livestock Improvement*. Washington, DC: Author.

——— (1984). *Honduras, Project Paper: Export Promotion and Services*. Washington, DC: Author

——— (1985). *Latin America and the Caribbean, Vol. 1* (Congressional presentation, fiscal year 1986, annex 3). Washington, DC: Author.

United States, Agency for International Development, Office of Housing (1980). *Urban Poverty in Guatemala* Unpublished paper, Author, Washington, DC.

United States, Congress (1962, October 2). *Congressional Record*. Washington DC: U.S. Government Printing Office.

United States, Department of Agriculture, Foreign Agricultural Service [USDA] (various years). *Attaché Reports*. Washington, DC: Author.

United States, Department of State (1983, April). "El Salvador's Land Reform." *GIST*. Washington, DC: Department of State, Bureau of Public Affairs.

——— (1984, January 26, February 6). *Report on Status of Land Reform in El Salvador*. Reprinted in U.S., House, Committee on Foreign Affairs. *The Situation in El Salvador*. Hearings before subcommittees on Human Rights and International Organizations and on Western Hemisphere Affairs. 98th Congress, 2nd session pp. 291–342.

———— (1985, February). "El Salvador's Land Reform." *GIST*. Washington, DC: Department of State, Bureau of Public Affairs.

UNITED STATES, HOUSE (1981a, February 25, March 24, April 29). Committee on Appropriations. *Foreign Assistance Legislation for Fiscal Year 1982: Pts. 1, 2*. Hearings before Subcommittee on Foreign Operations. 97th Congress, 1st session.

———— (1981b, July 14, 21, 28). Committee on Foreign Affairs. *The Caribbean Basin Policy*. Hearings before Subcommittee on Inter-American Affairs. 97th Congress, 1st session.

———— (1981c, July 30). Committee on Foreign Affairs. *Human Rights in Guatemala*. Hearings before Subcommittee on Inter-American Affairs. 97th Congress, 1st session.

———— (1982, February 2, 23, 25, March 2). Committee on Foreign Affairs. *Presidential Certification on El Salvador: Vol. 1*. Hearings before Subcommittee on Inter-American Affairs. 97th Congress, 2nd session.

———— (1984, January 26, February 6). Committee on Foreign Affairs. *The Situation in El Salvador*. Hearings before Subcommittees on Human Rights and International Organizations and on Western Hemisphere Affairs. 98th Congress, 2nd session.

———— (1985a, February 20). Committee on Foreign Affairs. *Developments in Guatemala and U.S. Options*. Hearings before Subcommittee on Western Hemisphere Affairs. 99th Congress, 1st session.

———— (1985b, March 5, 19). Committee on Foreign Affairs. *Foreign Assistance Legislation for Fiscal Years 1986–87:6*. Hearings and markup before the Subcommittee on Western Hemisphere Affairs. 99th Congress, 1st session.

UNITED STATES, SENATE (1978, October 4, 5, 6). Committee on Foreign Relations. *Latin America*. Hearings before Subcommittee on Western Hemisphere Affairs. 95th Congress, 2nd session.

VALVERDE, VICTOR, REYNALDO MARTORELL, VICTOR MEJIA-PIVARAL, HERNAN DELGADO, AARON LECHTIG, CHARLES TELLER, and ROBERT E. KLEIN (1977). "Relationship between Family Land Availability and Nutritional Status." *Ecology of Food and Nutrition*, 6(1), 1–7.

VALVERDE, VICTOR, ISABEL NIEVES, NANCY SLOAN, BERNARD PILLET, FREDERICK TROWBRIDGE, TIMOTHY FARRELL, IVAN BEGHIN, and ROBERT E. KLEIN (1980). "Life Styles and Nutritional Status of Children From Different Ecological Areas of El Salvador." *Ecology of Food and Nutrition*, 9(3), 167–177.

VEBLEN, THOMAS T. (1978). "Forest Preservation in the Western Highlands of Guatemala." *Geographical Review*, 68(4), 417–434.

VOLK, STEVEN (1981). "Honduras: On the Border of War." *NACLA Report on the Americas*, 15(6), 2–37.

WALKER, THOMAS S. (1981). "Risk and Adoption of Hybrid Maize in El Salvador." *Food Research Institute Studies*, 18(1), 59–88.

WALKER, THOMAS W. (1981). *Nicaragua: The Land of Sandino*. Boulder, CO: Westview Press.

WALKER, THOMAS W., ed. (1985). *Nicaragua: The First Five Years*. Boulder, CO: Westview Press.

WALLACE, SCOTT (1986, October 7). "In Policy Shift, Nicaragua Grants Peasants Ownership of Land." *Christian Science Monitor* (Boston), p. 12.

WARNKEN, PHILIP F. (1975). *The Agricultural Development of Nicaragua: An Analysis of the Production Sector*. Unpublished report, University of Missouri, Columbia.

WARREN, KAY B. (1978). *The Symbolism of Subordination: Indian Identity in a Guatemalan Town*. Austin: University of Texas Press.

WASHINGTON OFFICE ON LATIN AMERICA [WOLA] (1979). *El Salvador: Human Rights and U.S. Economic Policy*. Washington, DC: Author.

———— (1983). *Guatemala: The Roots of Revolution*. Washington, DC: Author.

242

WASSERSTROM, ROBERT (1975). "Revolution in Guatemala: Peasants and Politics under the Arbenz Government." *Comparative Study in Society and History, 17*(4), 443–478.

WEBRE, STEPHEN (1979). *José Napoleón Duarte and the Christian Democratic Party in Salvadoran Politics, 1960–1972.* Baton Rouge: Louisiana State University Press.

WEEKS, JOHN (1985). *The Economies of Central America.* New York: Holmes & Meier.

――― (1986). "An Interpretation of the Central American Crisis." *Latin American Research Review, 21*(3), 31–54.

WEIR, DAVID, and MARK SCHAPIRO (1981). *Circles of Poison.* San Francisco: Institute for Food and Development Policy.

WEST, ROBERT C., and JOHN P. AUGELLI (1976). *Middle America: Its Lands and Peoples* (2nd. ed.). Englewood Cliffs, NJ: Prentice-Hall.

WHEELOCK ROMÁN, JAIME (1980). *Imperialismo y Dictadura: Crisis de una Formación Social* (5th. ed.). Mexico City: Siglo veintiuno editores.

WHETTEN, NATHAN L. (1961). *Guatemala, The Land and the People.* New Haven: Yale University Press.

WHITE, ALASTAIR (1973). *El Salvador.* New York: Praeger.

WHITE, RICHARD A. (1984). *The Morass: United States Intervention in Central America.* New York: Harper & Row.

WHITE, ROBERT A. (1977). *Structural Factors in Rural Development: The Church and the Peasant in Honduras.* Unpublished doctoral dissertation, Cornell University, Ithaca, NY.

WILKIE, JAMES W., and MANUEL MORENO-IBÁÑEZ (1984). "New Research on Food Production in Latin America since 1952." In James W. Wilkie and Adain Perkal, eds., *Statistical Abstract of Latin America: Vol. 23.* Los Angeles: University of California Latin American Center.

WILLIAMS, DAN (1985, July 19). "Salvadoran Air War Intensifies With New U.S.–Supplied Planes." *Washington Post,* p. A27+.

WILLIAMS, ROBERT G. (1986). *Export Agriculture and the Crisis in Central America.* Chapel Hill: University of North Carolina Press.

WILSON, CHARLES MORROW (1968, reissue of 1947). *Empire in Green and Gold: The Story of the American Banana Trade.* New York: Greenwood Press.

WOLF, ERIC R. (1969). *Peasant Wars of the Twentieth Century.* New York: Harper & Row.

WOODWARD, RALPH LEE, JR. (1976). *Central America: A Nation Divided.* New York: Oxford University Press.

――― (1984). "The Rise and Decline of Liberalism in Central America." *Journal of Interamerican Studies and World Affairs, 26*(3), 291–312.

WORLD BANK (1978). *Guatemala: Economic and Social Position and Prospects.* Washington, DC: Author.

World Development Forum (1985). Washington DC: The Hunger Project.

WORTMAN, MILES L. (1982). *Government and Society in Central America, 1680–1840.* New York: Columbia University Press.

WYNIA, GARY W. (1972). *Politics and Planners: Economic Development Policy in Central America.* Madison: University of Wisconsin Press.

Index